Purbeck
Island

The quintessential view of the Purbeck that this book sets
out to celebrate – the quarrylands west of Swanage in the
closing years of the nineteenth century. Alfred Dawson made
this sketch, published in 1882, from above the slide at the
top of an underground working. A sledge, carrying stone,
is being hauled up by a mule which is plodding a circular
tow-path around the central capstan. Behind, a mason is
chipping out a trough, in front of one of the quarr-houses.

Goldingston Manor has a fortified rounded tower at the west end, with massive walls, which dates from about 1300. The building, at Ulwell to the north of Swanage, came into National Trust ownership along with the rest of Corfe Castle Estate, as part of the Bankes bequest of 1982. Cows may have been there when Alfred Dawson made his etching in 1882 but they are no longer welcome on the lawn. The house is leased under a farm tenancy and is not open to the public.

Purbeck Island

The industrial, social and natural
history of a corner of England

RODNEY LEGG

dpc

Dorset Publishing Company

at the WINCANTON PRESS

National School, North Street, Wincanton, Somerset BA9 9AT

THE FIRST EDITION WAS DEDICATED TO
Archie Strange-Boston

WHO WAS BORN IN WEST BUCKNOWLE HOUSE,
BETWEEN CHURCH KNOWLE
AND CORFE CASTLE, IN 1892. HIS FULL NAME WAS
LIEUTENANT-COLONEL ARCHIBALD DONALD
MACDONALD STRANGE-BOSTON
AND HE HAD SERVED WITH COLONEL T.E.
LAWRENCE IN THE DESERT REVOLT.

THIS REVISED EDITION I WOULD LIKE TO DEDICATE
TO
Iain Dean

WHO WAS BORN IN SUTTON COLDFIELD IN 1972,
WHEN THE FIRST EDITION OF THIS BOOK
WAS BEING PRINTED,
AND IS SWIMMING IN STUDLAND BAY THIS 24th DAY
OF JUNE 1988.

Copyright © Rodney Legg 1972-89

First published in 1972
by Dorset Publishing Company.
Published in this revised edition 1989
by the Wincanton Press,
National School, North Street,
Wincanton, Somerset BA9 9AT,
with distribution in Purbeck being
by Dorset Publishing Company.

Printed in Great Britain
by **WINCANTON
LITHO** *PRINTERS*

Typesetting originally carried out
for F & M. Naish & Co at Benfleet, Essex,
with revisions being processed by
Reg Ward at Holwell, Dorset, and output
by Wordstream Limited,
at St Aldhelm's Road, Poole, Dorset.

INTERNATIONAL STANDARD BOOK NUMBER [ISBN] 0 948699 08 6

iv

Contents

Symbol of Purbeck; one of Britain's rarest breeding birds. Delightful drawing of a Dartford Warbler, perched on a sprig of furze, from J.C. Mansel-Pleydell's "Birds of Dorsetshire" (1888). He laments that "it is doubtful whether we shall any longer see our heaths enlivened by this active little bird" – one hopes that some of the twentieth century's ecological concerns will prove to be equally over-pessimistic.

Foreword

WHEN IN 1972 I completed "Purbeck Island", my first full-sized book, I thought I had worked the Isle of Purbeck from my system. Some hope. Instead I have been drawn back to it a thousand times and felt compelled to sustain the scribbling into a surfeit of eight titles. Why anyone should go on buying them is absolutely unaccountable though I was surprised to find in 1986 that Rosemary Leontas is sharing my obsession. I compiled these reflections as a foreword to Rosemary's "Purbeck Poems" and am now expanding them into a self-justification.

It was the mention I gave "Purbeck Island" in Rosemary's book that triggered off a new spate of requests for what had been an out-of-print title since 1975. Stupidly, I never reprinted it – till now, that is – because there were always new things to be incorporated. What I failed to realise was that people were wanting it just because they thought it might recapture something of that lost age. "More people ask for it than any other book, local or national," Gareth Thomas told me from the St John's Hill bookshop in Wareham. "You seem to have produced something of a classic!"

From that came the realisation that I could now print it as a re-offering of my writings as a 25-year-old with occasional retrospective additions from the hindsight of 1988. The decision was clinched by the squirm of embarrassment I feel every time a television commercial for Yellow Pages features an elderly gentleman, J.R. Hartley, trying to obtain a copy of "Fly-fishing" which turns out to be his own book. I had been attempting and failing to obtain a copy of "Purbeck Island" though not for myself – my mother has one – but for my dear friend Merle Chacksfield of Swanage.

"We have a long waiting list for copies of your book," one shop told me. "And it will be expensive."

"I'll see what I can do to get the price down," I said. "It will be cheaper for me to reprint it!"

"Collectors will still want the first edition," she replied.

That from which the current printing plates have been made was obtained for me by Joan and Stan Rendell of Weston-super-Mare who picked it up in a jumble sale. They agreed to swap the copy for a box load of my other books which, I believe, went up into their loft.

Purbeck has been in my heart and mind since I first looked seaward with the eyes of a post-toddler and the uncertain beginnings of knowledge, from the sands of Bournemouth, across to the white shafts of Old Harry Rocks. Insight of an elementary sort came much later, at age eleven, and the hard-won access was a round trip of thirty-two miles on my bike. None of my friends would join me. The last I would ever ask was John Haig who lived in the best riverside bungalow at Northbourne. He alone among my contemporaries had parents who owned a slice of scenic England. Whatever his reason for declining, I had now learnt that most sensible people have normal interests and concerns, that would to me be be about as relaxing as living in a country under foreign occupation.

Commander Bowen of Corfe Castle was the first who caused me to reflect on the Purbeck factor when he observed that all its writers seemed to live elsewhere. "Property values," I replied. That is truer than ever; each move has forced me further inland.

Yet separation makes the attachment deeper. I experience a jump in my heart as I drive into Purbeck across the Wareham Causeway. There I find that loving planes can be as painful as loving people. Some of what hurts me you can see in the pictures to "Lulworth and Tyneham Revisited". I find it disturbing to open that book and route my trips to avoid reminders of particular cherished spots that have been destroyed. I wonder whether others are tormented to this extreme or if it is merely another of my abnormalities.

In Rosemary Leontas I found another of Purbeck's admiring outsiders who had come to terms with empathy for a landscape. Hers is a direct Purbeck descent, traced back through four centuries. So, too, is mine. My grandmother on my father's maternal side, Alice Kearley, was born at Stoborough in 1872. She taught in the old schoolhouse at Grange Gate. Her mother was Eliza Hardy, born in Wareham in 1829, who married John Kearley in 1850. It is blatant oneupmanship for a Dorset author to trace his roots to a cluster of Frome valley Hardys.

Rosemary found poetry to express the passion that I − these few words excepted − am as a male English native inherently conditioned to suppress. There is too much self that shows through a poem. I fudge the general presentation of my output through selective reflection on the achievements and tragedies of others.

Worshipping at Rosemary's "Purbeck shrine" has taken its toll mentally and left me with a body on its way to being as worked-out and exhausted as a vein of marble at Langton. It has many times returned sodden from Purbeck's weather which moves in the fast-lane, with quick successions from incredible clarity of landscape into daytime darkness preceding a big storm sweeping in from Weymouth Bay. "That magic touch of Purbeck which confounds," is how Rosemary explains, I think, a sense of frustration that life itself is not so clear-cut. One always comes home to a different reality.

The American television companies have converted world events into an armchair spectator sport. When I compiled the first version of these Purbeck ramblings, on the water returning from

The frog from Poole-born Thomas Bell's "History of British Reptiles" (1839). They are still quite common in Purbeck, as are toads, which unfortunately cannot be said of Dorset as a whole.

viii

Brownsea, which is a truly offshore part of the Isle of Purbeck, I returned in early 1986 to the most revolting report I have ever seen on television news. An Indian was shown slicing the legs off hundreds of frogs, on a circular saw, and tossing their bodies on one side to die, in order to provide a delicacy for Europeans. From that moment I have been a total vegetarian and have since shunned all meats and fish.

Purbeck is for me the obverse. The world here is worthwhile and it momentarily blinds me from a view that man is unworthy of his inheritance. If there were a god he would disinvent the human race. That is an expression of realism rather than pessimism as I delight in nice people of all ages and both sexes and strive for a proven theory of evolutionary meliorism of the sort believed in by Thomas Hardy. Unfortunately, as the Great War showed him, it is nonsense.

John Keats, too, was despairing of life when he unexpectedly put into Lulworth Cove for his last moments on English soil. The Purbeck magic broke through for a few hours as he controlled his mood and restrained the gloom to produce "Bright Star, would I were steadfast as thou art".

I used to regard both Purbeck and poetry as escapism but I cannot now see how we can have an escape from ourselves. Landscapes and words are as much part of the real world as the problems with people and the impossibility of reaching for the stars. The soul may be free but the body anchors it to positive discomforts. Yet we need our dreams to escape the vices that are for many the main dishes of life's menu.

Had I the means to give me the option of choosing somewhere to live from this potted selection of varied landscapes, I would still be dissatisfied. My softer moods are stimulated by the smell of peat and pine around Scotland Farm in the middle of the heath, but intellectually I need the austere grandeur of the coast. It was from a traditional cottage hearth that William Jeremiah Bower, better known as Billy Winspit, gave me tea in his ravine that opened on to the English Channel. I fear, however, that daily intimacy with either paradise would spoil the magic of Purbeck. You do not bring your bed into a place of worship.

R.L.

— written whilst coming back from
Brownsea Island in 1986; revised in 1988
while sitting on Black Hill, Bere Regis,
and looking south across the Frome
valley to a Purbeck where tanks
were at play.

ix

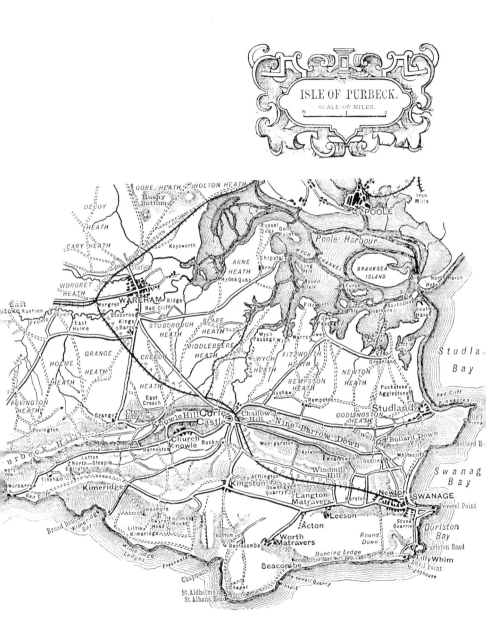

Map of Purbeck in late Victorian times with the "Swanage Railway in course of construction" (1883-85) and one or two spelling oddities, such as "Tineham" (Tyneham), "Kimeridge" (Kimmeridge), and "Bollard" (Ballard), though the author will later defend the latter as etymologically purer.

CHAPTER I

Inside The Borders

PURBECK ISLAND is some sixty square miles of England, its countryside as varied as any in these isles, and its name expressing a
feeling rather than a fact. The Isle of Purbeck is no island but the
inaccurate title is strangely apt in describing a land far different
from the countryside it abuts. Purbeck, correctly, is a peninsula;
the southeast corner of the mainland of Dorset.

Water is visible from most of the higher points of Purbeck.
Southward it is the misty distance of the English Channel where
waves merge with cloud. East are the sheltered waters of Swanage
and Studland bays, confused with the broader expanse of Poole
Bay, reaching across to the white rocks of the Needles, Isle of
Wight, where the horizon glints. To the north are the languid, silted,
salty reaches of a great harbour, statistically the world's second
largest.

From stretches of the twelve mile ridgeway across Purbeck, an
ancient grassy road along the hogs-back of the hills, all three sea-
scapes are visible. Each of these shores has a distinctive character
of its own. The other two boundaries of Purbeck are, in contrast,
nondescript. At high tide, the River Frome drifts into Poole Harbour at Swineham Point, but at low water its mouth is a mile
away across the harbour mudflats. Upstream the river twists
uneventfully through low, wide watermeadows.

Unworthy of being a boundary to anything is Purbeck's landward
flank, partly a tributary of the Frome called Luckford Lake, and
otherwise just sloping fields. Luckford Lake runs for little over a
mile as a reasonable stream before it mingles unnoticed with a
concourse of branches of the Frome at West Holme. Even its head
is disputable as the stream is a collection of smaller waters from
the ditches around ruined Whiteway Farm (below the west end of
the Purbeck ridge); from the road drains of East Lulworth; and a
trickle in Monkton Bushes, near the site of the recently demolished
sixteenth century Woodstreet Farm at Wool, which joins a ditch
from Coombe Lots. The only impressive source is the overflow
from The Lake, an expanse of water hidden in a plantation behind
Home Farm between East Lulworth and Coombe Keynes.

It is clear that no one took these 'lakes' seriously (the word is Old English: *lacu* 'watercourse') as they are only partially used for parish boundaries. Luckford Lake is simply an arbitrary border for Purbeck, and it even fails to cut clearly from north to south as the hilly spine of Purbeck thrusts decisively upwards across its path. On the other hand there is a positive and noticeable western limit of Purbeck as the landscape changes with the geology.

Purbeck really ends where the sands and clays of the Great Heath give way to the gently rising masses of chalk on a wavy line from the sea at Arish Mell, East Lulworth, and northward. A belt of woods lies where the soils mix and their names show how well popular etymology can describe the countryside—Long Coppice, Highwood (East Stoke parish); Monkton Bushes, Pepperclose Trees, Knap Coppice, Haremere Wood (Wool); Vicarage Coppice, Bramble Coppice, Eweyards Coppice, Kick Hill Coppice, Vary Clump, Ashy Drove, Duckpond Plantation, Kennel Wood, Lake Hill Plantation (Coombe Keynes); Gore Holmes, Seven Acre Withy Bed, Lodge Wood, New Barn Plantation, Bowling Green Wood, Botany Wood, Broom's Plantation, Marl Plantation and Maiden Plantation (East Lulworth).

The south coast of Purbeck starts at a small bay, Arish Mell, at the centre of a much wider bay and where the sea has found a path inland by eroding the chalky gap between Bindon Hill on the west and Rings Hill rising sharply to the east. Sadly, Arish Mell is completely out of bounds, being deep inside Royal Armoured Corps training ranges that were extended into Purbeck during the last war. Only a mile inland from Arish Mell, northward up the valley, stands amid trees the shapely grey mass of Lulworth Castle, impressive in silhouette, but with emptiness behind its walls. Built about 1609, and gutted by the fire of a single night in 1929, the castle is as dead as its history. Despite its appearance, Lulworth Castle was simply a grand house, built to symbolise strength but without any military applications whatever.

East Lulworth's thatched cottages, lying on the edge of the castle grounds, are all that have survived the devastation of this locality. Elsewhere the people have gone and tanks and fire have reduced their homes to shells or less. The strange appeal of depopulation is to watch farmlands deteriorate into a wilderness restocked by wildlife. Above Tyneham the buzzard soars daily in widening circles: it is one of the few places in Dorset where I saw this uncommon bird of prey maintain a continuous presence through the sparse years until the present day when its numbers are increasing dramatically.

On Whiteway Hill, whilst driving into Purbeck from Lulworth, it is often possible to count a dozen kestrels hovering in the wind above the overgrown escarpment and plunging frequently on to their plentiful prey. Roe deer, now common in woods throughout Dorset, have brought movement to Rook Grove and Tyneham Great Wood at the heart of a deserted parish. Wild land around Tyneham was created at the cost of people's homes, and yet it is possible to take some pleasure from the result. Natural habitats have recreated themselves in contrast to the diminution of such areas in countryside that is farmed properly.

A line of red flags extends from Charnel at the west end of Kimmeridge Bay and inland across the saddleback of the Purbeck Hills. It continues west of Creech Grange and over heathland to Holme Lane, the road from Stoborough that follows higher ground above the Frome meadows to East Stoke. This road, second of the road exits from Purbeck (the first drops into East Lulworth) is now tarred but it is remembered by older people as a rough track through fords and water splashes and between clumps of rhododendrons, firs and hazel thickets.

At West Holme another road runs north to cross the Frome by two bridges at Holmebridge. The oldest is largely mediaeval, with a modern brick parapet, and the recent takes the weight of military traffic. For practical purposes the Ministry of Defence land (the Lulworth and East Holme tank gunnery ranges cover about 7,200 acres) is the impenetrable western boundary of Purbeck. It is an effective border, spiked by only two public roads, and one of these is often closed.

The third and last road out of Purbeck is its main gateway, the A351 route through Wareham and across the Frome by the South Bridge. Until 1926 the river was spanned by one of the finest Dorset bridges, a narrow and ancient Purbeck stone affair with a noticeable hump, cut-waters and five graceful arches. The decision to demolish this historic bridge may have been generally welcomed but one professional man was concerned about the replacement. He was once the bridge engineer for the state highways of Virginia and is now retired in Louisiana. A native of Purbeck, he offered to design the new bridge, at no cost to the council, and made his offer through Gerald Bond MP.

His suggestion was declined and the new South Bridge arose tastelessly, though in full accord with the cultural barrenness of the twenties, and has a wide reinforced concrete main-span with two side arches, dressed white with paint that flakes into the water below. When the foundations of the old bridge were reached, workmen found the formation material of an earlier bridge, dating

3

probably from the eleventh century. In 1788 the bridge had been rebuilt at a cost of £2,932 and survived 150 years in its reconstructed state. The old grey stone, reused throughout the history of the bridge, was finally carted up to Trigon (on the River Piddle above Wareham) for housebuilding. A stone over a doorway to the garage at Trigon is inscribed: "This Bridge rebuilt 1788".

One writer of the twenties, Donald Maxwell, wanted to express his disgust at this destruction of "a priceless relic of old Dorset" but the laws of libel protected the guilty and he had to put his indignation in this way: "what I do say is that they [the local authorities] are a lot of dunderheaded, unimaginative, stupid, short-sighted jacks-in-office who, if they had a little more brains, would be half-witted—and that the people of Wareham have the government they deserve".

As late as 1800, Wareham was far from being a dependable gateway to Purbeck. The Frome filled with winter rain and by January it swamped the meadows. Flat-bottomed boats were used to reach Stoborough until the hard frosts came, and South Bridge was then a ferry point for sledges that ventured out across the wide table of steel-grey ice. Neither, at that time, was there a causeway through the Piddle flood plain on the other side of the town and the same makeshift transport had to be used to reach Northport where the railway station now stands.

It is significant that Purbeck—both originally in its role as a stone quarry for London and now as one of the major small tourist areas in England—has always endured poor communications with the outside world. Had the outlets been improved, its stone trade could have been on a greater scale, and the tourists would now come in still larger numbers if they were not faced with bottlenecks on the roads and a coast refusing to absorb them because it can only be reached by road at a handful of points. Just as some landowners resisted the expansion of the quarrylands, and at Kingston succeeded, there has been the same latent tendency to keep the holidaymaker away, especially from the main attraction, the sea.

Purbeck remained isolated throughout the period when the rest of Dorset was being opened up. Late in the eighteenth century, even Wareham would have seemed like foreign parts. An old soldier living at Swanage, Jos Rawles, became Purbeck's first postman. His job was to connect Swanage with the main mail network that passed through Wareham. Each Monday, Wednesday and Friday he walked from Swanage to Wareham and called at Kingston and Corfe Castle. On Tuesday, Thursday and Saturday he walked the other way. Mailbags were carried on each journey and letters and papers had to be collected and delivered on the way. The average was twenty-five items of post each day. Jos Rawles took his job seriously and walked with a pair of loaded pistols slung at his side. Later the horse was an innovation for the postman of 1800 who could then travel to Wareham and back each day. William Masters drove the first mail cart in the 1820s and did extra business by carrying passengers as well. By 1848 the number of items of mail reached a daily average of thirty, but the real stride forward came in 1850, after establishment of the penny post, when a mail coach joined the service. Regular departure and arrival times were maintained—it left Swanage at nine a.m. and was back by three p.m. The next change was the introduction of a coach-and-four, operating from the Red Lion at Wareham, to replace the first mail coach.

Before the mail service acquired a cart, Wareham and the outside world could be reached only on foot. The single form of public transport was owned by the Anchor Inn at Swanage and consisted of a gig-and-fly. Two horses were provided, together with the driver in leather and red coat, at the then colossal price of thirty shillings for a ride to Wareham. As the Anchor Inn also provided the first bathing machine, it had a motive in making it possible for visitors to come to the seaside. Everything was done in style and only those in the 'right class' could afford to pay for the one horse, a man, and a nurse that were needed—under the early rules—to make the bathing machine operational. Watering in Swanage during the early last century can only be compared with taking a world cruise today.

There used to be a yearly visit from six Bristol ruddle men with their donkeys and sacks of 'redding'. The red ochre they brought was used for marking sheep. Other visitors to Swanage were marine store dealers who came with china and other goods and left with iron, rags and bones. These dealers had dog carts, about three feet long, two feet wide and a foot deep, hauled by two or three bulldogs. William Masters Hardy remembered: "I have seen the carts overloaded and the dogs compelled to claw themselves uphill, with mouths wide open, tongues hanging out, panting like harts in the chase, and bodies nearly touching the ground."

Those dogs were British bulldogs of the old breed, fine specimens of the days before the animals were deformed according to the rules of breeding that have produced the present hideous malfunctioning creatures which carry a pedigree and win praise at shows. Today's fat, debased bulldogs would die under the strain of a dogcart and are lucky that Parliament outlawed the things in 1854.

It was the railway that brought the world to Swanage. The return ticket from Wareham to Swanage was 1s. 6d. and the fare was reduced to elevenpence in summer and on market days. All mail was taken out of Purbeck by train and Edwardian Swanage had sixteen postal workers handling a weekly total of 21,294 letters and parcels. The organisation moved in 1908 from its original home in the High Street to a new post office near the railway station. With the railway came the masses too, though Swanage regarded them as the respectable cream of quiet society, tasting the delights of the late developer on the Victorian coastal scene. Day trippers from Bournemouth were even a problem then, and were largely brought by paddle steamer. The main run was made by the *Lord Elgin* in 1881 and for more than thirty years it thrived. Minor summer services brought holidaymakers from elsewhere into Purbeck. From Poole, the *Telegraph* plied to Sandbanks and Swanage for a sixpenny fare.

Summer 1880 was when the steamer really discovered Swanage. It was the year that saw the opening of a new pier at Bournemouth and it was from there that most of the visitors came. *Heather Bell* had been the pioneer steamer in May 1871. Then *Lothair* took on the route between Swanage and Poole, with up to four journeys weekly, but 1880 was the season she was sold and left for the shores of Greece. *Telegraph* continued to run and came on Mondays and Thursdays. *Sunshine* arrived in March that year and brought sixty passengers, most of them bound for Corfe Castle. Later in the season there were protests of Sabbath-breaking by Sunday excursions and she gave up and returned to Liverpool. In June the Bournemouth Steam Packet Company introduced a new steamer, the *Carham,* to the Swanage route. *Princess* started to call whilst en route between Weymouth and the Isle of Wight. Lastly, there was *Florence*. She, alone, anchored at Swanage pier each night and was regarded as the town's own steamer.

In August it was reported from Swanage that "several hundreds are daily carried to Bournemouth or the Isle of Wight" but with winter coming the excursions ceased and the town felt its previous isolation. Deep snow in January 1881 prevented waggons loaded with flour arriving from Wareham, and Swanage was cut off for several days. An easterly gale tore planks from the pier and it was not until the wind changed direction that the *Telegraph* slipped into the bay and relieved the town.

The winters of 1880 and 1881 were long remembered. In the first, the bay at Swanage "was frozen over to such an extent that it was impossible to go out with boats. This has not occurred previously in the memory of the oldest person living". The following January brought a high snowfall and the news came from the north of the harbour that two children from Morden had died in a snowdrift whilst attempting to walk to school at Hamworthy.

In this century, Purbeck has lost much of its remoteness and become one of the heaviest visited areas in southern England. Most of the visitors, however, do not stay in Purbeck for their holiday, but are based in the larger centres outside, like Bournemouth and Weymouth. Purbeck has never developed into more than a satellite attraction of the Bournemouth conurbation, comparable with the New Forest as an ideal retreat for sunny days. In July and August the A351 main road from Wareham to Corfe Castle can be blocked for a couple of miles by bumper-to-bumper cars.

This lack of proper communications hinders any possibility of reintroducing some limited industrialisation in the future, or to revive the stone trade. It was the making of the Wareham to Swanage turnpike that gave Purbeck an adequate lifeline for the first time: but it is now choked by the volume of modern leisure traffic. The road through Corfe Castle is so constricted that the utilisation of the rail cutting for a by-pass through the narrow gap in the hills would be met with relief. But more foresighted would be a plan to cut a short road tunnel under the chalk ridge.

Corfe, however, is not the only part of Purbeck with a desperate communications problem. Though the existence of the Sandbanks chain ferry—the floating bridge for cars—since 1926 has prevented a remote rural backwater being left around Studland and Swanage, it now makes a limited contribution towards easing the traffic problem. Because the one ferry is operating at maximum traffic flow during the summer, there can be no expansion on this route. The fact that there is a toll is bound to cause some reluctance in using the ferry. More disheartening is the prospect that the ferry, although a direct link, will entail joining a queue of waiting cars at the water's edge.

There was once a plan to build a bridge across the mouth of Poole Harbour, from Sandbanks to Shell Bay, and had this taken place the whole development of Swanage would have been different. Had the town been brought within fifteen minutes driving time from Bournemouth the pressure for expansion would have been tremendous. It is fortunate for the character of Purbeck that the bridge was never built. The poor road connections guarantee the

7

region an artificial isolation from the full onslaught of the mechanised age.

One improvement deep inside the Purbeck road system which I would strongly advocate is the construction of a minor road across the island (from west to east) to allow local traffic to move about the countryside without involving itself in the Corfe Castle bottleneck. At present, all the roads from east to west across Purbeck pass through Corfe and add unnecessarily to its troubles. My suggestion is that a little known county road, running from Kingston to Smedmore Hill above Kimmeridge, should be tarred for the first time and turned from a rough stony track into a usable road for cars. This would open up a direct and impressive coastal route from Swanage to Lulworth, and involve no compulsory purchase orders as it would be simply an improvement of an existing public road. Furthermore, tarring the road would only be carrying out what was intended in the 1930s for the benefit of the motor car, but because of the shortage of money, it never took place. The term 'county road' is used for a highway that is "maintainable at the public expense".

For me, the quintessential appeal of Purbeck is a vague and inexpressible one, a feeling that its scenic variety and capability of producing so many surprises is unique for such a small area of country. Purbeck has inspired in me an impression of knowing and belonging that I have not found elsewhere. The land that I crossed in the day even drew me back once, by an evening steam train to Corfe, to walk westward along the ridge. I tramped to Kimmeridge on that dark, foggy and then frosty night to walk along the entire length of the cliffs to Studland—to pass immediately below a blaring foghorn at Anvil Point, and with the other lights of Portland Bill, Shambles ship and the Needles revolving low white beams across the waters as the cloud lifted a little. At dawn I was on Godlingston Hill where I heard my first cuckoo of the year, it was the third day of April, from somewhere down near Tom Burnham's Oak. Lambs were suckling noisily all around and I trod painfully on towards Corfe with half-a-shoe below me and skylarks persistently in front and above. At Corfe I fell asleep at the cross in the Square that commemorates Queen Victoria's diamond jubilee. The whole event was a performance I have not repeated, and if I did so again it would be spoilt by a fear of impending arrest, either for violating darkness on the seafront at Swanage or for some crime of loitering beside that cross.

CHAPTER II

An Age Of Marble

THE WORKING of Purbeck marble is an extinct and forgotten industry —yet its volume of production throughout the centuries of religious building is incalculable, and for every piece of polished marble surviving today in cold church architecture, there must have been another two bits that were smashed during the plundering after Henry VIII rid himself of the monasteries and dissolved God's earthly riches. Art and beauty carved in Purbeck marble continue to adorn the finest churches of England and show the extent that this, the primary Dorset industry, spread across the country. It was even used over the seas in Dublin and Normandy. Not that it is marble at all − Purbeck "marble" is a polishable fossilly limestone.

Marble working in Purbeck had a forceful Roman beginning, lapsed in the dark ages, and was revived in the frenzy of post-Norman England when the gloss was laid upon religion by the erection of the greatest churches ever built. The industry of Purbeck Island started again in the twelfth century when most of the first stone was carved into fonts, many of which are tucked away in country churches between Devon and Sussex and a dozen are still used in Dorset. Some marble was also shaped for altar tables.

The shape of the future was in monumental effigies, an immodest practice that soon became popular with the ecclesiastical hierarchy and knighted classes. The earliest marble effigies have survived inside Dorset, and these include Philip, a priest who died early in the twelfth century, who lies at Tolpuddle, and another marble figure—though less of him remains—the Abbot Clement, died 1163, at Sherborne Abbey. Earlier still, however, is Leofric, founder of the see of Exeter, who died in 1072, though his effigy was cut in the next century. He is carved in low relief and is the best preserved of the early figures. Two other marble effigies of this time are at Salisbury Cathedral (1186) and in the porch of Abbotsbury church. Each of these five examples is more than a simple incised slab, but they lack the shapely, full-bodied carving of the style developed in the following century.

Gothic churches brought marble into vogue for slender, polished shafts set in clusters, and the new phase of architecture flowered suddenly at Lincoln—torn by an earthquake in 1185—where vast quantities of Purbeck marble were used in the rebuilding. There had been an earlier, lesser experiment at Canterbury in 1174, and the outcome was the acclaim of the planners; decorative shafts rose in marble at Chichester, York, Worcester, Ely, Wells, Exeter, Winchester, London's Temple church and numerous other centres. Greater still was the growth of Salisbury Cathedral between 1220 and 1258 to reach the finest peak in Early English style and consume masses of Purbeck in the process.

Salisbury is only equal, rightly enough, to Westminster Abbey which was reborn out of the desire of Henry III and by 1269 had led to the establishment of an elitist colony of master marblers firmly in the heart of London. Many of these craftsmen had come from the quarries and workshops south of Corfe Castle and their jobs in London were a mark of complete royal acceptance; it gave Purbeck industry a place inside the closed-shop of building trades, a bandwagon that floated profitably on the waves of religious enthusiasm. With a footing in London, and major contracts in other cities, the marblers could travel to work at country churches and monastic houses throughout the provinces.

It is fitting that the earliest royal effigy in England, that of King John at Worcester, should have been carved in Purbeck marble about 1240. But though our marble had a part in the making of the tombs of virtually every member of the Plantagenet line, this is the only royal figure carved out of the material. At the lower end of the scale, the staple trade of the marble industry was in coffin lids. Business boomed as the big churches blossomed, with their requirements of thousands of tons of carved marble, but in the lull between building projects there was always a market for coffin tops. These were flat sheets of marble, broad at the top and tapering towards the foot, often with a plain polished surface or otherwise with a cross inscribed, and with carved edges. Perhaps some seven thousand coffin lids passed through Corfe and were carried by cart across the heath to Ower Quay and shipment out across Poole Harbour.

Throughout the mediaeval period, brasses were another common form of memorial in churches. These were always set in a stone slab, and the most favoured stone, yet again, was Purbeck marble. Considering the numbers that exist, and allowing for the proportion of such slabs that have disappeared, it is likely that the total Purbeck production in this line amounted to over ten thousand items.

Effigies became increasingly popular after the twelfth century and the Purbeck marblers led this field and set the fashion for others to follow. The output can be measured in dozens, and four of the finest military examples were the knights of Purbeck marble in Temple church, all badly damaged by fire in the blitz. These figures are shown in chain mail, and as with a few other effigies, were originally covered in painted colours and gold.

More examples remain of bishops and abbots, looking frail and pious, holding the staff of a crozier in the left hand whilst blessing the onlooker with the right. There are even a few ladies carved in marble, all of them from the thirteenth century, and the finest lies in Romsey Abbey, with the folds of her drapery flowing across her body, and the entire sculpture sublimely smooth and delicate, as if it had come from a mould rather than a block of hard stone. Abbots were generally unlucky, if they sought immortality, as their monuments fell during the collapse of the religious estates wrung by Henry VIII, and the Abbotsbury specimen was not rescued from the ground till centuries afterwards.

Shaftesbury is a typical abbey amongst those that suffered most, and today hilltop rockeries and flower beds are laid between the crumbling foundations of a great church. The abbey ruins became an open quarry for the town but in the heaps of rubble that survive there are still plenty of carved marble capitals and bases. More Purbeck marble fell later in the Great Fire of 1666, the greatest loss being Grey Friars in the city of London, one of the most magnificent of British churches and today a post office yard. Other grand churches, on the whole, have survived better than the mediaeval houses and castles, where there was a domestic use for the stone in great halls and windows.

Purbeck marble stood above its competitors until the fifteenth century when it was finally replaced by alabaster, though marble continued to be produced occasionally, mainly for local use in Dorset. Decline had come over many years as the choice, larger pieces of marble were taken from the quarries and only second-rate material remained. There was no longer the demand for thousands of tons to build towering shafts for abbeys and cathedrals; instead there was only the old line in effigies and for this the poorer stone could not be used, neither could the plentiful smaller pieces. A large, perfect, block was necessary for each effigy and the single thin vein of marble rippling across the Purbeck hillsides was only between eighteen inches and two feet in thickness. This accounts for the noticeable flatness of all Purbeck figures: it was a quality stone but with no scope for fancy adornments, or even big chested subjects.

Marble in Purbeck is confined to a wafer-thin outcrop running continuously along the middle of the northern slope of the limestone hills, from sea to sea, between Peveril Point in the east—where the exposed bed runs out into the waves—and the strangely conical Worbarrow Tout in the west. Choice of marble was restricted, the preference being for the reddish and most durable stone, found towards Swanage, as this weathers better than the blueish, less attractive, shelly marble found towards the Tyneham end of the outcrop. Even when good marble was found, and that of maximum thickness, it could only be worked easily on the surface; but as all Purbeck strata tilt downwards, it had to be followed underground and this was impossible for more than a few feet.

Alabaster offered a cheap, and easier carved substitute, brought from Nottingham and Derby, which took a growing proportion of the national market and caused a recession in Purbeck. Though the great industry had died, marble continued to be worked in small pockets until about 1700 and the redevelopment of the building stone trade at Swanage. In the hard times, business depended on the few sensitive rich who wanted their luxury work in something better, or different, from common alabaster. Even after all the quarries had closed, work could always resume when there was a customer willing to pay the price, as in 1842 when Woodyhyde was reopened to provide marble for restoration at Temple church.

A late episode in the long history of Purbeck marble occurred at the hamlet of Kingston, south of Corfe Castle. It was always a small place and is still counted as part of the 10,400 acre sprawl of Corfe parish. Its cottages, in prim terraces, date from its short-lived industrialisation at the end of the eighteenth century when philanthropist William Morton Pitt built a large rope and sail-making factory on the slope to the south of the old church at the east end of the village. It employed over 200, into the Napoleonic wars, but the bottom fell out of its market with the naval victory off Cape Trafalgar in 1805. John Scott, the first Earl of Eldon, son of a Newcastle coal trader, bought the Encombe estate in 1807.

On the east edge of the hamlet there was a chapel dating from the twelfth century. In 1833, Scott had it replaced by an uninspired and impoverished church of the Gothic revival. Its designer, G. S. Repton, used a little of the old masonry in the walls and rehung a bell, but otherwise only the position of the old chapel was perpetuated. Scott's interest in churches came late in life. One of his contemporaries, Cyrus Redding, wrote: "He had a sterile soul for all things earthly except money, doubts and the art of drawing briefs."

Church building, however, had become a family occupation and the third Earl of Eldon decided to give his village a second church. It is not clear why the first had proved insufficient, particularly as Kingston is one of the smallest Purbeck villages and would have found difficulty filling that—but another was to be built around the corner for £60,000. Perhaps the earl resented the cheapness of the edifice raised by his ancestor. Criticism was made at the time and included this comment by the City Press: "Lord Eldon is now spending an immense sum of money in erecting a church in a neighbourhood which, although it may be hereafter, is not at the present time actually overrun by human beings. If his lordship were to devote his attention to a railway for Corfe and Swanage he would vastly benefit the neighbourhood, and, it is needless to add, materially increase the value of his own property."

Whatever the reason for his whim, the earl did the job properly and hired George Street, a notable architect, as the designer. Street carried out his brief magnificently and gave Kingston a fine piece of revival architecture which successfully copied the style of the thirteenth century in many ways.

Stone and marble were used throughout and the building of Kingston's third church of Saint James gave the Purbeck quarrymen an easy job for seven years. Other work was dropped and most of the raw materials came from the old quarries at Blashenwell. Street's church was built during a recession in the stone trade but on balance it did not help the quarrymen because when work was finished in 1880 they found it impossible to renew normal business. While Kingston gives the appearance of being another quarrying village, it never was and missed out on the trade in the middle ages; there is still a lot of stone under the land around its neat houses.

Kingston may have been only a scapegoat for the difficulties of the stone trade in the 1880s. But just, or otherwise, the quarrymen's damning attitude towards it persisted. On the other hand, the Purbeck workers who visited Kingston left it with the greatest of the latter day examples of their craft.

Eastward from Kingston, turf and scrub now cover a succession of dips and mounds that stretch along the valley slope towards Swanage. At Dunshay, where the drive to the manor house winds through old marble workings, lived Alice de Briwere in 1219. She was the lady of the manor who contributed marble for twelve years towards the building of Salisbury Cathedral.

Afflington has now dwindled to a farmstead but in 1800 there was still a community of fifty people, and back at the height of its marble days, in 1270, Henry III granted a market and a fair. The remains of the mediaeval hamlet lie across ten acres of pasture to the east of Afflington Farm. Other lost settlements are at Lynch, Scoles, Quarr and Wilkswood in the valley south of Corfe. As well as marble, the mediaeval times saw immense quantities of building stone raised for the massive fortress of Corfe Castle, and the quarries also provided stone for the domestic buildings and churches of Purbeck and east Dorset. It is difficult to over-estimate the quantity of rough stone produced by the quarries as it was enormous and around Willwood, Quarr, Primrose Hill and Downshay Farm there are the earthworks left by some considerable extraction. Even the small settlements had their own local quarries nearby, like London Door Quarry a mile west of Kingston and the quarry beside the road on the hill above Kimmeridge. Stone for the building of Worth Matravers village came partly from the Old Quarry which lies on the north side of West Man, a short way from the track down the chine to Winspit. The quarrying of building stone and rubble in Purbeck during the middle ages is often completely overlooked because of the close attention given to marble and its more romantic uses. Stone tended to be used locally in Purbeck whereas the marble was invariably sent outside the Isle.

Surface workings and shallow quarries at Wilkswood are, some of them, among the most ancient workings in Dorset. Here the Romans worked marble, favouring the greyish-white variety, and used it to form a smart speckled background to the vermilion lettering in cinnabar. This style was widely used in Roman monumental inscriptions and such tablets of marble have been unearthed from Fordington in Dorset and as far afield as Chester, Chichester, Cirencester, London, Colchester and St. Albans. Another use of marble was for mortars, the stone withstanding hard grinding and pounding, and for panels and moulded decorations in important buildings—even, at Silchester, for large basins in the public baths. Roman marble workings in Purbeck appear to have flourished during two periods: from AD 43 to 200, and again between AD 350 and 400. Of all the many quarries opened for building stone in Roman Britain, the Purbeck sites were most specialised and existed solely for luxury purposes, which is why the trade thrived during times of extensive building and, later, had a second life during the country's economic revival. The Roman marble industry definitely had a working at Wilkswood but other possible sites, at Dunshay, Lynch, Blashenwell and Worbarrow Bay, are unconfirmed.

Geologically, Purbeck marble is a freshwater deposit, composed of the fossilised shells of the tiny *Viviparus*. Similar water snails still exist and are found in the deeper, sluggish, eastern rivers. Time and pressure changed the sediments of Purbeck into a smooth and compact crystalline limestone.

One single, distinguished slab of Purbeck marble in Dorset is at Sherborne Abbey, close to the entrance to the Lady Chapel, and stands nine feet high. This, like all of the marble, was hewn in a length roughly horizontal, though tilting out of the ground, and then shaped and polished. When brought to the church it was up-ended so that the natural grain now runs at right angles to the original plane on which it lay. It became a tall stone, and yet it is only about nine inches deep—this method was the only way in which the marble could be incorporated in high columns.

The greatest tribute to Purbeck marble is that it was considered to be the finest building stone, to be used for decoration inside the grandest architectural achievements. Little exterior work was attempted in marble, and though the reddish kind was better, other shades tended to flake when used on the outside of build-ings—as at Salisbury Cathedral and Westminster Abbey—but most facing stones also weather in time. The reason for Purbeck marble being restricted to internal use is that it is a decorative stone, al-ways highly expensive and limited in shape; a stone far too rare to be worked in quantity on the vast outsides of these churches.

Marble was brought from the quarries to Corfe on heavily laden sledges, hauled by horses, down deeply cut lanes from the hills to the valley. Such tracks, with thick hedgerows either side, over-hanging and meeting across the middle, can be followed, with diffi-culty, in the rough countryside south of Corfe Common. Burberry Lane, east of Blashenwell Farm, is one of the ancient marblers' routes. Another runs downhill from east of Afflington Barn to Woodyhyde. If you bend and untangle the brambles that get con-stantly in the way, it is possible to walk stooped underneath the canopy for a considerable distance. This, and all other old roads in these parts, heads eventually for West Street, Corfe Castle.

The old layout of the tracks came about because from the middle ages up to the making of the turnpike roads the main street at Corfe was West Street. This is now hard to believe as the old street is a deadend that disappears on to the common, where a track that heads for Blashenwell Farm and East Orchard is still a county road. The present major road through Corfe is East Street which takes the traffic from Wareham to Swanage—yet this was itself a backwater before coaching days. The bog at its south end had to be filled and the new road then continued across the common.

East Street became a by-pass to the principal part of the town, though virtually all fresh development occurred around it until, in turn, it became the new main street. Town's End, as it was called with meaning, became an area for expansion with two or three side streets. As new building retreated from the growing traffic, there was some danger of the common suffering, but it has come through unscathed and East Street's cottages still cease at Town's End, as they did in 1700.

If you walk along the now quiet West Street it is obvious that it was once the key road in the market town. For West Street is aligned directly on the castle gate, market place, and village square. It contains all the major buildings—Town Hall, Lock-up, Fox Inn, the old entrance to St. Edward's church, the ancient manor house, and Chaffey's where the leading stone merchant was based. All along West Street the old cottages huddle tightly and there are several ranges of dwellings. When the road reaches the common, it fans a dozen ways into southern **Purbeck.**

There is no evidence that any marble was carved on the quarry floor, but when it reached West Street there was a line of *bankers* waiting to receive the stone, and the whole street thronged with people employed in the trade. Much of the marble left Corfe unfashioned, though always in squared blocks, and some was partially carved. Other work, however, was carved and finished by the Corfe masons, including many of the effigies.

Documents prove that effigies were often sculptured at Corfe. In 1254, for example, the accounts of the Sheriff of Dorset record: "For carving a certain effigy of a Queen in marble stone, carrying it to Tarrant Crawford, and placing it there over the tomb of the Queen of Scotland, 100s." The friars of Mount Carmel in London were given a marble altar by King Henry III. It too had been made in Purbeck.

A bizarre incident happened in 1374 when some Poole men seized the ship *Margarete* of Wareham for use in an expedition against France. The keepers of the port of Poole received an order to release the forty-eight ton ship as she was loaded with two high tombs of marble for the Earl of Arundel and his wife Eleanor, together with "one great stone" for the Bishop of Winchester.

A little known fact is that the exploitation of Purbeck marble was one of England's first nationalised industries. The whole of Purbeck Island, with the great state fortress of Corfe Castle at its centre, was the King's hunting warren, and the quarries were crown property. A proportion of the revenues was passed to the considerable labour force who quarried stone, transported and worked on it; but a large amount must have gone to the royal purse. Others did have some rights, as with Alice de Briwere who gave marble for Salisbury Cathedral. Henry III himself financed the great work of enlarging Westminster Abbey and it is recorded several times that the surveyors purchased "the King's marble in Purbeck for the King's work at Westminster". It is obvious that Henry must have bought his own marble at cost price, paying only for the labour involved and the money needed to ship the heavy stone from Ower to London. Whoever the agents were who distributed Purbeck marble, they did a good job, as the material reached Ireland and the continent. The royal rake-off encouraged the patronage of marble, and the Westminster Abbey contracts meant a lot to the trade—at the height of this work in London, forty-nine marblers were employed and fifteen others to polish their work. The marblers from Purbeck had become some of the most sought-after craftsmen in Britain.

With so much work passing out of Corfe, it is to be expected that a little would remain in the village. Two carved panels, intended for tomb chests, are built into the walls of cottages in West Street, and in the church some mediaeval marble work has survived, including a hard reddish fifteenth century font. More important in showing the scale of the work done on marble in Corfe is the fact that for much of West Street, the road is built on a core of marble chippings several feet thick. This debris includes fragments of foliations and mouldings and other work that was fractured and discarded.

From Corfe the marble was carted the three miles across Rempstone Heath to Ower Quay, a wharf of timbers deserted today but with a few weathered blocks of marble left from the past. The Company of Marblers and Stonecutters of Purbeck has survived from these old days, and though they can no longer elect two wardens and two stewards to control Purbeck, they maintain other traditions. Their annual gathering and elections are held at the Town Hall, Corfe, on Shrove Tuesday and one custom is to kick a football to Ower. The ball is never touched by hand and is just trundled along. Finally, at Ower, it is kicked into the water and a pound of pepper sprinkled over it. The ancient custom preserves a memory that the once vital right-of-way was kept open by the payment of a peppercorn rent and a section of the track is known as Peppercorn Lane. This annual tradition has survived since the marblers' agreed in 1695 to pay John Collins of Ower a pound of pepper and a football but the practice may now be falling into disuse. In 1969, only one marbler arrived at Ower in the evening of Shrove Tuesday and he brought just the pound of pepper.

Ower had ceased to be a port when John Hutchins, the vicar of Wareham, was writing his county history: "Ower seems to have been formerly the chief port of the Isle of Purbeck, and it was the principal, if not the only, quay for the exportation of stone and marble. On this account the quarries pay on Ash-Wednesday yearly one pound of pepper and a football to the lord. The timber brought from the New Forest in Hampshire and used in the construction of Corfe Castle was landed here, and the remains of deep tracks and roads leading across the heath from Ower towards the town of Corfe Castle show that there must anciently have been considerable traffic carried on at this place. Since 1710 the exportation of stone has been neglected here, and that branch of the business removed to Swanage."

As Corfe Castle, the symbol of the Purbeck of old, was brought to ruins for losing the Civil War, the marble industry was also dying. Great churches were no longer being built and alabaster was chosen instead of marble for effigies of the dead. It is generally supposed that the stone industry moved to Swanage because Ower Bay had silted up. That is incorrect, but had it been the case there could have been a much easier move from Ower to Cleavel Point, only seven hundred yards away and directly on the South Deep, or to any other peninsula jutting into Poole Harbour.

The one reason for this change of location to the other side of Purbeck was that the high-class marble trade had died and in its place a new industry was founded to dig the building stone from the hills between Swanage, Langton Matravers and the cliffs. Marble and its former customers were gone, the workshops that carved effigies lay redundant at Corfe, and the basis of the new business was to export building stone in roughly cut blocks as directly as possible to the world outside. Swanage Bay lay below the scene of the new operations, and its sheltered shore had encompassed a fishing fleet for centuries—there was no competitor for the port of the revived stone trade. Swanage was the only choice.

A. Stone Cart
B. Stone lighter
C. Ketch

Loading Stone. Swanage, in 1875.

Thomas Hardy

CHAPTER III

The Great Stone Quarries

THE OLD men would have remembered it, but they be all dead. Their greatest stone quarry in the whole of the Isle of Purbeck was where you would today least expect to find one. Above the heart of Purbeck's holiday town, strung out above the High Street in a line for nearly a mile from Bon Accord Road westward to Belle Vue Farm at Herston are the vast disused workings of Swanage Townsend: the most intensively quarried part of all Purbeck it operated continuously from before 1700 to about 1905 when Cowlease was the last working. The creamish-yellow stone from this broad hillside long ago weathered to the familiar grey of Purbeck buildings, sometimes with a tinge of pink, and is one of the best known of British stones.

Although a quarry is normally an open pit, here was something quite different. Cowlease was only a small section of the workings but it was a full-scale stone mine with arms reaching 120 feet into the rock. These were the *lanes* and many were sunk in those two centuries of use. Each lane started with a *slide*—a steeply inclined shaft—and was a production line with carts taking fine limestone from passages that branched at various levels to the working faces on the *roach, thornback, cinder* (a bed of fossil oysters), *downs vein,* and *new vein.* Each deposit of clay or loose material parting the stone beds was known as a *shiver* or just plain *dirt.* The remains of at least twenty other abandoned shafts can be seen in other parts of the three hundred acres of the Townsend quarries. This method of working started about 1700 and was adapted in the year 1800. One of the first chain cables was then made by William Coombs, a blacksmith at Court Hill, Swanage, and used by quarrymen who found it far stronger than a rope. The mine shafts were called slides because they were originally at a low angle to the ground and the first carts had no wheels and were simple sledges. With the introduction of cables the mine shafts became steeper.

Though it caused draughts, the passages from two quarry lanes would occasionally connect together, making it possible to go down one shaft and surface at another hole. Underground, the ceiling was often only three feet high, though six feet was the ideal working height, and conditions were always clayey and damp. Good, hard stone had to be built up in pillars to hold the quarry roof—had a section of the earth been simply left, it would have crumbled under the weight and given way. With seams being worked at several levels, the *legs* had to be solid and strong to prevent *founders*.

There were times when pieces of Swanage fell through a quarry roof. In about 1895 the western house of Alexandra Terrace collapsed into an eastern lane from the Cowlease. But, generally, the workmanship of the old men is still standing surprisingly well and the quarry legs, even as they powder, hold parts of residential Swanage proudly in the sunlight. The spreading Townsend housing estate has covered the lower edge of the quarrylands and elsewhere it is blackthorn and brambles that obscure the openings to the slides. Ivy smothers old work huts and everywhere are the *scar-heaps* of overburden and *spawls*.

These mounds and craters cover the entire hillside rising above the southern side of Swanage. The larger hillocks mark the continuous surface workings and even at the top of the ridge you can look across to further pits beyond California Farm. Even to the west of the Townsend quarries—either side of the Priest's Way and the seemingly normal fields beyond the Swanage parish boundary at Verney Farm and to South Barn, and then along the track beside Leeson Park—most of this slope is undermined and the openings of fifteen shafts are still visible.

Above the High Street from Chapel Lane to Bell Street, the town's tentacles of bungalow development have moved up the hill, but a wasteland lies above. Because of the danger from old workings caving in, planning permission has been consistently refused for any building further up the hillside. This has been to the town's advantage as a natural, if pockmarked, skyline can be seen to the south of Swanage and it is better to look up at a green hill than watch buildings clamber over to the next obstacle. The view in reverse, from any part of the slopes, overlooks the entire Swanage valley with the town distended from right to left, strung out along the High Street from the shore to Herston.

It is hard to visualise this as the heart of a great industry. All of the workings are abandoned and the grass-grown spoil heaps that heave everywhere seem tossed imperceptibly together, and each dip is filled with dense clumps of thorn, bramble and elder. All the shafts have been partially or completely filled and the biggest hole that remains is a few yards from the bungalows, a short distance southeast of the end of Hillside Road and just east of the old stone wall that is now the boundary of Swanage urban council's caravan site.

This shaft is thirty feet wide and twenty feet deep with three sheer sides of the natural rock reinforced with drystone walling: a pit in which the body of a discarded car looks quite small. From the fourth side, the north, a wide and steep shaft rises from the bottom. A few feet northward from its head stands a perfectly preserved capstan with its stones complete but the wooden parts, as would be expected, have rotted away.

Around these historic stones, and hiding them from attention, is a thick clump of bushes. It was only after two days of searching, and when winter had lessened the screen, that I found this relic. A century ago, chains from its horse-operated hub were raising stone by the ton, but it is now the only remaining capstan in Purbeck. Nearby are the walls of quarry sheds, called *quarr houses,* and the two *crabstones* that supported a smaller capstan drum. All this, however, is little enough to see on the actual site of a great industry and Swanage council should be encouraged to preserve the Cowlease and its antiquities as a public open space.

In the other parts of the hillside there is less of interest, apart from the views, and a second shaft lying west of the spur off Manwell Road and a short distance beyond the buildings. This is a more delicate example of stone mine architecture with the hole having a diameter of twelve feet, its edges carefully rounded and the usual slanting shaft, seven feet six inches wide, projecting outward to the north where the hillside gradually falls away. The top fifteen feet of the shaft can still be seen and the rest is filled with earth and rubbish. Its walls are vertical, built upon the bedrock about ten feet below ground level and in a style similar to the drystone walls of Purbeck fields. The first stones were laid upright all round the shaft, except the slide part, and each stone is about twenty inches high and four inches across. On this line, smaller horizontal walling stones, roughly uniform in size, were placed carefully in level layers. The mine entrance is overhung by thick ivy and adjoined by the foundations of small square sheds.

It is timely to make this plea for the retention of the last capstan and its working as the whole of the Townsend quarrylands are facing a future of quick change—some of the area has been dug out by opencast methods; other parts have been levelled and covered with soil and refuse; one place conceals a caravan camp.

The picture was very different as recently as 1900 when a few lanes were still in use and blocks were tied to low, sturdy carts of elm and hauled by chains to the head of the shaft. Each lane then had its capstan, with a horse providing the power to pull a wooden bar which gave the leverage to turn the drum of the capstan. The bar was called a *spack* and required the horse or mule to plod endlessly along a circular towpath.

The Townsend quarries had the deepest lanes in Purbeck, the largest capstans and the longest spacks. For two hundred years it was the biggest production centre of stone in Purbeck and yet its situation came through simple convenience. Standing above the bay, at the back of Peveril and Durlston, the Cowlease and the other lanes were only yards from Old Swanage and its labour force of quarrymen. Here was the nearest place where stone could be lifted from the ground in workable quantities and they have left the most exhausted ground on the Purbeck limestone.

Lowest of the Purbeck seams to be dug was the *caps* and *new vein,* these two layers being separated by some dirt. At Swanage the caps has been greatly dug and this is the mark of an old quarrying area. The old men, when they worked the Townsend, reached all the seams of usable rock: while to the west at Langton Matravers, Acton and Gallows Gore it was exceptional for even two seams to be worked.

Throughout the eighteenth century the stone trade was concentrated at Swanage. Only when business became a struggle, with the danger of over-working the Swanage quarries, did the trade spread west to Langton. Ample stone was found under the new fields and within twenty feet of the surface. There was no longer the need to grope through twelve feet of useless *cinder* in the bowels of the earth to touch the caps. Langton men were busy enough with free stone and downs vein, and it was in just one place that they ventured to find the real hard stuff below. One of the most scarred hills, near the quarrymen's settlement of Acton, was called Mount Misery and it overlooked a greener rise in Langton— the latter is still known as Mount Pleasant.

Dr. C. le Neve Foster, inspector of mines for the west of England, carried out a postal survey of the Swanage and Langton quarrylands and reported in 1878:

> The Purbeck stone is a new feature of my statistics. In spite of a great many difficulties, I believe I have at last attained a fairly correct statement of the total amount raised from mines. There are nearly a hundred stone mines in the Swanage district, worked by one, two, or three men underground, who are in many cases the owners as well as the occupiers. Their work is often most irregular; if the men can find work as masons they abandon their quarries for a time, and do not return to them till other work is slack. As the quarrymen of the Isle of Purbeck have never been troubled

with Government forms till this year I had considerable difficulty in getting returns from them. Endless mistakes were made, requiring investigation by correspondence, and I may safely say that the ninety-two stone mines near Swanage, employing only 264 persons, gave me more trouble than all the other mines of my district put together. No doubt I shall have much less inconvenience in future years, as the men will soon get into the way of filling up the returns correctly. The following figures represent the number of tons raised during the past year [1877]: Purbeck stone and marble, dressed—11,816 tons 10 cwt. Purbeck stone, undressed—1,411 tons 10 cwt.

The creation of these quarries came about after 1650 when the mediaeval basis and traditions of the old Purbeck stone and marble trade were finally shattered. Corfe Castle, its castle in ruins, ceased to be its workshop and distribution centre. The ancient track to Ower Quay was abandoned and the trade no longer looked to Poole Harbour as its natural outlet. Instead the first major mines were sunk above the bay at Swanage and cliff quarries started within the next century at Durlston, Tilly Whim and Winspit. By the nineteenth century the coastal quarries extended to Dancing Ledge, Hedbury and Seacombe. The scale of the new operations was vast in comparison with the old and nearly 50,000 tons were shipped from Swanage in some years.

Swanage had been a town for centuries. Today it appears as a Victorian and Edwardian creation, looking rather tired in middle age, and this is true enough but the modern Swanage was only achieved between 1850 and 1940 by an unco-ordinated but systematic programme of destruction which removed most signs of both senility and charm. The result is a town dated by various periods and carrying a strong but tarnished Victorian gloss.

The town has much older roots and a defence map of the reign of Henry VIII shows Swanage, like Wareham, a major Dorset coastal town. In the same reign, the historian John Leland wrote: "From the mouth of Poole Haven, upon the shore by the southwest, is, in a bay about thirteen miles off, is, a fisher town called Sandwich and there is a peere and a little fresh water."

By the 1600s, a single narrow road, the High Street, wandered away from the shore—above a creek which had silted into a bog and is now completely gone—and for a mile was choked with houses. Here and there an odd building or two lay in the fields beyond. Most disappeared in the conversion to a seaside resort but a good cluster of the old survives around the parish church and mill pond. Yet the pond itself is of more historically recent make, being created around a spring in 1754 and later enlarged.

The first census, taken in 1801, records Swanage as a town of three hundred houses and a population of 1,382. Corfe, on the other hand, was then only half the size with 741 people living in 152 houses. Wareham, like Swanage, managed well over a thousand inhabitants and had 1,627 people in 381 homes. Villages like Studland, Stoborough and Kimmeridge each had about fifty cottages. The Swanage population had reached 2,100 by the 1871 census.

The typical Swanage cottage was small and low. Measuring the outside, it had a size of twenty-five feet by eighteen feet with one large room on the ground floor. Rough stone slabs covered the floor—which was often damp. At one side of the room was a pantry, and at the opposite end a large open inglenook fireplace was used for smoking bacon and had a large brick on the left and a staircase, or sometimes only a ladder, on the right. This led up into the bedroom which was partitioned into two rooms. The ceiling was only six feet high at the level part in the centre and considerably less where it sloped.

Four such cottages stood at the site of the Town Hall which was built between 1881 and 1883. There the ground fell away to the creek and the only doors to the cottages were at the back. The front bedroom windows were on a level with the High Street and people could look in; the cottages themselves extended three feet into the road. Between two of the cottages was a narrow passage called The Drong. Facing these were three old cottages on the other side of the road, demolished in 1959. Somewhat similar was another row of High Street cottages, one of which received John Wesley on his first preaching visit to Swanage in 1787. Only Wesley's Cottage survived and was shrouded by a luxuriant garden until it was blasted by a bomb in the Second World War and then pulled down.

Even in the far-off summers of the old stone trade it was no straightforward task getting worked loads of cut stone from the Townsend quarries to ships standing offshore. The blocks could be handled five times before they were sailing towards the customer. Old Swanage was a quarryman's town and the stone came down the cart tracks to the quarry entrance at Cowlease and was then hauled along the High Street, and through the close-packed lines of cottages at The Narrows to the stacks of stone, called *bankers*, by the shore.

One of the carters from the quarries was injured in an accident in October 1881. The Dorset County Chronicle reported:

> Last week as Mr. Grant's carter, named Pitcher, was coming down the hill from the quarries with three horses and a waggon and about four tons of stone, the tackle for tying up the hind wheel

broke and, the weight forcing on the waggon, the carter was knocked down, and the wheels going over both legs broke them. Fortunately the shafts of the waggon striking against the side wall checked and stopped it, or some of the horses might have been killed. The poor carter, in great suffering, is, we hear, progressing but slowly, though, we hope, favourably, under the care and treatment of Dr. G. C. Delamotte. We regret to hear Pitcher is not in any friendly society.

"The poor carter Pitcher" died two weeks later when "lockjaw set in".

The nineteenth century visitors to Swanage avoided the streets where these stone waggons raised clouds of white, choking dust throughout the best days of summer. Ruts were inches deep and in winter the streets became impassable quagmires of yellow clay. Horses hauled the carts to the quay where each load joined the vast piles of stone and was often later reworked. Sixty loads a day, each of about three tons, came to the water's edge. Many of the bankers stood ten feet high and these giant stacks of stone took up a wide part of the sea front and stretched around the southeast of the town from the Royal Victoria Hotel along to the White House.

C. E. Robinson described the bankers in his book published in 1882, "A Royal Warren: Picturesque Rambles in the Isle of Purbeck". His foresight was lacking somewhat for although the bankers have vanished they were replaced by bricks and mortar and not the seafront pleasure gardens that he visualised. Swanage in the early 1880s was still very much a town of the stone trade:

. . . its unsightly wharves, piled high with stone, which extend some hundred yards along the curve of the bay, directly in front of the principal terrace, and excluding all view of the sea from anyone walking on the pavement.

Here, on raised platforms intersected by waggon-roads, are stored the wrought stones of every kind, which have been carted down to the merchants from the quarries on the hill where they were dug, and here they remain until the day of shipment; when a cargo hurriedly leaves the bankers, only to be replaced by newly-collected loads. Even more destructive of the amenities of Swanage as a watering place than its narrow inconvenient old streets, are these bankers occupying and disfiguring as they do the very spot where pretty gardens, with broad gravelly paths, should be laid out as a public seaside promenade.

Hitherto the requirements of the staple trade of the place, the "chipping and shipping of stone", as it has been aptly termed, have almost necessitated this consecration to unlovely trade; but there is some hope now that the coming railway will lead to the transport of the stone instead of by ship, and set the bankers free.

The dependence upon boats to take the stone from the bankers out to the ships anchored in Swanage Bay gave the stone trade a shaky system of exportation. That it lasted so long, and only ceased after the arrival of the railway, is to some extent a reflection on the appalling condition of Purbeck roads. The first turnpike of 1768 was little improvement over the mediaeval road pattern as it went from Stoborough to Creech Grange and then linked with rough older roads to climb the ridge at Bare Cross and approach Corfe from the west. It did not even extend to Swanage. A proper carriage road followed a little later, running directly across the heath to Corfe and then through Kingston and Langton to Swanage, bringing the port into direct contact with inland Dorset for the first time. The toll houses and gates were at the north end of Stoborough village and at Swanage, opposite Jubilee Road, on the High Street, Herston. Another apparently existed at Gallows Gore, although it has left no official record, but the main building there was formerly called Turnpike Cottages. The course of the present A351 between Corfe and Herston did not become a through road until after 1862: it would inevitably have been utilised eventually by the stone trade but the railway's coming in 1885 had far more immediate and decisive effects. Had that arrived later then the steam traction engine might have provided an alternative for heavy haulage. The point, however, is that the operation of the Swanage stone boats up to a hundred years ago was not an outmoded custom from the past but because they were still an effective working system. So the bankers survived almost into living memory.

In those days, when buyers had been found and ships were waiting to take the stone, the blocks were loaded into high-wheeled stone carts. These waited at the bankers, were drawn by horses down to the beach and into the sea, and then the stone was transferred into boats. The stone barges plied between the wading carts and ships standing further out in the bay. Purpose built and pointed at stem and stern, the barges were cumbersome boats but they carried immense stones, some weighing half a ton. Manned by two men with oars, the boats also had a small lug-sail for when the wind was favourable. They ferried a load of six to nine tons on each journey. The stone was shipped differently from Durlston Bay. Stone boats were hauled close inshore and an inclined stage placed nearby. The blocks of stone were then slid down the ramp and lowered into the waiting boat, helped along by quarrymen who often stood waist-deep in the water for hours.

As well as taking stone out, the barges were also used as a lifeline into the town. They brought ashore coal and other supplies from coasters anchored in the bay. At the middle of the nineteenth century there was an average of seventy stone craft operating at Swanage and in an easterly gale and during the hardest weather all boats were hauled ashore and safely grounded. It was a wet and tricky job, only possible by using capstan rollers and chains, but a vital one because the barges would otherwise soon be overwhelmed and sink. The boats were also vulnerable to accidents, especially when meeting the cross-currents as they rounded the ledges of Peveril Point while bringing stone from Durlston to Swanage Bay. One such sad case happened there in August 1836 when young John Norman drowned after the sea swamped his father's craft. The following day he was to have been married.

The sight of tall carts being pulled by horses into the sea, out to the waiting barges, was not the only remarkable sight in Swanage during the first half of the last century. During the early 1800s the town was still using its own currency which was based on the ancient system of barter: emanating from the Townsend quarries, the almost unbelievable fact is that it came in units of 12 lb. and 144 lb. in weight. Coins that were pieces of stone were issued as quarrymen's wages and then traded across the counters of shops in the same way as the current legal tender, King George pennies. Tradesmen's counters had also to be slabs of stone in order to withstand rough treatment from the 'Swanage pennies' which were shaped like paving stone. Twelve pennies equalled, logically enough, one shilling and that was the second unit of the quarried currency, weighing as near 144 lb. as possible. Although this was a form of barter, the shopkeepers handled the stone as a direct fixed-price equivalent of the normal bronze coins and their counters were known as bankers, like the piles of stone on the seafront. Even the official pennies of the time were huge if compared with our late pennies and those outsized pieces of copper have themselves been abandoned.

Some Swanage traders did resist payments in stone, but only when they had a delicate business in such small items as snuff, pepper, vinegar and salt—and had a woman on the other side of the counter. William Masters Hardy remembered the Swanage pennies and wrote the following at the turn of the century: "I have seen quarrymen carrying stones on their backs from the quarries to pay for their beer, baccy, and other commodities. Land, coals, bread, boots, clothes and almost every article required for home consumption could be bought with stone currency."

Bowler hats are no longer worn by the quarrymen and moleskin trousers were discarded as opencast workings replaced the underground mines. Moleskin trousers are remembered by the old men who wore them as "fine things for underground" but they can also recall the surprising heaviness of their clothes after being caught above ground by a sudden downpour. Made not from the skins of moles, but from a strong cotton fustian, the pile of which is shaved, the trousers lasted for years. They can withstand much rough treatment and are still worn by foundry workers to protect their legs from sparks. Fustian (called *fuskin* in Purbeck) can be washed but never dry-cleaned, though it was always considered better just to leave it alone. Moleskins were a sort of baggy leggings of brownish-white thick cloth, and when worn to shape the trousers were usually hung 'at ease' and ready to be stepped into.

Nelson Thomson, one of the older quarrymen living and working at Acton, used to have moleskins and can also remember when the quarrymen were still wearing their traditional bowler hats:

When they built the sea wall down at Swanage in 1904, there's quite a lot of those men then [*he pointed to a photograph*] wearing a real hard bowler hat. You could take one and play football with it. I could remember my father wearing one on special days and I could go back to the early 1920s and there was quite a lot of the old men still wearing them. We did have a bowler hat dug up from one of the quarries up here when one of the men got out [*after an accident underground*] and never got hurted. But he did leave a bowler hat down there and later we went and touched it; it all fell to pieces. That was up here on top, opposite Gallows Gore, back in the 1920s.

I used to work with a man named Billy Brown back in 1922 and he used to wear a bowler hat. He used to go to church and Wareham market and wear his bowler hat. Billy Brown was living down in Langton village and he used to work up at the cliff quarries. He was nearly eighty when he died and he bin dead nearly thirty years. I went into the stone trade in 1925. I had to pay £5 7s. 6d. and a penny loaf and a quart of beer. Real tasty job in those days. In the little village hall at Corfe, and I had to go down and kick the ball up through Aves, [*The Halves*] as they do call it. I was the last one to be married into the trade and I had to kick the football—the last place to kick the ball, the villagers could go and pick en up and take en away. That was the quarryman's right for that day. . . .

Such ancient rights were the subject of a report by the government's inspector of factories and workshops, issued in March 1880. This was reported in the Globe newspaper and referred to the 'islanders' of Purbeck and Portland as remarkable in their habits and having:

a settled idea that the workings of the quarries in those localities is a privilege of their own, and they not only resent the intrusion of other workmen but go so far as to qualify the latter and, indeed, the whole world outside Purbeck and Portland, by the opprobrious title of 'foreigners'. The Purbeckians of Swanage maintain that this privilege is secured to them by an ancient charter providing that no person may establish himself in their trade who is not a direct descendant of some local quarryman.

This, however, is far from being the whole extent of the immunities claimed by the islanders. . . . Both peoples have a strong objection to being interfered with, the Purbeckians especially holding a sort of tradition that they are beyond all laws, and that they have a sort of right to make regulations for their own government, the general sum of which would appear to be to arrange that they should do as much, or as little, work as they please, have unlimited beer, and send their offspring to school, or not, at discretion, which would result in about ninety percent growing up uneducated as their parents boast that they are themselves.

So tenacious are both races of their individuality that they will not even contract matrimonial alliances with the foreigner, but intermarry amongst themselves so that nearly everybody in both localities is related to everybody else. Nothwithstanding this fact, it appears that the evils which are generally supposed to result from intermarriage are not particularly noticeable but, on the contrary, the health of the community is so good that no one could fail to be struck by their unusually fine appearance, and at Portland boys of thirteen or fourteen are often found to look as if they were two years older.

In a court case the same year, it was heard that a young boy, Jesse Stickland, was working full-time stone dressing at Swanage and had not been sent to school. In his father's defence, it was said that Swanage quarrymen were under the impression that "lads working in the mines do not come under the Elementary Education Act. They thought the inspector was carrying out the spirit of an obnoxious act which was hostile to them. They think that they can do what they like with their own children."

The case was found to be proved but no fine was imposed. The magistrates only "wished the defendants to comply with the law of the country" and ordered payment of costs. It was pointed out by the inspector that the stone workers could send their children to work at ten years old, providing they kept them at school half-time until they were thirteen. George Burt, one of the justices, remarked that Purbeck men were rather strong headed but he would advise them to look upon the inspector as a friend rather than an enemy. The inspector replied: "We are on the best terms except when it comes to keeping the law!"

The Earl of Eldon supported the backlash against the act and was in the chair at a meeting of the Wareham and Purbeck Union which came out in favour of ending "the compulsory sending to school by the labouring and industrial classes of children after the age of twelve, and allowing their full employment at that age".

It was a Dorsetman, W. E. Forster of Bradpole near Bridport, who had given birth to the monster that is now state education. For us at this point in time it is becoming increasingly difficult to understand the nature and extent of the child labour problem—and harder to accept the fact that ten year old boys were working a man's hours at a man's job in the stone mines of Swanage.

Equally, it is far from easy to envisage how a Purbeck mine shaft must have looked. These openings in the ground were sometimes more than mere work holes. Several of those around Langton and Acton were used up to 1930 as sources of fresh water for the cottages. Men and women queued for their turn to climb down twenty feet with a bucket. The old shafts are still there, though mainly stopped up at the entrance, and one was reopened at Webber's quarry and found to have air so foul that a candle would no longer burn there. Experiences such as this belong to an era that has vanished. There are still some quarrymen who remember cutting stone from holes in the ground and they know that the depth of an old shaft could have been gauged by the size of its capstan.

Langton's capstans were quite small to tackle the shallow workings, and unlike those at Swanage Townsend, could be worked by a donkey harnessed to the spack. An old pony could wind a ton up the quarry shaft as it walked at the end of a sixteen-foot spack round a six foot capstan of elm. Such an arrangement was said to raise a ton by six feet every time the animal went round. When a cart and its stone was lifted to the top of the slide, the pony would then be unharnessed from the spack and attached directly to the cart to pull the stone to the working floor. The usual place for the horse or donkey shed was beside the towpath, and adjoining the opening of the mine shaft. A capstan was a tough piece of machinery and only required an occasional greasing of the gudgeon. It would last a human lifetime and wear out several old mules in the process.

If a horse was not available, manpower could be used instead. Even as late as about 1850, two Swanage girls had to tread the spack "as their father was an old man and had no one to help him, his daughters were compelled to walk round and round in the mud and clay up to their ankles". In this century the capstans have rotted and there is only that one at Cowlease with all its stone intact, but I have sometimes found pairs of crabstones still standing. These supported the capstan drum and a hole at the top, through the sides of both stones, shows where a beam held the axle in place.

Money in Swanage last century found its way into two pairs of greedy hands, one belonging to John Mowlem and the other to George Burt, owner of the Cowlease. Burt died in 1894 and Thomas Hardy later called him "the King of Swanage" and said he was rougher in speech than he should have expected after his years in London "being the ordinary type of Dorsetman, self-made by trade, whenever one of the county does self-make himself, which is not often".

Surprisingly, it was Burt the stone man who saw the future of Swanage as a respectable watering place. One thing was lacking—there was no railway. The main line between Southampton and Dorchester had been completed in May 1847 and passed through Wareham. The Isle of Purbeck Railway, a branch extension, was proposed in 1862 and accepted by Parliament the following year. But nothing came of it.

George Burt applied himself again to the project after Mowlem's death in 1868. Then, when he had failed to bring the railway, he was astute enough to provide an alternative and bought a steamboat to run between Swanage and Bournemouth. She was the *Heather Bell* and operated between 1871 and 1877. Burt said in 1880: "Bournemouth people were originally rather jealous of my steamboat, but in the course of a year or two they found people said, 'Is that steamboat running now? If she is, I shall come to Bournemouth. If she is not, I shall not come.' There is no doubt about it—Bournemouth people now say if more people could get over to Swanage they would have more visitors come to Bournemouth."

George Street, the architect who built the Law Courts in the Strand and a second church at Kingston, told a colleague about his use of the burr, Purbeck's building stone, and added: "Let the rail or tram go to where that stone is, put it on the rail at once, and I will undertake that six churches out of seven shall be built with that material."

Street had enjoyed using Purbeck stone and his son described the new Kingston church as "probably one of the most complete things my father ever did". During the progress of the work, the architect wrote in his diary "the church is looking well. I hope the interior may be beautiful. It ought to be for they have already spent a large sum of money on it. It will be difficult to find, even among old buildings, anything more thoroughly elaborated, I believe. It is a real pleasure to work for such a man as Lord Eldon." Subsequently, Street wrote: "It is a pleasure to be allowed to make work so much after one's heart as this will be; I think it is the jolliest church I have built."

Burt's heart was in the cause of bringing the railway to strengthen the commercial potential of Purbeck. He held meetings to push forward the idea that the railway's coming was inevitable. He repeated Street's views and said: "Swanage has been a place of stone for many years, but the great place now is a little to the west where there is an immense quantity of stone that could be carried to a profitable market if only they would lessen the cost of carriage. If Swanage is to move ahead and you are to get out of the dirty streets into a more wholesome and profitable atmosphere, you must have a railway."

Railway engineers surveyed Purbeck in 1880, and the following year, despite opposition from Wareham, an act was finally passed for the second time to enable the building of a railway to Swanage. There was no objection from the Earl of Eldon who owned much of the land across which the line was to run. Capital of £90,000 was authorised for the project and work started on 5 May 1883 at Wareham. Ten miles further on, with the date 5 May 1885, the line was completed. A year later, the Swanage branch was bought by the London and South Western Railway and the town became a holiday resort. There was a scheme for a 1,338 yard spur to connect Swanage station with the stone bankers and a tramway leading to the old pier, but no progress with this was made.

The pier had been built in 1859 and is now a skeleton, though the rails of the original narrow-gauge tramway are still embedded in the road by the pier head. The second pier was built in 1896 for the paddle steamers and visitors but the first is of most interest as it was constructed when Swanage was still an industrial town. The tramway ran from the pier to the bankers. Teams of horses pulled carts along the rails to the ships but the pier was in operation for only the closing years of the stone trade at Swanage. Even after the new pier was built, the old structure did not degenerate into a second life as a visitors' plaything and was only used until the 1920s for coaling steamers. Its planking has now gone and the supports are rotting and disintegrating into the sea. The first Swanage pier was heavily criticised in its early years and one visitor's complaint was printed in an east Dorset newspaper, the Poole Pilot, on 1 March 1869:

Swanage is a charming place; its praises are in many mouths, and it cannot help rising in public favour if fair chances be afforded it. Its inaccessibility is one clog which retards its progress. The appear-

ance of its Pier is by no means an attraction; its baldness and inconvenience discredit every inhabitant in the place.
A more ugly, bone-breaking trap I have never looked at, especially for weak or invalid people. No side walk where passengers may go without fear of tripping between the open transverse planking, and iron tramroad projecting upwards four inches; no seat on which tired or weak people may rest whilst waiting to embark; no protection, not even a handrail, to prevent a child from falling overboard and being drowned.
First impressions are, we all know, the most enduring, and I believe many a person has condemned Swanage immediately upon viewing this construction.
Let me implore the Swanage inhabitants to bring their Pier Company to book during the present spring. . . .

The stone trade at Swanage died between 1885 and 1896 and Burt's stone-weighing office is now a travel agency. The bankers were still high with stone in 1880, but by the turn of the century, The Parade and Institute Road had risen from their remains. Seaborne trade from Swanage finally ceased in the 1890s and one last stone barge retired to Chapman's Pool where it rotted.

Change was brought by the railway which has now itself been phased out. Old ways ended in 1964 when the M7 0-4-4 tank engines and their push and pull methods were withdrawn. The line has been run by three-car diesel multiple units since 1966 and had a busy summer in 1969. Through workings were resumed on Saturdays when some trains left Swanage packed with 350 passengers for Waterloo. The end of the Swanage branch line will only dissuade a small minority from visiting the town but it will be the destruction of the original mechanism that brought the whole resort into being. Closure of the line, however, will not affect the stone trade as all the loads have left Purbeck in lorries for years.

Another plan by the Burt family for improving Purbeck's communications was revealed in 1904 but was killed by small-town politics at Poole and Bournemouth. The ambitious idea was to convey tramcars across the water between Sandbanks and Shell Bay by means of overhead cables. Others suggested a suspension bridge instead. The Bournemouth Graphic reported:

We are enabled to publish this week the official announcement that the plans and arrangements for an important development of the tramway system to Canford Cliffs and Swanage are practically complete. This is the first announcement that has been made on the matter, and we are in a position to give authentic details of the scheme in so far as present arrangements permit.
A private company has been formed, and among those taking a prominent part in its working, we believe, are Sir John Burt, of Swanage, and Mr. Bankes, of Corfe Castle, to establish a system of

trams, which will start from the Westbourne Arcade, and run through Seamoor Road and Branksome Park, across Canford Cliffs, to Sandbanks. Here it is proposed to erect a tower on either side of the water, and by means of a cage and chain arrangement, to swing the cars across to the opposite bank and thence continue the system to Swanage. We understand that it has not yet been decided whether the line of route will pass through Studland, though the whole scheme is complete in all but one or two minor details.

The capital of the company is to be £68,000, and we are informed that practically the whole of this sum has already been privately subscribed. No appeal will therefore be made to the public.

Westward from Swanage, among the empty, treeless hills above the sea, are the cliff quarries whose growth and decline is a separate story from Townsend and the shafts further inland. The whole cliff from Anvil Point to St. Alban's Head is sheer, solid stone. At St. Alban's, the best seams lie near the top, and are otherwise found halfway down the cliff face. The ideal place for a cliff quarry was where the sea had cut across a valley opening. A gallery was then made outwards along the cliff, mid-way down, and inwards along the flank of the hills that held the valley on each side. Winspit and Seacombe are the most extensive examples, but Tilly Whim Caves and Dancing Ledge show the same principle.

Directly below the ceiling of a quarry such as Winspit—where workings spread up the valley on both sides from the sea—was the *underpicking cap.* This was holed by hand or, later, by pneumatic drills, and charges laid. Explosives blasted through two feet of stone and this was cleared. Then the work started on using wedges, called *gads,* to carefully cut blocks of stone from the bottom of the gash. This stone was removed till the quarry floor was about ten feet below the roof, and the process continued up to about two hundred feet into the hillside with the galleries some twenty-five feet wide. As the cliff was solid stone, legs of living rock were left to support the hills and these have survived the quarrymen's day. Where the roof was sufficiently strong there are even some great open caverns without any supports.

Usually the legs of untouched stone are square, with sides about three feet wide, and regularly spaced at ten foot intervals through the galleries. Other supports had to be built up with blocks of stone. The care taken in their size and placing has meant that most of the quarries still stand: but here and there a support has collapsed and the hill fallen to fill the gap. All the quarries at Winspit and Seacombe are derelict and deserted, with water constantly dripping from the roof and, now and again, the intrusion of a cow or two lazing in the gloom. Seacombe's quarries have roofs about twelve feet high and are mainly only supported with a few huge pillars. Blocks of up to fifty tons were taken from the cliffs and cut into manageable sizes. The quantity of the stone was matched by the problem of transport as away from proper roadways and the rail link, the sea was the natural exit from the cliff face. The method used during the peak years of cliff quarrying is shown in a Victorian lithograph of about 1870 depicting Hedbury Quarry, a wide quarry shelf above the sea about halfway between Dancing Ledge and Seacombe. A *whim* was mounted on the edge of the cliff—this being a normal derrick made of timbers, and similar to those used today for lowering boats into the sea near Portland Bill. Wood for the whim came from the timber of shipwrecks. In the drawing, a ship's wheel was used as the winch and was obviously geared to minute precision for lowering a heavy block of worked stone into a barge waiting on the calm sea below.

The delicacy of this operation, and the fact that the stone barge had then to make Swanage, shows why the cliff quarries could only function during the summer. The print also shows a stone being worked and the quarry operator, Thomas Chinchen Lander. Another whim was at Tilly Whim Caves, the cliff quarry near Anvil Point, which was still being worked during the Napoleonic wars. The whim gave the quarry the second part of its unusual name and Tilly was probably the name of the quarry owner.

Some written record of Tilly Whim has been preserved. The quarry is mentioned in a letter of 13 April 1813:

> There is so much room in this quarry for any assignable number of men to work, and so great a facility, in summer, of shipping the goods, letting them down at once by a crane into the vessel, that men of industry and enterprise ought to command almost the whole market for the species of articles which this quarry produces. . . . The sort of goods which this quarry yields are of what is called the Portland Purbeck, a sort of freestone; much like the Portland only harder, and much used for building in bridges, harbours, fortification walls, troughs, columns, rollers, staddle stones, etc.

Calculations of the output of Tilly Whim have been made from a series of accounts dated between 1805 and 1812. The total production of the quarry for the five-year period ending on Ladyday in 1810 appears to have been:

> 37 setts of brigs and caps.
> 14 setts of rink stones.
> 83 pairs of staddle stones.
> 340½ pecks of sinks and troughs.
> 318½ feet of rollers.
> 2305 tons of backing.

97   tons of blocks.
133 tons of pitchers.

Further along the coast, at Hedbury in 1960, I clambered down to the quarry floor and found a direct reminder of the French wars on the ledge above the sea. Lying amongst blocks of stone was a rusting cannon; a twelve-pounder of the Napoleonic period. Though I have passed the quarry since, and looked down from the cliff, I have not noticed the gun again but there was some ironwork set directly above the waves and showing the site of the whim.

One mile west of Hedbury is the cliff quarry which was the last to be worked. It is Winspit, in a chine above the straight cliffs, a mile from the village of Worth Matravers. Workings on the cliffs at Winspit probably started after 1673 and the evidence for this is in the name of the place. The word *spit*, meaning a point of rock, is unknown before then, and the second part of the name refers either to the *wind* or is a corruption of *whim*. Work ceased at Winspit about 1945 and the nearby Seacombe had closed between the wars. Up to the time Seacombe closed, fifteen-ton blocks of stone were still being taken from its galleries and cut with hammers, punches and wedges. A breakwater at Poole and other projects were built with Seacombe's rock, which provided larger blocks and a better class of stone than Winspit.

But the coming of war was to give Winspit a respite: thousands of tons of stone were taken as hardcore for roads and airfields, though most of this rubble was removed by opencast rather than underground workings. In the traditional ways, two layers of fine stone were cut from the cliffside galleries of the quarries, the base-bed and the whitbed. The whitbed was seven feet thick at Winspit and eight at Seacombe. One of the special jobs accomplished with Seacombe's thick seam was the making of a three-and-a-half ton trough for North Woolwich Galvanising Works in 1871. The great stone produced at A. Bower's quarry was eight feet long, four feet wide, and four feet deep.

These coastal beds are truly Portland stone and from the uppermost stratum of the Jurassic system. Portland stone is marine in origin, whereas Purbeck is a freshwater limestone. The difference is shown mainly in the types of fossil but has a practical importance in that the Purbeck beds yield rubble, while the Portland beds have provided the finest of stone used to face the fronts of London's public buildings. The *whitbed* lies under the *roach* and provides the commonest of Portland oolitic limestone. Light brown when cut, it eventually weathers to the traditional whitish grey. Below the whitbed is the *basebed* which, though harder and less shelly, has basically similar characteristics. Beds at Winspit were described in 1895 as having the following local names: *burr, shrimp stone, blue stone, pond freestone, flint stone, listy bed, house cap, underpicking cap, under freestone* and *cliff beds* (chert). There is one change in this list from the original. Quarryman Billy Winspit confirmed the word 'listy' to be correct and not the named 'nist bed' of which he had never heard. Listy was so called, he thought, "because it breaks easily". The word means streaky and originates from OE *liste,* meaning "a border, strip or band".

John Smeaton, who started work on the new Eddystone Lighthouse in 1757, surveyed stone quarries throughout the West Country. He found the cliff quarries near St. Alban's Head, probably those at Winspit, and wrote:

> The strata of merchantable stone lie here in the upper part of the cliffs, as they do at Portland, but having more cover they are in some measure worked underground. This stone is of the like nature, and puts on so much the appearance of the Portland that it is often used in lieu of it. It is, however, inferior in colour, harder in work, and, according to the information I then got, not in general so durable. But what seemed to me like for ever to prohibit this field of stone from coming into competition with Portland is that, as it cannot bear the expense of land carriage down to Swanage to be shipped, the workmen are obliged to let it down with ropes from the place where it is wrought, to the surface of the sea, either into vessels lying at the foot of the cliffs, where there is deep water, or where there is a dry strand at low water; but there being but little shelter from the winds and seas, this can only be done in very moderate weather, and particularly winds; wherefore the shipping it must necessarily be somewhat precarious.

The last man to work Winspit was named William Jeremiah Bower—and always called Billy Winspit. He was born in the grey Purbeck stone cottage one hundred yards from his quarry and it was there that he died, only days from his eightieth birthday, on 9 August 1966. I called two weeks before his death and found him in his garden workshop chipping away at the centrepiece for a stone fireplace. He stopped to sharpen some tools as he had done since the age of sixteen when he was the quarry's blacksmith. Billy Winspit had started quarrying when he was 11-years-old and he looked back to the year of 1907 when pay in the quarries was twenty-five shillings a week and £11 was the weekly wage bill for Winspit. Till his death, oil lamps gave the only light in the cottage which was without either gas or electricity.

The old man told me: "My father before me worked the quarries like I do, and granfer worked on the cliffs and his father. When I was a boy, father and I worked underground. In the old fashioned ways you moved the stone out, cut it and sent it to London in blocks. But that is all finished with now and I only do a carving job as a part time. Once I had a fourteen-foot boat and went fishing in the summer as well. You couldn't do it in winter as we have some terrific weather here—seas fifty feet high. I have seen the waves come over the cliffs into the quarry."

When quarryman Billy went fishing, his main catch was shell fish, which were profitable, but apart from lowering lobster pots he also went after wet fish like mackerel and herring. Mackerel shoals were watched from the cliffs and followed as they broke up. Instead of a seine, a *set* net was used—a hurdle affair with lead on the bottom and cork at the top which floated upright close to the surface. Now fishing is declining and in Purbeck can only be found at Swanage, Kimmeridge and the sheltered inlet of Chapman's Pool. All the old fishermen, as Billy put it, are in the 'boneyard'.

Sixteen cubic feet of Billy's cliff is one ton of stone, and if there was ever demand again, vast quantities are still there waiting to be worked. In the corners of the old quarries are even blocks of worked stone—left by the old men who never managed to clear their last loads. Inland, their work is often finished by today's quarrymen who enter an old quarry at weekends to clear the remaining stone. There is a word for everything on Purbeck, this operation being called *ridding* and the quarry being reworked, a 'ridding hole'.

Some of the old names for coastal features are remembered in the former quarrying areas, like Molly's Garden for the thorny undercliff of Houn's-tout, and Buttery Corner where a quarry shelf is eaten out of St. Alban's Head. Other names have faded with the passing of the old quarrymen. There was a Crab Hole below West Man, and a host of names at Seacombe—Mike and Willy's Caves, Cliff Field Quarry and Watch Rock among them. Further east, between Hedbury Quarry and Dancing Ledge, was Topmast Quarry, Green Point and Bower Rock.

Purbeck has now reverted to the original ancient methods of opencast quarrying. From the time when the Romans picked at greyish-white marble at the surface outcrops of Wilkswood, to the quarries of Langton and Acton today, the principle is the same. The idea is a hole in the ground, gouged bigger to reach the better stone below.

Stone quarrying in Purbeck has declined since before the war, when there were 550 full-time employees, and in 1961 there were only a hundred workers. Purbeck is still used as a building stone in Dorset, with Corfe Castle village a particular example, though it tends to be marred by over-careful dressing which can leave the natural stone looking like moulded concrete. Special commissions have included use of stone to restore major historic buildings like Temple church and the Tower of London.

Demand for garden rockeries, crazy paving, bird baths and non-plastic gnomes is often greater than that for building stone. There is even a tendency for some quarries to specialise exclusively in the production of ornamental ephemera for the window dressing of suburbia. Daily in the quarry huts, and workshops that hide in Swanage town, come the chinks of fat stone owls in the hatcheries. The industry that built Corfe Castle and raised churches for a kingdom is surviving by adapting to the needs of a bungalow generation.

Its mechanised methods of digging stone are despised by the last of the older generation of quarrymen. To Nelson Thomson, the modern way is both wasteful and destructive. He considers that opencast workings are devastating the landscape around Acton:

> There is no mining up here at all now. This yer machinery comes in and they just go down and lift the stone up on top. They go down and get a stone, perhaps three-ton, brings him up and stick him up—and the next time they've got three-ton of dirt and clay to stick down beside him. You've still got to pick at it. I've had to go and get out some crazy paving today and, oh dear, I'd rather go down to the natural stone and dig it.
> It's all pushed and crumbled together on top, see, and smashed about and broke. You've got to muddle through and get what you can.
> Ten or twelve year ago, this place up here was a little field planted into swedes and corn—now it's all turned upside down and inside out. And that's what they've done right the way round, right up nearly to the cliff. When we did used to work on the top we used to pick out everything and all the soil went back in the hole. You'd hardly knew we bin there. But opencast is awful destruction to me. It's beating a lot of the ground about unnecessarily and they take the stone out and put it on the top of the good land. This machinery costs so much money that they say you have to keep on and hump all the stone out.

Bob Harris, a Langton quarryman and fisherman, is another concerned at the treatment of the land. Some quarrymen, he said, leave the land in a poor condition after they have finished working it, and many make no attempt at reinstatement: "There is more stone left in Purbeck than has ever been dug out. But they won't let you get at it. You can understand a landowner saying 'no' when you see how some quarrymen leave the land."

Reserves of workable stone are limited in the present restricted areas of extraction and the only important quarries today are around the quarrymen's own hamlet of Acton at Langton Matravers, and Sheepsleights Quarry operated by Swanworth Quarries Limited on the south side of Coombe Bottom between Kingston and Worth. Aside from the building stone trade, W. J. Haysom, operators at St. Aldhelm's Quarry, tackle specialised orders and have even reopened an old marble quarry at Lynch, to the south of Corfe Common, to lift the raw material for historical reconstructions.

There is still a lot of stone under the cliffs between St. Alban's Head and Anvil Point, but even if demand rose again there would be a strong case for resisting extraction along this lonely and unspoilt coast. Only Swanworth Quarries and the small St. Aldhelm's Quarry, a mile south of Renscombe Farm on the road to the headland, now dig the Portland beds. Even these two quarries take the Portland stone from its most exposed levels in the region between Chapman's Pool and Worth Matravers—and the stone industry has completely died out along the cliffs to Swanage. Dock walls were once built of Purbeck cliff stone but today concrete is mixed on the site: no one now thinks of moving the contents of a hill from Dorset to make a breakwater, and it is becoming difficult to visualise that once it was done.

Staddle stones for all the South

Hindsight Subsequent research has shown that the majority of late eighteenth and nineteenth century farm granaries in southern England were built on Dorset staddle stones (see page 35). Only a small proportion of these granaries survive – examples of timber, the real rarity, are at Manor Farm, Sixpenny Handley, and at Hurnbridge Farm, Hurn – and of these some 95 percent have either nine or twelve staddles.

Charles Vancouver reported to the Board of Agriculture from Hampshire in 1813: "An excellent practice seems to be fast gaining ground in many parts of the county, of building wheat barns, as well as corn stacks in general, upon stone stands or staddles, the stones, or *legs* and *caps* (as they are usually called) are supplied from the quarries of Purbeck and Portland, and cost at sea ports or wharves at the head of the marine navigation, about seven shillings per pair."

CHAPTER IV

Clay From The Heath

EXTRACTION OF Purbeck ball clay has been one of Dorset's major industries for the past two centuries. The whole gargantuan operation has slithered across the heath over the seven miles between Creech and Newton, carrying with it men, cranes, sheds and railway engines to lift new seams; and leaving behind a lunar landscape of sticky white hillocks that were soon reclaimed by the tough heathland flora and stand full of wild colour above the former workfaces. These, the claypits of Purbeck, filled with water and now have their own charm, especially in late summer when red, yellow and white water-lilies flower across the shallows, but also at all times because the waters are translucent with strong shades of turquoise refracted from the clayey bottoms.

The best-known abandoned claypit, the Blue Pool at Furzebrook, was dug by Watts, Hatherway and Burn of Newton Abbot in about 1846-50. The boys who removed the overburden of sand were paid twelve shillings a week and given a hot meal each day. Their wheelbarrows, called *rubblers,* had to be pushed up planks to the top of the pit. Clay from the Blue Pool was supplied to Royal Worcester, Minton, Wedgwood and the other leading pottery manufacturers. Its railway, to Ridge, was sold in 1850. Walter Pike bought the Blue Pool pit in 1874, though not from Watts but the Brown family, who had been digging Purbeck clay since before 1699. Pike's business expanded into Pike Brothers, Fayle and Company which is now absorbed into the giant combine of English China Clays. In 1960, before the takeover, Pikes celebrated their bicentenary: "Apart from grading, turning and weathering, it is doubtful whether, in the early days, the clay was subjected to preparation. But it must be remembered that the blue clays of the Bagshot beds are the finest in the world. They fire a near white and their small and uniform grain size and consequent unequalled plasticity make them an important ingredient of bodies for the manufacture of most earthenwares and pottery."

Though they were unaware of it, the Pike brothers revived an industry that had flourished long before them—in the hands of Celtic potters during the Roman rule. Clays were collected on the heath and taken to a string of workshops and pottery kilns along the shorelines of Poole Harbour. Two kilns, a short distance south of Shipstal Point, lie on the very edge of the saltings and the old shore can still be seen. Whilst the kilns are now over a hundred yards from the high tide mark it should be remembered that the mud-flats have been reclaimed by the rampant growth of *Spartina townsendii*, the grass of the salt-marshes, since the early 1800s. The kilns were carefully sited where their wares could easily be removed by boat. Similarly, kilns at Fitzworth Heath and Cleavel Point—the west spit of Newton Bay—are beside the safe harbour beaches. Remains of a hut, probably the home of a potter, have been found nearby on Fitzworth Point.

Up the Frome at Stoborough, north of Nutcrack Lane and close to Redcliff Farm, another group of potters had their wheels and the discarded sherds of pots that misfired have been frequently found. These wasters, substandard work rejected by the potters and smashed on a heap, can sometimes be found in large quantities and it is a scattering of broken pottery that usually betrays the existence of a kiln below the ground. Because of the dense ground cover along almost the entire line of the old coastline, which is both lonely and long, deeply indented and hard to explore, it is likely that many more Romano-British pottery kilns are awaiting discovery. Samples of the pottery already uncovered can be seen in the more comfortable surrounds of the County Museum at Dorchester.

In 1952 it was noticed that some molehills beside Nutcrack Lane to the east of Stoborough contained fragments of pots. A small excavation revealed a vat of puddled chalk with a clay lining, four feet in diameter and two feet deep with a central plughole at the bottom, together with five or more holes in the rim. There were more potsherds amongst its ashy filling and these dated from about the end of the first century. The whole basin-shaped tub was carefully lifted and taken to the museum at Dorchester where it was displayed under glass for many years. But the vat—a potters' pit for puddling clay—unfortunately disintegrated in 1970 whilst being moved to a new position inside the museum.

Such dating evidence as has been scrutinised points to these potteries having been worked by native Britons during the first two centuries of Roman control and then abandoned by the craftsmen who moved to the valleys of the New Forest uplands where a larger and more sophisticated pottery industry was developing. After this decline the local craft virtually ceased until an industrial revolution in the outside world opened the real era of Purbeck clay in the eighteenth century.

Clay brought the first prosperity known to the poverty stricken Purbeck heathlands and came, ironically, from the most barren parts of the landscape. Its latter day exploitation largely started with the Hyde family of Poole who dug clay from under cotton-grass bogs at Arne. Their operations started in the late 1600s and they became leading exporters of pipe-clay. The time was right for speculation in clay as imports of tobacco and tea were becoming substantial and this meant demand for pipes and teacups. As pewter was at the same time being replaced in public houses by earthenware mugs there were prospects of steady growth in several directions. Thomas Hyde, born in 1731, was the notable member of the family and the man who dominated the politics of Poole corporation for twenty years. The doors and windows of his Poole house were "all smashed" in an election riot in 1769 and Hyde's colourful history is given in Barbara Kerr's "Bound to the Soil". By the 1770s, Hyde was living at Arne and paying £30 a year for mining rights. His contracts included an agreement to supply Josiah Wedgwood with 1,400 tons yearly of potters' clay from the Rempstone estate. Thomas Hyde's business fell in the slump of 1792 and the extraction of clay ceased at Arne. Few signs have survived his operations and nothing remains of Hyde's Quay where a projection of firm land touches the Wareham Channel on the west side of the Arne peninsula. Clay was shipped from there to Poole. Russel Quay at the seaward end of the long road from Stoborough, reached by a track of white sand across the heath from Arne, is another survival from the early clay trade.

Donkeys carried those first loads of commercial clay, the raw material, to the quays at Arne and from the early pits at Furzebrook to the river at Wareham where it was also loaded into small sailing boats. At Poole the clay was transferred to sea-going vessels and shipped to the Mersey ports and from there overland to Staffordshire where, in 1759 at Etruria near Stoke-on-Trent, young Josiah Wedgwood had started a business. Other major customers were in London and at Queenborough in Kent. Clay for the Thames estuary was carried up the Channel by sailing barges. After 1770, when the Trent and Mersey Canal opened, Staffordshire increased its capacity and demand for raw clay, leading directly to the growth of new pits and clay works in Purbeck. The importation by the pottery towns of china clay from Cornwall had also started.

The abortive Dorset and Somerset Canal, as envisaged in 1793, would have connected Poole Harbour with the Bristol Channel and had as its two main prospective sources of income the Somerset collieries and potters' clay of Purbeck. It was intended to build the canal to avoid the passage round Land's End by cutting across the southwest peninsula of England and that, for the clay boats, would have provided a far easier access to Bristol and the route from there to Staffordshire. Part of the canal was actually constructed in the colliery district but the entire illfated scheme ran out of money in 1803. Its owners had already abandoned the intention of reaching the Dorset coast and were going to stop at Shillingstone on the Stour. A result of the collapse of the Dorset and Somerset Canal Company was a meeting in the Red Lion Inn at Wareham on 26 November 1825, chaired by John Calcraft MP, that supported moves to build a railway costing up to £300,000 and running from Poole Harbour to the collieries at Radstock. Nothing came of this project either: the effects of canal mania and the subsequent growth of the early railway system had failed to arrive in Dorset.

Sailing barges remained the basic means of distribution until radical changes followed the successful cross-Channel voyage of the tiny vessel *Sirius* in 1837 when she became the first ship to complete a voyage under steam alone. On land the first stages of an efficient distribution system were created by Benjamin Fayle, a London potter, who bought the claypits at Norden, a scattered heathland settlement a mile from Corfe Castle. It seems the workings had been established by a man named Chiffney in 1795. Fayle avoided the Pike family embarkation point at Wareham and used instead an old cart track across two-and-a-half miles of heath to reach Middlebere Lake, an inlet of Poole Harbour.

Benjamin Fayle learned of the early railways from his customers in the Staffordshire potteries and considered one might provide a workable alternative to sending poorly laden donkeys and horse and cart transport across the rough heathland roads. He obviously found a railway engineer to undertake the project as the line he established in 1806 has graceful sweeping curves, shallow cuttings and low embankments, and a skilfully gentle gradient that maintains the steady fall of land from one hundred feet to sea level. This ancient mineral railway, working more than forty years before the first main line crossed into Dorset, survived in use until 1905 when it was finally abandoned. Even its closure was not caused by the more attractive proposition presented by the Swanage branch of the London and South Western Railway but because Fayle and Company had completed its own replacement line, no less than six miles long, to link the Norden pits with Goathorn Pier.

Because of its historic significance—it was Dorset's first—the railway of 1806 merits close attention, particularly as it allowed Purbeck ball clay to be marketed in quantity and enabled its creator, by his foresight, to compete effectively against the Pike family, his monopolistic rivals.

Mineral railways were one of the first technical innovations to be accepted in mines and quarries. In 1803, at a time when their construction was increasing in the North, the Surrey Iron Railway opened and became the first line to carry public loads. All these lines, until the widespread introduction of narrow gauge steam engines in the 1850s, were powered by simple horse traction. Nonetheless it was still a bold venture by Fayle to cut a railroad across the wild heathland and connect his claypits with an isolated jetty in one of the remotest regions of Dorset.

The railway was originally called the New Line to distinguish it from the old cart track but it later became known as Fayle's Tramway. The gauge was 3 feet 9 inches and the method of construction was to peg three-foot lengths of L-shaped rail to stone block sleepers (a so-called plateway) the trucks having flangeless wheels. William Stevenson, in an agricultural survey of Dorset in 1812, described the 'trains' as being made up of five two-ton waggons drawn by a horse. There were three such trains when the railway opened, each normally making the journey to the quay three times a day, though more trains had to be run as the tonnage increased.

Even though the building of the Swanage branch of the national railway system was to cut directly through the Fayle claypits in 1885, the private railway was still maintained, chiefly for the exportation of foreign orders for clay. These shipments started in barges at the jetty on Middlebere Quay and were transferred to ocean-going vessels at Poole Quay. Middlebere is tucked away in the far reaches of the tidal estuary of Poole Harbour with extensive mud-flats and never a possibility that the vast banks of silt could be dredged to make a wharf for deep water ships.

Shortly before the arrival of the mainline, Fayle's railway had been mechanised by the introduction of *Tiny*, a steam engine built apparently by Stephen Lewin of Poole in 1868. It was an outside cylinder 0-4-0T, looking small and box-like, appearing as a cross between a modern tractor and a child's toy. The driver had an open cab. *Tiny* survived in regular use for over seventy years and was scrapped about 1948.

In 1905 this first engine was joined by *Thames,* a locomotive built by Manning Wardle (an outside cylinder 0-4-0ST) which had been made in 1902 and used for a short time by the London County Council at the Barking outfall sewer. The year 1905 sadly meant the end of Fayle's Tramway, discarded after virtually a century of continuous use. Some stone sleepers can still be seen at Middlebere and a few retain the iron pegs that held the rails. There are also the decaying timbers of the jetty together with a ruined building. On the heath east of Hartland Moor there is a cutting and a long low embankment then carries the line over some marshy ground. Near Langton Wallis cottage is a gap where a short section of steep embankment across a stream was swept away when the culvert blocked after the railway was dismantled.

It is possible to trace the line today from a pair of tunnels under the main Wareham to Corfe road a short distance south of the bridge over the Swanage branch line. Patrick Henshaw has drawn my attention to one of these, about six feet wide and seventy-five feet long, as it is still open right through and the west portal has a stone inscribed "B.F. 1807". Through the tunnel, on the east side of the road, the line passes Norden Cottages, Hartland's Farm, New Line Farm (preserving the original name of the railway), Langton Wallis—and then stretches away from the scattering of valley settlements in gradual descent across Middlebere Heath, along the low ridge above Slepe, and lastly to its final curve round Middlebere Farm ending at the quay and jetty.

With the redundancy of one railway, Fayle and Company embarked upon the creation of another: a surprising project to cut a new mineral line across six miles of the solitary and desolate heaths over which Thomas Hardy and his pen were then brooding at Dorchester. This century has seen the cessation of railway building with the advance of the internal combustion engine and the second decisive Fayle project was one of the last but most extensive private plans to be undertaken in this country.

Years before, in 1852, the Admiralty had given permission for a wharf at *Goat Ord Point*—the tip of Goathorn Plantation—and by 1868 a fresh series of claypits at Newton were in full production and a railway ran from there to the South Deep of Poole Harbour at Goathorn Pier. Newton Clay Works was a sizable concern and with its opening the labour force of Purbeck clay workers reached a total of 350 men, earning between twelve and seventeen shillings per week on piece-work.

The effect of the building of Fayle's Tramway had been dramatic as it created new jobs and enabled the claypits to expand across hundreds of acres. It allowed Fayle to break the Pike monopoly in Purbeck clay. The growth of the industry is shown by the statistics for three indicatory years: in 1802 the output of clay from Purbeck was only 14,796 tons; in 1808, when the tramway was operational, it had risen to 22,000 tons; and by 1859, with the establishment of new clay workings at Newton, the quantity shipped through Poole had reached 50,000 tons a year. Potteries were appearing during the nineteenth century on the furzey hills between Poole and Wareham, producing glazed earthenware drainpipes, bricks, tiles, pots, cups and saucers. A growing market for domestic goods followed the boom years when the demand had been for mass-produced building materials for the Victorian new town of Bournemouth and those endless sprawling red-brick suburbs of older towns across Britain.

All this led to the second ambitious burst of railway building by Fayle and Company. Their Norden pits were using Fayle's Tramway to Middlebere Quay and the Newton Clay Works had its own wharf a mile to its north at Goathorn Pier. Because of the costs involved in maintaining two outlet routes to separate jetties on the shore of one water, Poole Harbour, it was decided to dispense with the tramway—nearing the end of a century's service—and cut five miles of new railway across the vastness of the heath to link the main workings at Norden with Newton Clay Works, its own little railway and the ships at Goathorn Pier which, as it became a timbered jetty reaching out from the point of a peninsula into deep water, was not at the mercy of the tides to the extent of its silted predecessor at Middlebere.

The Goathorn Railway opened in 1905 with the same unusual 3 feet 9 inches gauge as the tramway. It had engine sheds at Eldon Sidings, to the west of the Corfe River at Norden, for *Tiny* and the new locomotive, *Thames*. From there the track crossed the small river and passed uneventfully through small fields on the edge of the heath to Bushey without nearing a single building and then east away across the lonely wastes of Brinscombe, Claywell and Newton Heath. The line here is now a public bridleway and hard pressed on both sides by conifer plantations which have transformed the region since the war. At the east end of the forest, where the line comes out on to a remnant of the Great Heath, there are traces of a siding and a limeworks. The Goathorn Railway, the longest mineral line in Dorset, was abandoned in 1937 with the decline of Newton Clay Works. During its short life the railway was worked by *Tiny* and *Thames* with about twenty-four waggons and an improvised coach for taking children from Goathorn and Newton to school at Corfe. On several occasions the railway was used to transport Purbeck stone. In 1924, for instance, much of the stone for the Training Bank, a breakwater at Poole, came on the Goathorn line to the wharf. Each train had ten trucks, and each truck three tons. At Poole the rubble was dumped from ships for the middle core of the breakwater and settled on top of ten-ton blocks already lowered for the base. Among the last of the old sailing ships that came to Poole Harbour for clay were some graceful wooden vessels from Italy. The barquentine *Patria* and a brigantine, *Avvenire,* arrived in the 1920s to load ball clay for Savona in northern Italy. At the present time about 12,000 tons of ball clay a year is exported from Poole and other ports are also used but on a much smaller scale.

A Poole man, W. H. Froud, recalls the clay industry at Goathorn and Newton during the early part of this century:

> The Dorset Iron Foundry used to look after Fayle's two locomotives and my father and grandfather worked on them regularly. On some occasions in the years before 1914 I went to Goathorn with them. In those days the pier was regularly used for steamers that called to take the clay to London. They were generally Henry Burden's boats from Poole.
>
> There was one cottage at the pier, then occupied by the foreman, William Tubbs. This has now been modernised. The hamlet of Goathorn consisted of a number of cottages occupied by workers at the clay works, a small school and a locomotive shed. There was a resident schoolmistress and the school was attended by the small number of children who lived at Goathorn. On Sunday afternoons a church service was conducted in the school by a visiting parson and organist from Swanage.
>
> The only communication with the outside world, except by boat, was along the railway to Corfe Castle and I believe that on Saturdays the people were taken on the railway for shopping—and the nearest public house.
>
> The ships ceased to call at the pier in 1930 but the works continued some years longer. In the 1930s the school was closed because of the decline in the number of children, and the remaining ones were taken to Corfe on the railway. One of the waggons was covered in as a passenger coach and the county council had to pay the clay company for the service. The hamlet and works, together with the railway, were abandoned by 1939.

The closure of Newton and Goathorn was made irreversible during the latter half of the war when the area was occupied, shelled, bombed and devastated by the allied armies as they waited to be unleashed on the French coast. In more peaceful times, the ruins of the old buildings have been pulled down and at Goathorn a farmer, J. P. H. Warner, has rebuilt the least damaged cottage and lives there now. The shape of the claypits can still be seen at Newton: the pier juts into the harbour from Goathorn, and embankments and cuttings are all that survive of the dismantled railway.

After the war, in 1948, the remains of Fayle and Company's railway system was reduced to a couple of miles of track at the worked-out heart of the old Norden pits and in fresh ground on the other side of the main road, at mines south of Little Coppice immediately below the Purbeck ridge at Knowle Hill. With the scrapping of the two old steam engines, the small remaining length of railway was relaid on the more common 1 foot 11½ inches gauge in 1948 and the *Russell*, a 2-6-2T built by Hunslet Engine Company in 1906, was bought from a disused iron mine in Oxfordshire. It had originally worked on the Welsh Highland Railway. At the same time, the old waggons were replaced by V-shaped, all-metal side tipping trucks. *Russell* was withdrawn in 1953 and replaced by diesel tractors. Five of these were still in use and housed in a shed at Eldon Sidings until 1969. Trains of metal trucks full of white clay continued in operation, and occasionally crossed the main road, though several pieces of rolling stock were abandoned and rusting on overgrown arms of the railway. The railway closed in 1970 after a long period of decline and the last lengths of track have gone. *Russell* survives – on the Welsh Highland Railway.

In 1949 the two Purbeck clay companies merged into Pike Bros., Fayle and Company Limited. At Furzebrook, nearly two miles northwest of Norden, Pike Brothers had developed their mines —and as the Fayle enterprise stretched eastward to Goathorn, they had moved in the opposite direction to the rich deposits at Creech and Povington. The Pike railway to the sea, opened in 1866, runs north from Furzebrook in a dead straight line across two miles of heath to Ridge Wharf on the River Frome. Barges holding about fifty tons of clay were towed by steam tug down the Wareham Channel to Poole. Sidings and the clay works itself were built near Ridge Farm and later moved from there to Furzebrook. The railway gauge was 2 feet 8½ inches (a section of rail is still embedded in the Arne Road) and the first locomotive, *Primus,* was an 0-6-0T having a low boiler, high chimney and bought from Belliss and Seekings for the opening of the line. Then the line took a different course from later years and extended southward on its same straight course at Furzebrook, by Railway Cottages, finally turning west to avoid the Blue Pool and finishing in pits north of Blackhills.

Another 0-6-0T engine, *Secundus,* cost £690 when it came to the line in 1874 and had a long working life, becoming a spare engine for a number of years and finally being taken to a transport collection at Birmingham; it is the only other Purbeck clay locomotive to be preserved. By 1886, when a third engine, *Tertius* (an 0-6-0WT built by Manning Wardle) joined the line, the Pike railways extended southwest from Furzebrook to the pits around the prehistoric Icen Barrow and John's Plantation in the rough country towards the Grange Road. These workings, and others dug at the turn of the century are now lakes and have become the most beautiful gems of the Purbeck heath: they have wide sheets of water smothered with the colour of water-lilies in July and August, and are remote and lovely.

The Pike railway system was still expanding towards new pits in 1889 when *Quartus,* a four coupled engine 0-4-2WT, was bought secondhand from a Leeds company. About this time the greatest of the Purbeck pits was being dug, a deep hole behind Old Bond Street at the Grange Gate. Today it too is filled with water, has a resident flock of Canada geese and many ducks and is overhung by the dense foliage of the Breach Plantation. The great open lake is surrounded by impenetrable undergrowth and trees, and even where the water comes within forty yards of the Grange Road you are unable to obtain more than a poor glimpse.

Further extensions of the line took it to the region of small, old fields held by numerous belts, woods and banks of trees to the north of Creech Grange. The railway then reached to Povington where today there are extensive pits inside the army ranges, and still in full production, though without their original life-line. It was also during this century that the railway threw an elaborate offshoot with several sidings extending south through the remains of earlier pits to Blackhills, Cotness, East Creech, and as far as the eastern slopes of Creech Barrow. A couple of pits at Cotness are still in use.

Other engines working the railway system in its heyday were *Quintus, Sextus* and *Septimus.* The first was a domeless 0-4-0ST made by Manning Wardle in 1914 and the other two were 0-4-2ST types built by Peckett in 1925 and 1930. Wooden waggons were used all across the Pike network and at one time over a hundred were in regular use. All the steam engines were ousted by diesel tractors in the 1950s and the entire railway closed in the 1960s. The Pike railway system had extended three miles from Furzebrook to West Creech and also developed numerous sidings including that intricate layout to Cotness and East Creech.

Opencast claypits are now less fashionable and the inconspicuous underground mines have become far more important. There are many of these in unlikely positions such as underneath the well known viewpoint of Creech Barrow, and each has a narrow gauge (about 1 foot 10 inches) incline railway with cable-hauled trucks operating between the workface and the surface. Underground the men wear blue boilersuits and miners' helmets, and cut the clay with pneumatic spades. Waggons are winched up long tunnels to the sheds which are partially visible and set at an angle at the head of the mine.

Traditionally, the clay used to be cut in chunks about a foot square and transferred at the head of the shaft into the larger trucks of the mineral railway. Trains went to the weathering grounds and along the top of hillocks of clay, to tip their loads on to great heaps. There it stayed for six months whilst it was frequently turned over and aired to improve the plasticity of the clay. This has all been done away with by modern methods which also remove the necessity for trains. The name of the clay, 'ball' is also an echo of the past, deriving probably from *tubal*, a type of spade used formerly in the pits.

Having closed their railway, Pike Brothers use lorries to transport clay—most of it coming from under the army ranges at West Creech—to the processing works, a collection of sheds covering ten acres at Furzebrook. There are still sidings of the Swanage branch of British Railways at Furzebrook but road transport takes most of the clay out of Purbeck. The processing methods crush and shred the clay, remove moisture and put it through various stages of dry mixing, before turning it into a fine powder blown through air flotation mills. After shredding, blending, drying and granulating, the clay is artificially weathered—subjecting it to alternate cutting, soaking, pressure sprays, moving and further soaking. The effect of two years' weather on the clay is achieved in only a matter of weeks.

These processes have greatly speeded the output of clay from Purbeck and with the exploitation of the extensive deposits under the Lulworth and East Holme Ranges at West Creech and Povington, the total quantity leaving Purbeck is currently well over a hundred thousand tons each year. Only a quarter of this comes from the few remaining opencast pits and these are opened only where the over-burden above the clay seams is under thirty feet deep. Underground mines provide the bulk of the production, and operate mainly on a mining principle that starts with a shaft being bored into the ground at an angle, then becoming a 'drift mine' following the seams under the heath. Clay seams are usually found two or three together in veins that the workers call *lenses*. Each lens covers several acres and can be between fifteen and fifty feet thick. In common with other strata in Purbeck, the lenses lie at an angle to the land above, and are covered by an over-burden of sand and loam anything from a few feet to more than two hundred feet deep. The output of the Purbeck ball clay industry was 130,856 tons in 1965 from nineteen workings and the total workforce numbered 201 men. The principal workings were drift mines and shafts beneath the north face of the Purbeck Hills where, according to the Dorset County Council's planning department, "estimates suggest there may be as much as four million tons of clay". Ball clay, despite this, is a rare substance and John Cooper, managing director of E.C.C. Ball Clays Limited, told me reserves are definitely not adequate for the foreseeable future. Suggested reserves for the security of the industry and its customers were given by the old Ministry of Housing as at least sixty years' supply. The 1971 price of high quality ball clay was £5 to £10 a ton depending on the degree of processing.

Purbeck claymining, unlike many other traditional mineral industries in southern England, has not suffered a decline. This is because the deposits of the raw material, much of it having the finest grain size and therefore the highest plasticity, still lie in quantity under the Great Heath. Layers of clay are consistently similar in texture and sufficiently thick to allow the use of pneumatic spades on the workface. The two old Purbeck clay companies were able to adapt to the full mechanised methods necessary for any historic industry to continue working in a competitive world where vast imports from overseas have caused many of Britain's traditional mineral extractions to cease. Local ownership of the Purbeck pits ended however in 1968 when English China Clays paid £30,000 cash and £1.2 million in shares to acquire Pike Bros., Fayle and Company. In June 1971 E.C.C. Ball Clays Limited gave me a list of its present workings: *Mines*—Aldermoor, Creech Barrow, East Holme, Grange, Greenspecks, Killwood, Norden 6, Norden 14, Ridge Heath and North Trigon. The last is outside Purbeck and lies in the Piddle valley two miles from Wareham. *Quarries*—Holme Priory, Gadle Nap, Povington, Norden, Trigon, Aldermoor and Squirrel Cottage at Holme Lane. *Works*—Furzebrook Clay Store, Furzebrook Shredders, Furzebrook Drier, Furzebrook Mill and Control Laboratory.

Dorset ball clay continues to be used at home in old established works like Poole Pottery and the potteries of north Staffordshire. The British pottery industry stays concentrated in that one district and fifty years ago it was calculated that no less than seventy-two percent of the country's male pottery workers were living there. Demand for ball clay from Dorset had developed originally when other Staffordshire potters imitated the new skills found by the Wedgwood family and from their studies came salt glazing, the use of moulds, and the realisation that more care had to be taken when selecting clays for their colour and consistency. Ball clay fires white, or near white, when heated in an oxydising atmosphere to between 1,000 and 1,400 degrees centigrade.

Although the Staffordshire potteries still take considerable quantities of ball clay, over sixty percent of the Purbeck output is now either directly exported from Britain as a raw material or leaves as finished articles produced by the ceramics industry. Exports go to almost every European country, America, Australia, India, South Africa and many smaller nations. About two hundred workers are now employed in the Purbeck mines, pits and clay works. They are maintaining a wealthy industry that has enjoyed success for two centuries and left us a physical legacy in the very shape of the land. The effect of the old methods of working has been to create on the Great Heath between Povington and Norden a landscape unequalled in Dorset.

Industry on this scale was bound to upset the geography of the region but it displaced surprisingly few people in the process. The area was poor and extremely thinly populated. The only habitations were such as Killwood: a lonely cottage beside a spring and amongst some small and ancient fields on the mixed soils of sand and chalk to the north of Knowle Hill. It has now disappeared but went probably because of the extinction of the heathland crofters rather than through the ramifications of nearby pits and shafts. On the other hand the destruction of Arfleet Mill on the Corfe River to the north of the castle was a definite loss, especially as fifty-five years ago corn was being ground in the old building, continuing an industry which had been carried on at that place throughout the middle ages. *Alfledesmulle* was recorded as its name in 1318. Even after Arfleet was demolished, the area was only lightly scoured but it was needed mainly as an access to deeper workings beside Rollington Wood. The sluices, mill pond and traces of a picturesque setting are gone and the Corfe River itself takes a miserable, overgrown course through the only depressing corner of the Purbeck clayfields.

In the future it is likely to be conservation aspects that cause most controversy. E.C.C. Ball Clays Limited holds a lease to the whole of the Arne peninsula and inland as far as Stoborough Green. Drilling started in March 1971 as part of an extensive geological exploration of the area to establish its potential reserves of ball clay. Industry will inevitably return to the region of the Roman pottery kilns and the rushy ponds where Thomas Hyde had his clay pits two centuries ago.

Pike Brothers, Fayle and Company obtained a lease at Arne

53

from Colonel Harold Scott of Encombe in 1950. Planning permission was given in 1957 for clay extraction at Froxen Copse, an attractive belt of old woodland, on the extreme north of the peninsula between the Wareham Channel and Arne Bay. This mining consent has not been taken up and English China Clays now prefer to have a co-ordinated plan for an extensive exploration of the Arne clayfield before starting any operations.

The main conservationist opposition is on the ground that the wide areas of furze at Arne are the habitat of the country's principal colony of the Dartford warbler, *Sylvia undata dartfordiensis*. This is one of Britain's rarest breeding birds and it has been on the verge of extinction for most of the last hundred years. Apart from the natural threat of snowy winters, at Arne it has also had to survive the devastation of the region by battle ranges, used by allied troops rehearsing the Normandy landings. The Royal Society for the Protection of Birds holds a reserve to the south of the Shipstal road, specifically for the conservation of the warbler. English China Clays will not do any prospecting in this area and the completed mining proposals, when submitted for planning permission in 1972, will not touch the reserve. No less than 3,016 acres, however, of the heathland at Arne has been scheduled by the Nature Conservancy as a "site of special scientific interest" and forms "an outstanding example of Dorset lowland heath". The Conservancy gives the ecological rating of most of Arne as "nationally important".

The coming objections to the Arne clayfield will not be about the bird sanctuary itself but the wider issue of whether the existence of suitable habitats elsewhere at Arne is essential for the survival of the birds. It is ironical that the clay surveyors, having for so long changed entire landscapes completely as they wished, are now faced with having to ensure the conservation of about a hundred tiny birds.

"The Night-Jar. Goat-Sucker, Dor-Hawk, or Fern Owl." One of the more unusual denizens of the heath, with folklore to match, as is indicated by the country names given it in the caption to this woodcut by Thomas Bewick. Nationally it is a rarity, but nightjars are still common on the Arne peninsula and other heather-clad parts of Purbeck.

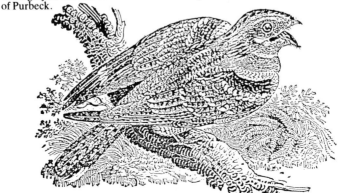

CHAPTER V

Cement, Shale And Oil

EXTENDING THIS account of the mineral wealth of Purbeck to lesser known extractions gives this book an industrial bias such that it paints an unreal picture of Purbeck Island. Whereas the countryside was, and is, comparatively remote and empty the extent of the removal of raw materials has not been sufficient to mar the landscape. Many of the marks of thriving industry of one hundred years ago have in fact now disappeared completely.

Creech Brickworks and its kilns have vanished in the cover of Cotness Wood. To the southeast, where the county road from Furzebrook climbs a pass in the Purbeck ridge to the hairpin bend at Bare Cross and the hillside settlement of Cocknowle, there lies a fainter trace of the past. Some of the quarries that fringe the south top of the hill are popular for Sunday picnics. But there is something else that nobody realises is a piece of industrial archaeology.

Southwards from the modern chalk quarry dug into Stonehill Down, which produced five hundred tons a year for the processing of ball clay at the Furzebrook works of English China Clays, is a grass track to Victorian workings at the top of the Purbeck Hills. The modern tarred road takes an easier course up the coombe. Straight uphill from where they part there is a fence.

One hundred years ago it was an operational cable-worked incline railway. Loaded drums descending hauled the empty ones back. Marl is decayed chalky soil from surface layers and was widely used as a fertilizer during the past two centuries. The chalk pits where it was dug can be found along the entire base of the Purbeck chalk ridge, especially on the south side and between Corfe Castle and Godlingston.

Cocknowle quarries, however, were different and the tramway took the chalk northward—away from the Purbeck farmlands—to be hauled by carts across the heath to Ridge. Here, on the mixed soils between the heath and the Frome marshes, plots of land were given to the homeless after that vast tract of common land, the heath between Stoborough and Corfe, was enclosed in the second half of the eighteenth century and cleared of its inhabitants.

At Ridge, T. P. Powell built Wareham Cement Works in the third field west from the Pike clay works. Comparisons with old maps indicate that he probably diverted a stream on Stoborough Heath to bring water running beside his works. The local correspondent for the Dorset County Chronicle visited Wareham Cement Works in 1881:

> The marl is passed through a mortar pan and worked into a plastic state, then it is mixed with a dry ground marl and put through a pug mill, coming out in the shape of bricks, which are wheeled into the yard and stacked on hacks for drying. There are four kilns used for burning these bricks, which are laid alternatively with coke, taking about thirty hours in the process, during which the bricks become reduced about one third in weight and rendered into clinkers. These are passed through a powerful Blake's crusher and reduced to about the size of walnuts. This is raised to the hopperbox above the mill stones by means of an elevator.
>
> I am told that the sieve, through which all the cement passes, has 1,600 meshes to the square inch. That which does not come up to the crucial test passes below to a small pair of stones, and is carried up again to the sieve. After undergoing this process it is run down into bins to the floor below. Here there is a very large stack in bulk, as well as on the ground floor, and it is from this that the men are weighing it in bags and putting it into casks ready to be sent away.
>
> The machinery is worked by a powerful horizontal condensing engine, the fly wheel of which weighs four tons and measures twelve feet in diameter. This and the double-flue Cornish boiler was supplied by Messrs. Lewin, of Poole. The qualities of this cement were afterwards tested with a Michele's machine—briquetts were placed in it.
>
> The first (two months old) stood the test of 1,400 lb. to the $1\frac{1}{2}$ inch by $1\frac{1}{2}$ inch section. One at one month broke at 1,000 lb. and the third (only six days old) stood the test of 1,000 lb. and did not break. All these were immersed in water when only a day old. This, I believe, is equal to any cement that is made, being considerably beyond the Government requirements, and is spoken well of in a number of testimonials.

Far longer ago, there was another Purbeck industry that has now vanished. The Domesday survey of 1086 records that the Count of Mortain, King William's half-brother, owned thirty-two saltpans (*saline*) at Studland valued at forty shillings and part of a manor worth £8. Another thirteen saltpans, held by Milton Abbey, were at Ower. The University of London commentary to the translation of the Dorset section of the Domesday Book states:

> Later evidence records saltcotes in the same areas. Robert of Lincoln, in his charter founding the priory of Holme as a cell of Montacute, gave to it one tithe of salt from his saltcotes adjoining the manor of Langton Matravers, and Robert's son Alvred in confirming and extending his father's grant mentions a tithe of salt from his saltcotes in Purbeck. In the second survey of Shaftesbury

Abbey's lands (dating from the later twelfth century) there is an account of Arne in Purbeck, which consisted of a hide of land devoted entirely to the production of salt. Since all the places named are on the seaboard, it is evident that the salt was refined from sea-water and not from brine-pits, and the account of Arne mentions the *plumba,* leaden vessels used to collect and boil the sea-water and isolate the salt.

The boiling of sea water for salt was practised in Purbeck centuries before Domesday. Debris from Roman salt extraction operations has been discovered north of Bank Gate Cottages, just east of The Moors at Arne, three hundred yards from the present shoreline of Wareham Channel. The area was being ploughed for conifer planting and the ground was strewn with briquetage: fragments of brick-like clay containers used in the manufacture of salt. More extensive remains have been found across a wide shelf of land on the edge of the scarp bordering mudflats to the south of Shipstal Point. Other evidence has come from Fitzworth and Ower. There is also debris from Roman salt making at Kimmeridge, beyond the pier at the south end of the bay, where briquetage lies in a deposit four feet thick just above the high water mark.

Manufacture of salt was later to be revived near this point. It is recorded from the 1620s that salt was being extracted from the sea at Kimmeridge Bay by Sir William Clavell who obtained white common salt "in great abundance, by boiling it out of the sea water". The site of these operations was probably at an area known as Cuddle on the northwest side of Hen Cliff. The name has now been transferred to an area of clifftop above the west end of the Kimmeridge Ledges. "Cuddle" is given in Wright's "Dialect Dictionary" as a Cornish miner's word for a "thick, muddy fluid".

Kimmeridge is also of industrial interest because of a thin layer of bituminous shale less than three feet in thickness that runs through the greyish masses of the bed known to geologists as Kimmeridge clay. This shale is called *blackstone* or "Kimmeridge coal" and the story of its exploitation is a chequered piece of history, though its first phase was a considerable success. It all started with hand-cut imitation jet armlets made from shale about 400 BC.

Later in the Iron Age, and to a far greater extent in the Roman period, the bracelets of Kimmeridge shale were mass-produced by Celtic craftsmen working with wooden lathes at a large number of sites across southern Purbeck. The output of the industry was vast. An indication of its extent came in 1859 at Povington when J. H. Austen found flint tools, broken bracelets and more than six hundred shale cores from two small excavations of only about a yard in diameter. Substantial quantities have since been found at other sites but the worked shale soon disintegrates on exposure to the air and laboratory treatment is necessary if it is to be preserved. The cores were the waste product of the process and have chuck holes which were made to enable the pieces of shale to be held in the lathe. These cores are also circular and this led to their local name of 'coal-money'. David Calkin of Langton Matravers has turned a number of shale armlets by using flint tools and he cleared up many of the technical points which had puzzled archaeologists. His father, J. Bernard Calkin, has fully investigated the industry and the extract below comes from a paper on "Kimmeridge Coal-money":

> When the shale is freshly quarried, its texture and hardness closely resemble those of slate. Cleavage planes form a low angle with the bedding, and often prevent satisfactory splitting. If struck sharply the shale develops a conchoidal fracture. It is light in weight, and greyish-black or brownish-black in colour. Of a dull and uninteresting appearance, it at once comes to life if smoothed and polished with beeswax, and then looks very much like jet.
> Shale quarried in ancient times and consequently weathered has undergone a profound change. It is generally found to be much cracked, and upon drying, the cracks open. It becomes brittle, is inclined to curl and shrink, and may slowly break away in small pieces. This change of condition, which is reflected by a lowering in its specific gravity, is perhaps the result of loss through oxidation of its oily content. Anyone who is only familiar with the shale in its weathered condition can have little idea of its original toughness and strength.

This material was also cut and carved into sheets for panels, flat dishes, floor tiles, spindle-whorls, small carvings and furniture. Shale table-legs have been found at Silchester and in Dorset at Frampton, Preston and Colliton Park. The best summary of this aspect of the Kimmeridge shale industry is by the late Ian Richmond in his "Roman Britain" where he wrote that the "table furnishings were modelled upon metal prototypes, just as were Victorian trays of papier-mâché, though the hardness of the shale suited the treatment better. Even furniture was thus made, table-legs with claw-feet and sea-horse or sea-lion shoulders being known and widely distributed in southern Britain, though not common. Furniture of this kind must have been difficult and hazardous to manufacture, and consequently both expensive to buy and frail to maintain, though it could be kept in good condition by oiling".

Richmond added that the patterns on this type of work were always run on strictly classical lines, which shows a surprising degree of Roman influence for what has always been looked upon as a native industry. Obviously, it had to adapt to Roman tastes but the majority of villas and town houses were owned by Romanised Celts and some traces of British culture did survive. The absence of such traditions from Kimmeridge implies that the native workers of the shale industry were directed by a Roman management. At any event manufacture of shale commodities ceased completely at the end of the Roman period. The Saxons made no attempt to revive an industry that had flourished for eight centuries. Only another use of Kimmeridge shale was maintained and lasted into more recent times. In his "Observations on the Western Counties", published in 1797, W. G. Maton wrote: "It burns very strong and bright; and emits a sulphureous smell. When exposed to the atmosphere, it soon falls into pieces; but in the cliffs, or under water, it is very hard. The price is about eight shillings per ton; it is chiefly used in ovens and by the poor people."

Only the poor ignored the vile smell and used the shale as fuel. The story of latter days at Kimmeridge is nothing if not a study in failure until this century brought the highly successful drilling for oil. The saga of the later history began in the 1560s when Lord Mountjoy discovered that the land at Kimmeridge was "full of allom myne" and he obtained a patent to make alum there. In this usage the word 'mine' has its older meaning as the 'ore' of a material and refers to the 'alum shale'. Alum is a double sulphate of aluminium and potassium which is widely used in medicine and the arts. Mountjoy's plan was unsuccessful but it was taken up again by Sir William Clavell, the owner of Kimmeridge, around 1600. When Clavell had perfected the production process, his alum works was seized by a group of London merchants who had been granted King James I's sole patent for making alum. They took possession of Clavell's "houses, furnaces and cole pitts" and only left when he agreed to pay them £1,000 'rent' each year.

Months later, however, they returned and systematically ransacked all the alum houses and sold off all Clavell's chattels. Sir William retaliated by spending £4,000 on litigation at the same time as turning Kimmeridge into a port by building a pier one hundred feet long, fifteen feet high and sixty feet wide. The height of this quay is given on one document as fifty feet but that is obviously a mistake as a structure of such height would be totally unusable as a pier or anything else. This pier was described in the 1620s as a "little key in imitation of that at Lime" (the Cobb at Lyme Regis) and it was apparently allowed to fall into disrepair, finally being destroyed by a storm in 1745. Its remains, large blocks of squared stone, can be seen at the east side of the bay, together with a ruined section of sea wall that was also built by Clavell. A later wall, built in the nineteenth century, has survived in better condition.

Clavell's next venture was glass making, an industry modernised about that time by the use of coal instead of wood for smelting. Admiral Sir Robert Mansel sold a concession in 1617 to Abraham Bigo, glassmaker, allowing him to set up a glass-house to make green drinking glass in the Isle of Purbeck. Bigo went into business with Clavell and used shale as fuel on a site at Kimmeridge. By 1621, Clavell himself was on the edge of the law and challenging the terms of the concession. Royalties were unpaid; glass sold in London against a clause in the agreement; workers forcibly removed from Mansel's Newcastle works to one Clavell had involved himself with in Scotland. After two periods in prison, Clavell was released in 1626 with a free pardon given on condition that he discontinued glass making. His losses were above £20,000 and he died in 1644 without recovering his financial position.

Industry ceased at Kimmeridge until the short lived Bituminous Shale Company which between 1848 and 1854 produced varnish, grease, pitch, naphtha, dyes, wax, fertiliser and other coal by-products from its works at Weymouth. The raw material was shale from Kimmeridge and the company appears to have built the earliest tramway at Kimmeridge, a short section of about six hundred yards running a short distance east of the Clavell Tower, keeping to the contours of the hill and descending in a cutting at a gradient of about one in forty. It stretches from the south end of Hen Cliff to a terrace on the cliff above the boathouses. An Act of Parliament in 1847 had given authority for the construction of "railways, inclined planes, causeways" at Kimmeridge.

Another and longer tramway was built to link a mine shaft half a mile east-southeast of the Clavell Tower with a short siding that ran into an opencast working north of the 'D' Plantation, and then down the valley, below the old coastguard station, on to the rocky beach and along a short length of wooden pier that has now disintegrated. Part of the line of this tramway can be seen as a scattering of stones in winter and as a crop-mark across the fields in summer. It was probably built by Wanostrocht and Company who obtained a contract in 1858 to light Paris with gas refined from shale oil. Fifty tons of this oil were produced each month at its Wareham works and fertilisers were also exported to America but the company failed because of the rapid competition presented by the development of other products. After an attempt by another concern in 1876 to make a filter from Kimmeridge shale for the purification of sewage, which also came to nothing, all attempts to exploit the shale beds ended until the search for oil.

In a recently published booklet "Kimmeridge and Smedmore", J. C. Mansel fully documents the industrial history of this section of the Purbeck coast. He writes:

> The most obvious remains of the nineteenth century enterprises are to be seen in the cliff at Clavell's Hard, a mile to the south-east of the bay. Here were tunnels running into the cliff about thirty feet above the shore level. One such tunnel still remains, though its mouth is gradually being closed by falling shale. They were connected by a ledge, presumably artificial, which still remains, though in an unsafe and dilapidated condition. Along the ledge once ran a railway from tunnel to tunnel. Below the ledge, at low tide, one can find circular cuttings in the flat rock, usually covered by seaweed or full of stones. In these are the metal bases of uprights of which the purpose was presumably to carry some sort of pier.

Donald Maxwell mentioned these workings in his "Unknown Dorset", a book published in 1927:

> . . . our guide made us ascend the cliff at a point where this was possible, and we came to a ledge about halfway to the summit. This, he explained, was the track of an old tramline that carried the trucks from the tunnels to the quay. At the end of this gallery was the opening to one of the workings, still accessible and not, as is the case of all the others, barred by debris. . . . It is now so irregular and so cut into by the weather and consequent landslides that it is hardly recognisable as the track of a railway.

Exploration for oil at Kimmeridge was started by a geological survey team at the end of the First World War. Maxwell predicted in his book: "The possibilities of shale oil are the best hope of resuscitating the industry". Borings for oil in the Kimmeridge clay beds were continued in the 1950s. The main hope lay at Kimmeridge Bay itself where the beds show their fullest development and depth. These exploratory rigs found the formation there has a maximum downward extent of 1,651 ft. (almost entirely beneath sea level) compared with a thickness of little over eight hundred feet at Ringstead nine miles to the west. The national Geological Survey stated about Kimmeridge in 1948: "Tests here have been made from time to time with a view to its exploitation as a source of oil, but hitherto the high percentage of sulphur is one factor among others that has prevented its being used."

By 1959 the difficulties were overcome and Britain's most successful 'on shore' oil well established above the sea a short distance west of Gaulter Gap and only a few feet from the boundary of the army ranges. The well is operated by British Petroleum and takes from a point in the Cornbrash at 1,850 feet below the ground. The labour-force comprises four men: two drivers and two pump attendants. All the crude oil is carried by road tankers to Wareham station where it is pumped into railway tankers. Each holds thirty tons and I am told that a train of around twenty waggons runs to Ellesmere Port, Cheshire, each week. The oil is refined there. Official figures are difficult to obtain but 13,132 tons of crude oil left Purbeck in 1964 and it was said to be of a high grade. On 21 October 1968 Kimmeridge became the first English oil well to produce more than 100,000 tons of crude oil. The tale of Kimmeridge has at last lived up to its ancient beginnings and prosperity.

Dorset's Texas: Wytch Farm

Hindsight The above chapter ending now sounds as if it is from a past century, as indeed it is poised to become. The sea-change in Purbeck's oil fortunes came in the autumn of 1973 on the opposite shore from Kimmeridge Bay, on the inland side of the Isle of Purbeck beside the placid backwaters of Poole Harbour, at Ordnance Survey map grid reference SY 980 853. Petroleum production licence PL 089, operated by the British Gas Council, had hit the bullseye beneath a field beside the pine plantations of the Rempstone Forest.

Oil-site 'X' for exploration took the obscure placename Wytch Farm into national currency. A whole oil-field would follow. As I wrote in *Purbeck's Heath — claypits, nature and the oilfield*, more oil was "discovered in Purbeck in 1974 than was found that year in the whole of Texas", and the reserves were estimated to be around nine billion tonnes of top quality crude.

The Wytch Farm field taps the oil impregnated sandstones of the Jurassic and Triassic ages, between 144 and 248 million years old. The oils of the North Sea are thought to have been generated in the deposit that carries a Dorset name, the Kimmeridge Clays, being the result of organic decay of liptinite, exinite and vitrinite materials at temperatures between 95 to 105 degrees C. The North Sea oils are probably a little earlier than the Purbeck kind, being dated to the late Jurassic and early Cretaceous ages of 100 to 200 million years ago. Despite the strong sulphurous smell of the Kimmeridge coast, the oils from this deposit are sulphur free and of the finest quality, known as "British light sulphur-free", needing minimal refining though they are mixed with Arab oils for the manufacture of the end products.

CHAPTER VI

Channel Wreckage

THE SEA and the harbour comprise three of the four sides of Purbeck. Those waters of the English Channel have been one of the world's busiest highways since before the advent of written history and, as would be expected, the sea has had a disproportionately great effect on the lives of those living behind the rocky headlands that project seawards from the Dorset mainland. St. Alban's Head, Kimmeridge Ledges, and the sheer stone cliffs that form an unclimbable wall to Durlston Head have all seen countless shipwrecks and drowned life. The news of a wreck once spread fast between the villages, farmsteads and cottages, and people came not to help or watch, but with ropes and gear from the quarries because each new disaster brought fresh impetus to the local economy.

Thomas Bond told an antiquarian meeting at Corfe Castle in March 1867: "The Purbeck peasants appear to have been not less addicted to the lawless practice of wrecking than were, at that time, the inhabitants of other sea coasts, and perhaps if anything could palliate such enormities on the part of the peasantry, it might be, that they were countenanced by the gentry of the area."

In the year 1371, during the reign of Edward III, a special commission was called to try no less than a hundred persons for their part in robbing the ship *Welfare* of Dartmouth which had been sailing from Devon for London. The ship was in difficulties off Portland and was driven ashore at Kimmeridge. Her freight included thirty-two pieces of cloth of gold, bales of richly embroidered silk, and other merchandise to the value of £2,000 in the currency of that time.

The trial was at Sherborne, at a considerably later date, when many of the accused were found guilty of robbery. Robert Knolles, the owner of the vessel, had been "insulted, wounded and maltreated" and the plunderers had been encouraged and assisted by no less a person than Thomas, Abbot of Cerne Abbas, who had the freight taken and stored in buildings at Kimmeridge. As the owner of the manor of Kimmeridge, the Abbot had a right of wreck to the shore there, but the *Welfare*—because she beached and was held by her crew—was not a 'legal' wreck.

The right to the wreck of the sea has legally gone with the manor of Kimmeridge and this has not yet been forgotten. Eustace Mansel, of Smedmore, recalled: "In about 1872, I saw a spar washed into Kimmeridge; it was afterwards found to measure three feet thick and seventy feet long. The admiralty claimed it. My father produced the deed of 1554 and it was allowed that it was his right to claim it if not claimed by the rightful owner within a year and a day."

Among those convicted when the verdict was reached in 1377 were not only the Abbot and one of his monks, but members of the landed gentry of Purbeck who included William Chaldecote; John Anderbode, of Brinscombe; William Wyat and his son, of Kimmeridge; John Russel, of Tyneham; John Swanland; and Thomas Gerard, of Corfe Castle.

Even in the slightly more civilised year of 1786, when the *Halsewell*, an East Indiaman, foundered below the cliff between Winspit and Seacombe and was dashed to pieces by the sea, some of her fittings were salved and became part of the furnishings of Purbeck homes. Slanting against the cliff at the east end of the Winspit cliffside quarry gallery is the Halsewell Rock. Some survivors struggled up this rock and were rescued by ropes lowered by quarrymen; but on that sixth day of January, 168 of those aboard were drowned. The Gentleman's Magazine reported: "The few men who escaped were most terribly bruised, and some had their limbs broken from being dashed on the rocks. The East India Company's loss is valued only at about £60,000. Captain [Richard] Pierce was the oldest captain in their service, and proposed to retire, had it pleased providence to permit his return from this voyage."

The ship was described as a total loss, having been reduced to driftwood, but there is evidence that a hasty and competent salvage operation was carried out as the gale abated. Even an item as delicate as a large green hour-glass was saved and can now be seen in the County Museum at Dorchester. A mirror from the wreck hangs in the parish church at Worth Matravers. In 1786, the year of the wreck, a house standing near the New Inn at Swanage was rebuilt and in one of the bedrooms a cupboard was fitted in the wall. This small cupboard has glazed doors, a semicircular top, and has been identified as the private cupboard of the captain of the *Halsewell* who died with his ship.

Rev. M. Jones, the vicar of Worth, recorded the disaster in his parish register: "On the fourth, fifth and sixth of January, a remarkable snow storm, sometimes a hurricane, with the wind at south. On the latter day, at two in the morning, the *Halsewell*

East Indiaman, 758 tons burthen, commanded by Captain Richard Pierce, bound for Bengal, was lost on the rocks between Seacombe and Winspit quarries in this parish. Never did happen so complete a wreck. The ship long before day-break was shattered to pieces, and a very small part of her cargo saved. It proved fatal to a hundred and sixty-eight persons, among whom were the captain, two of his daughters, and five other young ladies. Eighty-two men, by the exertion and humanity of the inhabitants and neighbouring quarriers, at the imminent hazard of their own lives, were saved. The East India company, to reward such merit, sent a hundred guineas to be distributed among them."

The dead from the *Halsewell* were buried beneath low mounds in Seacombe Bottom and their graves marked by guns recovered from the ship, but these had disappeared within fifty years of the shipwreck. The lasting memory of the tragedy is not to be found on the ground but among the old men, a dying race of hardy fishermen, who included figures like Billy Winspit. He told me to walk round East Man, along the clifftop path, to the first stile and there stop and look down more than one hundred feet to the rock on to which the sixty-eight survivors climbed and clung. In 1967, three Swanage divers found a cannon from the wreck of the *Halsewell* and they recovered coins, cannon balls, lead shot, tackle and glass.

Almost every gale in Purbeck claimed casualties by sinking small craft, and less often but more seriously, lives that were lost. Both happened at the end of January in 1866 when hurricane force winds swept the island and blocked the lanes around Studland with dozens of fallen trees. In the village itself, no less than sixty-three large trees were uprooted, and on the other side of the ridge, many more fell at Whitecliff, Godlingston and in a line across country to Encombe. The roof of Afflington Barn was lifted off and a window blew in on the Sunday congregation as they prayed at Kingston church, less than a mile away. At Corfe the gale even demolished part of the castle when it toppled a large part of the octagonal west tower, called the Dungeon (now known as the Butavant Tower), at the top of the steep slope above the old West Mill.

A gale of this intensity had to take lives: and they came from three schooners dashed to pieces on the usually peaceful shore of Studland Bay. Only two people survived and eighteen hands were believed to have drowned. Later that year, on 11 July, the French barque *Georgiana* was driven ashore at Chapman's Pool but her crew and passengers were saved by a line fired to the ship by coastguards. A few months later, a newspaper announced the decision to build a lifeboat station at Chapman's Pool and commented, "the great loss of life and property on this part of the coast have at length aroused the attention of the government and we are happy to say that preparations have commenced for placing a lifeboat in this little bay". The boathouse was built only a few yards from the spot where the *Georgiana* was broken up by the sea. The lifeboat station at Chapman's Pool was short-lived, however, and closed in the 1880s. This was because there was no settlement near the water to provide men for the boat with the speed that an emergency demanded.

A Kimmeridge lifeboat station had been established in 1868, also as a result of the disasters of the 1860s, and its 28-foot, five-oar boat saved many lives in the next twenty years. William Stickland was chosen as coxswain of the boat, *Mary Heape,* at the opening of the station. During a gale on 8 December 1872, she rescued seventeen men, the crew of the German ship *Stralsund* which struck Kimmeridge Ledges. Stickland, a fisherman, was the hero of the rescue and saved many more lives before he retired. He was buried at Tyneham churchyard in March 1881 at the age of sixty-four.

The Chapman's Pool station is now an ordinary boathouse, unusual only for its position beneath the tumbling undercliff and the four hundred foot contour of Emmetts Hill, buttressed at the top by a curtain of yellow stone. Below on the boathouse slipway are the lobster pots of Percy Wallace who has two boats there: he is now a fisherman after retiring as a coastguard at St. Alban's Head.

In January 1879 "the boom of guns quickly made known the fact that the American old three-masted vessel, the *Constitution,* had in the haze and mist of the night" found herself aground on shingle near Old Harry Rocks. The United States frigate was carrying products from France for the Paris Exhibition on the other side of the Atlantic. When morning came, guns, chains, cable and other heavy articles were removed to lighten her and about five steamers spent several hours trying to pull her clear. Eventually a Government tug arrived from Southampton, helped the steamers to release the *Constitution,* and towed her to Portsmouth where only minor damage was found.

Exactly a week later, a 500-ton Norwegian timber schooner *Annie Margretta,* ran into the headland within a few hundred yards of the spot where the frigate had been stranded. The Norwegian vessel had also left France for America. By afternoon, however, she was a total wreck. The Swanage lifeboat itself had found difficulty getting down the Peveril slipway against the force of a heavy sea driven in by easterly wind. The Lifeboat Institution decided to build a groyne to hold back the sea. As for the wreck below Ballard Head, that was auctioned for £45.

The lifeboat, *Charlotte Mary*, was launched from the boathouse at Peveril Point in 1875. Trinity House followed this lead and work started on the Swanage lighthouse in 1880 when a road was pushed forward from Sunnydale to Anvil Point. On Saturday, 29 April 1882, after the lighthouse was operational, a hurricane swept the south coast and when it had subsided the 1,250-ton sailing ship *Alexandrovna* of Liverpool was found to be missing. In the afternoon the ship was blown in towards the lighthouse with her topsails in ribbons and only a staysail set. No crew were seen and in minutes "the fated ship was among the broken billows which covered the sea with foam for hundreds of yards from the rocks". She struck the perpendicular cliff at the Ragged Rocks to the west of Round Down. In ten minutes, when the rescuers had run along the clifftop to the spot, she was in pieces and nothing was seen of the crew of seventy-seven. All were lost and many bodies were later found "jammed in among the rocks, or floating in the waters of the Channel, most of them bearing marks of frightful injuries— inflicted, it is to be hoped, after death".

On the following Thursday evening the steamer *Empress* brought a large party from Bournemouth and Swanage round Durlston Head "to see the remnants of the sad wreck of the unfortunate vessel". They saw "immense quantities of wreck" including two large sections of the ship. One body was found naked with a lifebuoy in its arms and others were picked up "much bruised and disfigured". Describing the hurricane, C. E. Robinson wrote that year: "The phenomenal violence of the gale may be judged from the fact that sea-salt is recorded to have been blown by it more than a hundred miles inland; and that it completely stripped all the trees in exposed situations on the coast of their young green leaves, which the spring had just brought out. The elms at Swanage were not covered with leaf again until past midsummer."

Later, at the other side of Swanage Bay on a fine summer day shortly before the outbreak of the First World War, two pleasure craft were involved in a tragedy off Ballard Head. Vyvyan Floyd recalled the day for me and described how she was out in a sailing boat. There was a second boat nearby. The paddle steamer *Stirling Castle* had pulled away from the pier at Swanage and was gathering speed for Bournemouth—it approached, swamped the Floyds' boat with spray and "suddenly rent the air with its fearful din".

The other small yacht had been sliced in half by the steamer and four of its occupants, including a mother and her two children, were drowned.

That afternoon their father, an Australian, arrived at Swanage by train and was met by the vicar at the station. The Australian was carrying a doll, a present for his small daughter who had been enjoying her birthday in the boat. The doll was buried with the little girl at Studland and Mrs. Floyd, who remembers the sad day so vividly, has never sailed again. To her, the most tragic thing of the whole affair was that the body of the mother was washed up on the beach in front of the house in which the father was staying.

It was not the only accident involving the *Stirling Castle*. She was one of the fastest of the paddle steamers and during 1913 and 1914, her two seasons on the Bournemouth, Swanage and Poole service, she also sank two other yachts. The *Lord Elgin* had previously given many years to the run—introduced by the Bournemouth Steam Packet Company in May 1881 she continued to 1912 without a break—but the *Stirling Castle* followed with a short and undistinguished career off Purbeck. A large paddler (length 175 feet, beam 24 feet, draught ten feet) she was returned to Southampton in October 1914 at the outbreak of the Great War.

After the war, the worst Purbeck shipwreck of this century occurred at 9 p.m. on Friday 9 January 1920 when the freighter *Treveal* (3,226 tons) foundered on Kimmeridge Ledges and thirty-six men, including the captain, drowned. The ship carried a cargo of jute and manganese ore and was on the last leg of her maiden voyage, returning from Calcutta to Dundee. She went aground when nearing St Alban's Head in a heavy sea and sent distress messages by radio and flares. Her wireless signals were received at Portland and a dockyard tug was sent to her assistance.

From this point, the rescue services themselves foundered and were routed by the weather. The tug was beaten by darkness and turned back for Portland. By the morning, two tugs were ready and sent out—one towing the Weymouth lifeboat—but by this time the gale had intensified and tremendous seas were running off St. Alban's Head. It was then feared the lifeboat would be swamped; but instead she was swept away from the stricken steamer and embarked upon her own flight to safety! Having failed to turn into Swanage Bay, the lifeboat eventually passed into the quieter waters of Poole Harbour.

With the rescue operation abandoned in disarray and the sea tipping over the *Treveal*, the captain considered she was on the point of breaking up and ordered the crew to abandon ship. Of the forty-three sailors leaving the ship in two boats, only seven reached the shore. Both boats had been swamped and the men thrown into the sea. The seven who lived were thrown up exhausted by the sea and pulled from the waves by Frank Lander and Rev. M. Piercy, the vicar of Worth Matravers. Piercy held on to a jutting rock and grabbed the sailors as the sea washed them towards him.

The two men from Worth had not been alerted as part of the rescue operations but had heard the endless wailing of the ship's horn and went to Egmont Point at the west end of Chapman's Pool. Had they not gone, the seven sailors would probably have all been dragged to their deaths by the backwash. That those seven survivors were taken to the Anchor Hotel at Swanage was remarkable, but the day is remembered locally for its tragedy: a few witnesses are still living who can recall seeing the bodies of the drowned being carried to the Reading Room at Worth where they were laid out.

Today the *Treveal* lies eight fathoms down, a mile off shore, with her hull still holding together and the cargo of manganese ore remaining intact.

One of the sights of this century was also in a January, that of 1933, when the French liner *L'Atlantique* was watched from the Purbeck cliffs as she blazed from stem to stern in the Channel. Her position, as recorded by one of the onlookers on St. Alban's Head who had a sextant, was about 50° 34′ N—2° 3′ W. The burnt-out liner, which had cost £3 million, was recovered by Captain Schoofs, the commander, and some of his crew. They hoisted the French tricolour and the ship, with upper decks fallen in, was towed to Cherbourg.

A more distant disaster and its repercussions threatened the Purbeck coast in April 1967 after the oil tanker *Torrey Canyon* had broken up off the Cornish coast. Part of her cargo had been ignited by napalm bombs dropped by naval strike fighters, but the bulk of her spillage drifted up the Channel and fouled West Country beaches. It seemed likely that Purbeck would suffer the same fate but the weather changed and northerly winds took the oil slick away towards the French coast.

Poole Harbour had been sealed across its mouth by a thousand-yard boom costing £15,000. It was a novel idea, recommended by Sir Solly Zuckerman, the Wilson Government's chief scientific adviser, and the work was virtually completed in time. The force of the tide at the Haven was then a problem and some of the buoys, anchoring sections of the boom, began to drag their moorings. That difficulty was overcome but the fabric of the boom started to tear and it was hoped to strengthen it with nylon ropes to avert the impending break-up. Northerly winds then came and the boom, in seventy-five feet sections, was dismantled with relief.

The *Torrey Canyon* oil killed countless thousands of sea birds and had long term effect on marine life along the western shores, though these were not as enduring as had been feared. Constructively, it also prompted swift government action: an attempt to destroy the wreck and its oil; a series of official reports and international repercussions − the first glimmer of global awareness that even the immensity of the oceans cannot absorb endless pollution. The English Channel is still one of the world's busiest waterways, and geography has given Purbeck an involvement with the sea greater than that endured by most other coasts − but the waves and tide can no longer guarantee the old fashioned quality of isolationism.

Sinking of the 'Aeolian Sky' in 1979

Hindsight The major Purbeck pollution of recent times came in 1979. The 6,540 ton *Aeolian Sky*, carrying insecticide and other toxic drums, was in collision with the German coaster *Anna Knuppel* on 3 November. The crippled *Aeolian Sky* was towed towards Portland Harbour but she was taking in water at the bows and in the early hours of the following morning she sank in a hundred feet of water about five and a half miles south-west of St Alban's Head.

Studland's Armada wreck

Hindsight Some ancient Spanish timbers were found off Old Harry Rocks in 1984 and caused excitement that it might be the wreck of the great Armada ship *San Salvador*. A chest from her is in the museum at Weymouth.

She carried the Spanish Paymaster-General and most of his gold. On 21 July 1588 she exploded in Lyme Bay, either in an accident or sabotage after an argument on board, and was abandoned as a smouldering hulk.

After being patched up in Weymouth she was fit for a journey to Portsmouth in November 1588 − or so her repairers thought. In Studland Bay she began to sink and the British crew either abandoned ship or drowned.

GATEWAY TO PURBECK. The old South Bridge at Wareham before its demolition in 1925. It was one of the most graceful bridges in Dorset. This route, now across an undistinguished bridge over the River Frome, remained the only main road into Purbeck until 1988 when the A351 was diverted westwards and provided with a motorway style bridge across the meadows in the middle distance.

THE BRIDGE. A closer view of the mediaeval South Bridge over the Frome at Wareham. Standing on the foundations of a bridge probably of the eleventh century, it had last been reconstructed in 1778. The grey Purbeck stone was at that time used again for the cutwaters and five arches seen in this photograph.

THE HARBOUR AND THE HEATH. The Purbeck heathlands rise slowly from the southern shore of Poole Harbour. This view across Arne Bay is dominated by the modern landmark of Poole power station, two miles away, at Hamworthy on the other side of the Wareham Channel. Inland, the Great Heath stretches four miles to the base of the Purbeck ridge at Norden.

HEATHLAND WOOD. Slepe Copse at Arne is one of the few deciduous woodlands on the Purbeck heath. Three thousand acres at Arne have been designated by the Nature Conservancy as the largest "site of special scientific interest" in Dorset.

MINERAL RAILWAY. *Quintus,* a steam engine made in 1914, lay
damaged and abandoned on the Pike Brothers' heathland railway
at Furzebrook in the 1950s. She has since been scrapped and the
entire Pike railway dismantled.

STUDLAND BAY. [Above] The beach at Studland is one of the widest and sandiest on the south coast. On the other side of the bay are chalk cliffs with Old Harry Rocks projecting at the far left.

ANCIENT STONES. [Left] Part of the prehistoric stone circle at Rempstone, dated around 2000 B.C. and erected by Bronze Age man. The woodland in the background is on the northern slope of Nine Barrow Down.

AN OLD MILL. Inside Arfleet Mill on the Corfe River to the north of the castle. Corn was still being ground when this photograph was taken but the building has now long been gone and replaced by the sprawl of Norden clay workings.

WEST MILL. One of the most picturesque settings at Corfe Castle was the old West Mill, photographed here before 1900. An eighteenth century bridge still spans the Corfe River near this point and carries the road to Church Knowle but the mill has been demolished. Some ruins and sluice-gates remain.

CORFE CASTLE. This photograph was taken from Oliver Vye's Lane
which follows the Corfe River below the southwest side of the
castle hill. The tilting outer tower of the Southwest Gatehouse (left)
is eleventh century and the ivy covered Fifth Tower was added
about 1215. Behind looms the Keep with its South Annexe showing
clearly.

CLIFFTOP FOLLY. The circular Clavell Tower above Kimmeridge Bay is a folly built by Rev. John Richards in 1831. It was later used as a lookout by coastguards. The cannon muzzle in the foreground dates from the Napoleonic wars.

TYNEHAM HOUSE. The east front of Tyneham House, one of the finest domestic buildings in Purbeck, was built in 1583. This, the main section of the house, was demolished in 1968 and the remainder of the building lies derelict.

LULWORTH CASTLE. Despite its appearance, Lulworth Castle was
simply a grand house, built to symbolise strength, but without any
military applications whatever. It was built about 1609 and gutted by
fire in 1929. The building is of brick faced with Purbeck and Portland stone.

WORTH MATRAVERS. Typical Purbeck cottages with stone-slated roofs surround the village pond. The parish church is partially obscured by trees towards the top right.

LIMESTONE SCENERY. Mediaeval strip lynchets, part of the open field system of the manor of Worth, cover both sides of the deep valley between the village and Winspit. This track to the sea passes through some of the most impressive scenery of the limestone hills in southern Purbeck.

SEACOMBE CLIFF. The entrance to one of the many extensive underground galleries at Seacombe. This cliff quarry produced finest quality building stone and was in operation up to about 1930.

CLIFF QUARRY. The sea and cliff below Tilly Whim Caves, a cliff quarry worked at least until 1812. Durlston Head projects to the right. This is an old picture of one of the best known corners of Purbeck.

COASTAL DEFENCE. Men and guns of the Dorset Artillery Corps at Peveril Point in the 1880s. The old Swanage pier is in the background.

STONE BANKERS. The bankers were a vast stoneyard on Swanage sea-front, seen here about 1880. Institute Road and The Parade arose from their debris at the turn of the century and this is now the busiest part of modern Swanage.

SWANAGE TOWNSEND. One of the last of the Swanage quarries was still functioning in about 1903. The capstan is in the centre, the towpath shows plainly. and a cart can be seen at the head of the mine shaft, just to the left of the shed.

BURT'S QUARRY. George Burt's quarry, Swanage Cowlease, photographed probably in 1891. Left, in white shirt, dark waistcoat and moleskin trousers, is Sammy Norman. With him is 'Single' Downland and they had just drawn up a block of freestone and disconnected the horse from the spack, attaching it instead to the stone cart. The beam has been replaced across the slide to keep wandering cattle out of danger. Next to the slide is the horse's shed, and then two quarr houses, facing due east. This site is now ruined and overgrown on the edge of the Townsend estate.

THE END. Another part of the Cowlease: but impending desertion is suggested by this photograph of 1910. The spack had been removed from the capstan, stone appears to have blocked the towpath, and Fred Meader and his colleague do not seem to have been working normally.

THE NARROWS. The constricted passage of Swanage High Street through the Narrows has now been entirely opened up. Virtually all the old cottages have been demolished since the taking of this photograph, about 1910, and no one can now remember when stone was hauled through here on its short journey from the quarries to the bankers on the seafront.

THREE COTTAGES. These old cottages, standing in the High Street opposite the Town Hall, Swanage, were demolished in 1959. The two on the right (Hendon's shop and the building with the right-hand chimney-breast) were built in the seventeenth century. The other low cottage, projecting on the left and with the posters, was added in the following century.

The High Street, Old Swanage

TOWN HALL. The building that supports the clock is the Town Hall with its tall, two-storey frontispiece, made for the rebuilding of London after the Great Fire of 1666. Virginia Cottage, on the left of the postcard, dates from the early eighteenth century. The group of old cottages shown in the previous plate can be seen on the opposite side of the High Street.

COURT HILL. One of the prettiest parts of old Swanage, this road branched northward off the High Street. John Mowlem was born in one of the cottages on the left. The scene, however, is now unrecognisable, and only one historic building still stands on Court Hill.

OLD SWANAGE. This used to be the junction of Station Road and Institute Road. The photograph was taken around 1890 and since then the creek on the left has been filled and the stream piped underground. The bridge is gone and so too are all the buildings. Instead there is a maze of lofty Edwardian brick and the Post Office has risen above the stream, on the left. Forte's cafe is now the dominant building on the corner.

HIGH STREET. Since this photograph of 1899, the old houses on the right have been swept away and replaced by Lloyds Bank and other buildings. The only lasting link with the past is the White Swan inn which may be seen behind the horse and cart.

ROUND HOUSE CORNER. This part of Swanage has been known as The
Square since the demolition of the three-storey building. Other old
buildings that can be seen continuing to the right have also gone.
Again, it is the White Swan inn that alone survives. The part that
can be seen jutting out is eighteenth century.

TWO PIERS. Swanage had two piers that were joined together. The old pier (right) was built in 1859 and is now derelict, having rotted apart from the new pier which was added in 1896.

NEW RAILWAY. Swanage Station seen shortly after its completion and the opening of the line. The engine is a Beattie 2-4-0 well tank, No. 209.

CHURCH HILL. [Overleaf] St. Mary's parish church, Swanage, and old cottages on the east side of Church Hill. The house immediately left of the cross has a round arch with the date 1793 and this photograph of about 1920 shows its appearance before it had to be partially rebuilt after bomb damage in 1940.

Smugglers And Coastguards

A BRIEF disturbance on a Lulworth cliff that ended with murder rated only the following short paragraph in a local newspaper of 1832: "An encounter at Lulworth between a Preventive Officer named Knight and his assistant and a party of smugglers resulted in the officer being thrown over the cliffs. He died soon after being found."

The story is told more fully on a gravestone from Weymouth's Bury Street cemetery, now in the town museum:

> Sacred to the Memory of Lieut. Thos. Edward Knight, RN, of Folkestone, Kent, Aged 42, who in the execution of his duty as Chief Officer of the Coastguard was wantonly attacked by a body of smugglers near Lulworth on the night of 28th of June, 1832, by whom after being unmercifully beaten he was thrown over the cliff near Durdle Door from the effects of which he died the following day. By his untimely death the public service has lost a valuable and universally respected officer and sincere friend and his wife and family an affectionate husband and kind father.

That memorial comes from the closing years of the smugglers' era: two centuries of heavy taxation on spirits that brought prosperity to those in a position to evade the excise—the fishermen of the south coast, and those in the manorial homes who financed illicit cargoes, gambling on the fact that four out of five runs came safely through the coastguards' net. The job of landing the kegs and distributing the goods fell to a wider section of the community who played their part in a national network of secret routes and caches. Most of the Purbeck cargoes were shipped out again, across the waters of Poole Harbour, to avoid risk of leaving by the island's easily guarded land exit. Landings were made on the northern harbour shore at Keysworth, West Holton, Lytchett Bay, Hamworthy and Parkstone. The waggon routes inland lay open from these lonely places.

Some loads, however, did go out through the front door of Purbeck. W. M. Hardy recorded in his "Smuggling Days in Purbeck" a rare occurrence of boldness in daylight: "In the year 1796 my grandfather, then a boy ten years old, and living at Wareham, was an eyewitness of a stroke of astonishing bravado and reckless defiance of the law in broad daylight. Well did he remember one day seeing two waggons pass through the main street of the town, coming from the direction of Purbeck and going on to Northport. They were loaded with tubs and the devil-may-care smugglers, with great sticks in their brawny hands, were seated on top of them, evidently ready to defend their property should occasion for doing so arise. . . ."

Frequent landings were made on the cliffs and bays of southern Purbeck, especially Worbarrow, Brandy Bay (an appropriate name), Kimmeridge, Chapman's Pool, Winspit, Dancing Ledge, Tilly Whim, and Durlston Bay. Easier for operations was Studland Bay with its wide sandy bottom and ample areas of dense cover. Often, kegs were hidden temporarily under seaweed that had been dragged up the beach for fertiliser. From there the tubs were carried across the heath to Brand's Point, Greenland or Redhorn Quay and loaded into flat-bottom canoes to be rowed to the other side of the harbour. The closely watched entrance to the harbour at the Haven had to be avoided.

The last person who remembers the smugglers of Purbeck is probably Walter Miller of Chaldon Herring who was born in Rose Cottage on the Burning Cliff at Ringstead, 24 June 1890. He looked back for me to those figures of the past:

My grandfather, Joseph Miller, was born at Worbarrow. He died at West Lulworth in about 1911, aged about seventy-eight. All the Miller family were smugglers before the Crimean War. The landowners and gentry smiled at this as it wasn't considered a crime. If they were caught with their gear and their boat and all that, they had six months imprisonment, but not hard labour.

One of my great uncles did his time at Dorchester. He was unlucky to be caught, and when he came out of jail, he was met by the squires and whatever and taken to the Kings Arms for a good meal; because cellars were getting low, you see. They condoned it in a way.

We have a grapple, used to grapple up the barrels when they were sunk at the bottom. Grandfather, Joseph, had to give up smuggling in 1854 because the Russian war broke out and all the coastguards were called up to serve in the Baltic fleet. Then they recruited all the smugglers to be extra-men, as they called them: that is, coastguards.

Old Harry Vye and my grandfather and a few more had to sit on the cliff and watch for the smugglers who didn't come! They couldn't risk doing the two jobs at once. That's George Begg [*he pointed to a photograph*]. He didn't like me; he used to think I was too mischief-full or something. There was a story of a coastguard who accused a smuggler of doing something, pulled out a revolver and shot this man. What comforted the smugglers was that this coastguard was called up to the fleet in the Russian war, got frostbite —and both his ears fell off. They said it was retribution.

George Begg was at Ringstead and had a boat of his own and went to Cherbourg to get a load. He had a twenty-two foot *lerret* [*Dorset dialect word for a type of fishing boat*] and built a house at Ringstead to conceal it. The boat wasn't on the beach: when he wanted to he just had to slip it out and go to France.

He was a clever old fellow. He used to wear these white trousers when I was a boy: I suppose he died about eighty-five in 1898. Dr. Good from Dorchester came twice and said he was finished, but George Begg got up and went to sea again. He had another bout and this time the doctor said: 'I think he will do.' He died! Dr. Good was wrong in all his predictions. It didn't enhance my father's opinion of doctors.

These memories cover the closing years of the smuggling trade. Another account survives from the opening period of the history of organised illegal importation of spirits and wines, tobacco, pepper and other taxable luxury items. By 1727, the state's annual income from excise duty had reached nearly £2,500,000. Already the business of evasion was far more successful and sophisticated than the inadequate machinery established to ensure that duties were paid.

Phillip Taylor, Collector of Customs at the port of Weymouth, wrote on 11 April 1719:

We have from Sunday last searched Lulworth Castle belonging to Mr. Weld, a Roman Catholic, and many other suspect houses in East and West Lulworth. In the house of Edward Bagwell, a tennant of Mr. Weld, we seized about four gallons of Brandy and about 12 lb. of pepper, from whence we proceeded into the Isle of Purbeck and places adjacent where we seized one anchor of red wine and two anchors of vinegar. And knowing it is the constant practice of smugglers to carry their goods off the coast as soon as possible after landing, as Blackmore [Vale] is the most disaffected part of the county abounding with the greatest numbers of dangerous rogues, two whereof we hear were Thursday last committed for declaring themselves for the Pretender, and consequently a place very fit to be searched, we have accordingly narrowly searched several houses and there seized yesterday in the home of Jacob Fox two anchors of Brandy.

A year before, Taylor had written in despair to his superiors:

The smuggling traders in these parts are grown to such a head that they bidd deffiance to all Law and Government. They come very often in gangs of sixty to one hundred men to the shoar in disguise armed with swords, pistolls, blunderbusses, carbines and quarter staffs; and not only carry off the goods they land in deffiance of the officers, but beat, knock down and abuse whoever they meet in their way; soe that travelling by night neer the coast and the peace of the country are becoming very precarious; and if an effectual Law be not speedily passed, nothing but a military force can support the officers in discharge of their dutyes.

In 1766 the Government increased the scope of smuggling when it banned the importation of foreign made silks and velvets to placate British weavers. Fifty thousand workers had marched on Westminster a year before to protest that their trade was collapsing under overseas competition. Rioting and attacks on the houses of importers continued into the night and the outcome was a set of restrictions that gave smugglers a new job.

A correspondent to the Gentleman's Magazine in 1763 said that one smuggler in the West Country cheated the customs of about £20,000 a year. By 1779 it was calculated by the authorities that thirty-one smuggling boats, between twenty and seventy tons with crews numbering up to twenty, were operating from the Dorset coast. These vessels had, during the previous three years, brought 163,000 gallons of spirits and 780,000 lb. of tea into Britain. In fact, Dorset scored high in the smuggling stakes and only one English county operated more boats. As for productivity, Dorset was beaten by two other counties in the spirits figure and by three for tea. In 1822 a confidential report to the Board of Customs in London commented cryptically: "Much must be doing on the Dorset coast. Brandy is offered at Yeovil at eight shillings a gallon."

Later the officials assessed that no duty was being paid on two-thirds of the tea and half the brandy consumed in the country. Only an insignificant proportion of the trade was intercepted and seized: about 2,000 hogsheads of spirits in Devon, Dorset and Hampshire in a year. This was probably about a tenth of the total brought across the Channel to the three counties.

Six Purbeck smugglers appeared at the Lent assize which opened at Dorchester on 14 March 1834. They were aged between sixteen and thirty-five, and their entry in the "Calendar of Prisoners at Dorchester Prison" reads:

> Committed by the Reverend Nathaniel Bond and the Reverend George Pickard, Junior, charged on the oaths of Lieutenant Henry John Carr, Chief Officer of the Coast Guard stationed at Kimmeridge in the Isle of Purbeck, and others, at a place called Gadcliffe, in the parish of Tyneham, in the said Isle of Purbeck on the evening of the 31 January, they being then and there assembled in order to be aiding and assisting in the illegal landing, running or carrying away, prohibited goods.—Warrant dated 10 February 1834.—*Death recorded.*

That record is misleading: at the Midsummer sessions on 1 July that year their death sentences were commuted to hard labour for a year in each case.

For the coastguards, their work was even more dangerous than that of the smugglers. In the churchyard at Kimmeridge there is a line of gravestones which catalogues the misfortunes of a small band of coastguards. None of them died directly as a result of the smugglers themselves. Nearest to the sea is the headstone of Thomas Lavery, a boatman in the coastguard, who died aged twenty-six after "accidentally falling over the cliff in the execution of his duty" on the night of 7 October 1839.

His headstone, like the next which is to John Perren, was erected by "fellow officers and boatmen". Perren was a boatman who drowned whilst on duty, at the age of twenty-six in Kimmeridge Bay on the night of 14 April 1838. Boatman Alexander Simpson also died aged twenty-six: "killed by his own firearms" in the execution of his duty on the morning of 9 February 1841. Finally, there is a stone to boatman Henry Thomas who died—the stone does not say how—on 13 January 1811 and again at the age of twenty-six.

Walter Miller, whose memories of smugglers are printed near the start of this chapter, also told me about the legitimate old-time fishing industry of Purbeck, Lulworth and Ringstead. He was once advised by his friend Llewelyn Powys: "When you see an old man, ask him all you can." This I did when I was with Miller and he explained how the old fishermen lived and worked by pot-fishing in the shallower offshore waters:

Lobsters used to be caught more than crabs, as those change their skins and are slim before they do so. The saying is that crabs are good when there is an 'r' in the month. But in May, June and July they aren't much good.

There was fifteen fishermen at Lulworth, and now there's only two. There were around six at Worbarrow. There was Jack and Tom, and another called Tarry and his mate, and then there was old Charlie. All were one family originally but Henry Miller, the last one, had two sons, Jack and Tom, and both died during the war after the occupation.

At Ringstead the catch was rowed to Weymouth. That at Worbarrow was taken by fishmongers who used to come down over Tyneham hill from Wareham. They came the same to Lulworth. Father and them, when they couldn't come, they carried their catch on their backs to Weymouth and that was never considered any trouble. The fishmongers at Wareham, when they had too much, put what was over into a packing case. The lobsters were live with seaweed over them. They put them on a fast passenger train to London and they were sold at Billingsgate.

When mother had two lobsters, a pound-and-a-half, she would cook them, cool them down, put them in a basket and I'd take them and sell them at ninepence a pound. That made your mouth water! Everyone would have a feed of lobster sometimes. Good sirloin beef was then eightpence a pound. Visitors would come down and get the lobsters fresh, cooked on spatches.

All these fishermen were rabbit catchers in the winter. They had to because you couldn't make a living out of fishing alone as you couldn't earn enough; there wasn't enough gear. Sixty pots was as much as you could do. Now they work four hundred and the Lulworth Grounds, a huge triangular shape off Lulworth, is prime fishing. They come up from Swanage and down from Brixham. But the lobsters aren't there now and we consider it's overfished. In the old days everything had a chance to live.

Mrs. A. Moulder recorded a conversation with an elderly, weather-beaten Lulworth lady, in an issue of "Dorset, the county magazine", during 1969: "Talking one day about fishing, she told me that since the coming of the Gunnery School lobster fishing had been severely restricted. Many years before, there had also been flourishing, profitable oyster beds. Oyster fishing was done on quite a large scale and an oyster pond was made on the west side of the Cove, where the fish were kept till wanted. She pointed to the outer wall of the pond, which could be seen at low water, though few people knew its origin."

The old lady was one of the last to remember that a fair was held on a broad stone jetty at Lulworth Cove each Easter Monday. This construction was washed away and the last fair stall was then pitched near the hotel. The memory of a forgotten fair at the water's edge; oyster shells that are now always empty; a smugglers' grappling-iron and tub that were discovered at Kimmeridge and hang from a wall in the museum at Dorchester—all these are reminders of the lives of old-time fishermen.

"Meups Rocks and Bay, Warbarrow Bay, Bindon Liberty, Dorset" by Philip Brannon, 1862. – "Mupe Rocks" they are called on twentieth century maps, though locals still talk of them as "Mupes", and "Worbarrow" is the current spelling for the bay. For "Bindon Liberty" read "Lulworth".

CHAPTER VIII

The Hard Old Days

THE ELITE of the old Purbeck working class were the quarrymen and the fishermen. For those born inside the families who made a closed shop of such crafts, the way of life was hard and demanding, but at least it had some of the security denied to the lower classes. Life was tougher and offered less on the north side of the range of hills that separates the richer limestone landscape from the arid barrenness of the heath that spreads across the acid sands to the shore of Poole Harbour.

North of the hills, the faces of the people, the intonation of their tongue, the shape of their clothes, and the state of their stomachs were all different from those of the inbred elite who held the lands above the Channel. The people of the north were called 'heath-croppers' and they were the old peasant stock of Dorset, poor crofters eking a bare existence from the heath and living in dilapidated cottages that were hovels.

Their homes had walls of mud, the yellow cob of east Dorset, under thin roofs of ageing wheat thatch. Each cottage was an oasis of small fields and poor grass standing by a stream or water source amid the empty desolation of the Great Heath which pressed relentlessly with furze and bracken at the pocket of cultivation. As the occupant aged and withered, then could the heath win back its former property and the walls of the cottages were known to crumble to nothing in only three years.

All this created another world, far from the solid strength of the grey stone walls and roofs of the buildings in the quarrying belt of Purbeck. Hubert Smith was born on the wrong side of the hill in 1872 in a thatched cottage at North Castle, in the very shadow of Corfe's ruins. The cottage has since burned down, which is somehow fitting in that the life and times of the era of the underprivileged multitude have also passed.

His mother's rent was ninepence per week and this was paid half-yearly at Rempstone Hall. There, on those two red-lettered days of the year, the tenants would gather for a hot meal in winter and a cold one in summer. Hubert was an elder child and he paid the rent as his parents could not spare the time to visit Rempstone. A member of the staff would inquire of each tenant how many children were living at home—and for each a chunk of bread pudding was cut and wrapped, the traditional treat for the poor.

Young Hubert was brought up to show his respect when the third Lord Eldon's carriage passed through Corfe on its way to Encombe House. Hearing the blare of the postilion's horn, the inhabitants would run to their doors or gates to curtsey or bow. The vicar and three curates at Corfe also expected similar respect from the working class. Hubert Smith's daughter, Mrs. A. F. Riches, described the family's life in a cottage at East Street, Corfe:

> My grandmother had a fire on the hearth and a long iron rod came from the back wall. On this, a gypsy-pot hung and all the food was put in nets and cooked together in the one pot. If my grandmother needed to make a cake she used to get the hearth fire red hot, spread the cinders and make a well. The cake was put in a tin with another tin on top and then sunk into the cinders.
> My great-grandfather built a back-oven in which he used to roast Sunday meat and potatoes for sale in the village at a penny a tin. There were also jam or fruit tarts for a ha'penny. My father was sent out on Saturdays to gather faggots from the woods to heat the oven.
> It was from these pennies that my ancestor earned sufficient to buy his first cow. My great-grandfather worked in the claypits and the social status of the working class in those days depended not on whether you owned your house, but whether you owned a cow. The cow was turned out on Corfe Common during the day, and to be milked it had to be brought home and walked through the passage of the house to a shed at the back.

Sticks were still being collected in the woods for fires at Corfe, as Hubert Smith had done, into recent years. Bread was baked in faggot-heated ovens at Batterick's Bakery as late as the 1950s. This is a disused eighteenth century mill building on the Byle Brook below St. Edward's Bridge at the north end of the village.

The elimination of the Purbeck peasantry from the heathland wastes had started with the enclosure acts of the eighteenth century which enabled vast acreages of common land to be stolen by the gentry. Several parcels of unwanted land, as at Ridge, near Stoborough, were given to the homeless to build hovels but that was scant return for independent crofters who had been driven off the wilderness where their ancestors had learnt the ways of survival. Even the lonely pockets of remote cultivation that did outlast the enclosures have been dispersed during this century.

Clearance and the wartime occupation of the Purbeck heaths by the military have together removed most traces of former life. Up to 1943, inside the present limits of the army ranges, there were homes on the heath at The Cat, north of the Heath Gate on the turnpike from Lulworth to Holmebridge; Povington Farm; White-way Farm; Farwell's Cottage. Eastward, to mention barely a hand-ful of the lost names, there was Churchill's Cottage on the shore west of Arne; Sharford Cottage on Wytch Heath; New Mills on the Corfe River; Thrasher's Cottage west of Bushey; Milford Cottage near Ower Farm. One cob and thatch cottage, immediately south of the white slopes of clay wastes that mark Thrasher's Pit, was dilapidated in the 1960s and by the end of the decade its roof had fallen through. Unlike the others, however, it is being renovated and in 1971 its conversion from a derelict cottage to a country retreat was being completed. The crofters' spiritual retreat was a Wesleyan chapel hidden in the outback of Rempstone at Foxground—a small thatched cottage with the upstairs floor taken out. It was destroyed by fire about 1920.

Shell Bay too has been devoid of habitation since the inn at South Haven collapsed into the sand dunes before the First World War. Nearby were Gotchabed Cottages, likewise gone—as have Curlew Cottages which lay between Brand's Bay and the Little Sea.

Benjamin Pond, who lived in a clay company shack at Goat-horn in the 1920s, saw the decline of the Purbeck heath-croppers:

There were a number of crofters living on the north side of Ballard Down and around the heathland. They were very poor folk who found it difficult to sell their produce. Eventually they found a new market by using a wheel-barrow and pushing their butter, eggs and pork all the way to South Haven [Shell Bay] where the produce was dumped at the inn, which became a ruin between about 1896 and 1914, to await a sailing brig which would convey it to Portsmouth for the naval officers' mess.
You can well imagine what it was like, pushing a loaded barrow five, six or seven miles as the case may be, over rough land. The wheels of these barrows were unusually large, varying from four-teen to eighteen inches in diameter. Even today, if you walk the heath, you can come across the remains of a broken wheel, charred by a past heathfire.
Often it was the womenfolk who pushed these loads. The men had to stay behind and work a ten-hour day to get a return from the desert-like soil.
The last person to walk to the ferry was Mrs. Guy of Greenland Farm. She would carry two big baskets and sometimes a lad would help. She did this once a week until 1929 when I took one of the baskets.

On the other side of Purbeck, where Luckford Lake issues from the overgrown hedgerows of Whiteway and Povington, was the largest and most orderly of the heathland communities and that with the longest history. Most of the small, irregular fields surrounding the hamlet of Povington were created in their present shapes before the Norman Conquest. Half a mile to the north of the chalk ridge, a rough road ran from East Lulworth to Creech Grange and linked tiny farmsteads that grew out of the mixed soils in the long, narrow belt below the hill. Somewhat fertile and watered by ample springs, the settlements were nonetheless constantly pressed from the north by the wide plain of desolation of the dreariest, most uneventful of the Dorset heaths.

To people like Mrs. S. B. White, the thought of returning again to see her former home was too painful to be contemplated. Her mother's homestead on Povington Heath "can just boast a pile of stones, part of a chimney stack and a lonely and gruesome-looking yew tree". She recalled her grandparents for me, and their life at Povington, and this story of the end of one family of heath-croppers shows the disruption caused by military occupation. It was recorded in 1970:

My mother lived in a little house called Whiteway. It seemed large to me when I was a child but I daresay it was really quite small. Whiteway lay almost in a line with the round, scooped out, hollow of chalk in the hillside.

I must have been very young when I was there with my mother, so my recollections are bitty. But I can remember it had a thatched roof and walls of that gritty mud substance; very thick with wide window sills. The large living room had a massive scrubbed table and an open fireplace with a mantelshelf along the top. Mother told of sitting on the stone slabs inside the fireplace, putting on fircones and roasting potatoes during the evenings. A large, black smokey kettle hung on a chain, and you could look up the centre of the chimney and see the sky. Apparently they used to sweep the chimney by letting a faggot of furze (*fuzz,* they called it) down on a stone.

Grandmother was a large, comfortable woman, with a soft singing voice. I only ever saw her with a black dress and enveloping white apron. She smiled a lot and worked very hard. I think she had fourteen children, although I believe some of them died at birth.

The family became very scattered: I think I still have an aunt in Canada, and an aged uncle at Poole. The grandparents could neither read nor write and my mother used to correspond with her two brothers who went to the 1914-18 war. She was forced to convey the news that they were both killed in the battles in France.

I remember a garden with a stream, and lots of outbuildings with chickens and a few cows. There was also a little house down the garden with numerous horseshoes on the lintel of the door and a double-seated lavatory. Mother spoke of having to scrub the seats until they were gleaming white wood. She also told of going up to the chalkpit to clean the knives.

They apparently also had bees. I was always interested in the tales about them, and heard fascinating stories of Grandma telling her bees all family news, both good and bad. Mother often had to go and listen to hear if the bees were singing and if the queen was calling. One of the younger girls, Edith, worked at Tyneham House. She married but her husband was also killed in the war and she was left with a little boy. Later she died and was always discussed in grim whispers (galloping consumption and a broken heart) but Gerald was brought up by another aunt at Hollow Ditch, a smallholding northwest of Creech Grange. I spent many happy holidays with them and am more familiar with that part.

This was a sturdy little house with little windows and thick walls. Large cupboards by the fireplace housed hams and smoked bacon. Breakfasts there were marvellous meals—my aunt and uncle having done hours of work fetching the cows and milking by hand, had by this time developed large appetites. Hence we had masses of eggs, thick slices of bacon and chitterlings and soft potato cakes. Sometimes they cooked eels which cousin Gerald had teased me with early in the morning.

Mother's name was Beatrice Bessie Balson, and you can imagine how she was teased about that. Her sister, Susan, who lived at Hollow Ditch, married Matthew Charles. Grandfather Balson worked at Tyneham House. He had very bright, blue eyes and I remember I was a little in awe of him. He was such a silent, gnome-like figure with his white beard and sideburns.

Little things drift back as I try to recollect. I can remember singing around the old harmonium, which we eventually had in our home, and many times I wept whilst mother sang and laboriously played sad songs. Her mother had taught her songs about little Mary dying, becoming an angel, and similar sad laments—always most tragic, but I suppose it was a pleasure for them.

At Hollow Ditch there was a large russet apple tree, large wooden butter-pats with intricate patterns, and rows of lovely golden butter laid on a tray ready to go to Wareham market. Once a lady named Elsie Cake called on a straight-up, no-nonsense bicycle with a fancy chain-guard. She hopped off in a most graceful manner, in spite of long skirts and button boots. I later tried to do the same but came a cropper. In the evenings I would go across the heath to Marepool and watch the deer drinking at dusk. It was also from this spot that I watched Lulworth Castle burning. My grandparents are buried at Tyneham churchyard but Aunt Susan was buried at Steeple. She ended her days in a cottage at Kimmeridge, having been moved there at the time of the evacuation. But she always hoped to return to Hollow Ditch. . . .

One of the most far-flung of the tiny heathland settlements is at Ower where James Churchill was born in about 1845 at the thatched cottage by the shore. He married Jane Batter, from Claywell, a mile away on the stream that skirts Rempstone Heath. Churchill worked for forty years at Newton Clay Works and

earned twelve shillings a week by piece-work. He took off the
covering of sand and then dug a hole twenty feet square. Seven
rubblers would work in a gang and cut the clay into chunks, some
seven inches across, and others eight by nine inches. Their spades
weighed twenty-five pounds and had a straight handle with a blade
six inches wide. It was found that a spade at Newton was quickly
worn by sand particles and lasted only a couple of years whereas
twenty years' use could be had from one at the Norden claypits.
When James Churchill started at Newton, before the introduction
of the first steam engine to Purbeck, horses pulled the clay trucks
along the tramway to Goathorn Pier.

Part of his earnings went towards the £4 10s. paid to the Rempstone estate on the first Wednesday in October when tenants
gathered at Rempstone Hall for a feast. H. P. Smith recorded
Churchill's story and how it was that the pig helped pay the rent;
it was bought for twenty-five shillings and fattened for killing
shortly before rent-day. One half was cured and sold in Poole
and the remainder kept at the cottage for the winter. They also kept
a cow and heifer, three dozen chickens, six ducks, and took the
chance to shoot wildfowl on the saltings when birds flocked in
the winter. The Churchills also subsidised their income by exercising the right to cut three thousand turves on the heath each
year. In this, and other ways, their twelve children were both
necessary and useful: no family of heath-croppers could survive
without plenty of children. One son, Tom Churchill, remembered
being paid half-a-crown per thousand turves which he cut in
May and June and left to dry until September when a *turf-pook*
was made in the shape of a beehive. The turves from Russel
Quay at Arne were about two feet by one foot and a foot thick—
and very *pethy* (peaty). They were burnt through the winter as
fuel.

Other heathland fuels were *nitches* (bundles) of furze, used for
baiting (stoking) the oven, and *blackstalks* (burnt furze) gathered
after the heath had been fired in April to allow grass to grow for
the cattle. One nitch of furze weighed two hundredweight and
was cut with a *vuzz-hook*. Fern also was cut, on Green Island,
for use as animal fodder and brought to the mainland on two
canoes tied together.

There was a brick oven beside the open fireplace in the cottage
and dough was slid into place with a *pale* (a long-handled wooden
bakers' shovel known generally as a 'peel'). The wooden door
to the oven was sealed with damp cloths but many poorer heath-
croppers used cow-dung instead. Seven six-pound loaves could be

baked at a time with a few cakes as well. Outside the cottage was half an acre of land used for growing potatoes and a little corn. The *droshin* (threshing) of this was done by laying a sail on the ground and strewing it with corn. Two sticks seven feet long were fastened together with leather for the flail. The *wimming* (winnowing) was then done with an ordinary sieve. Such was the primitive life of the heath-croppers of Purbeck at the turn of the century; with their extension of the Dorset dialect to give them a descriptive language that was their own.

When the heathcroppers of north-east Purbeck went to market they often took their own tiny craft to Poole. The Poole Pilot newspaper recorded a fatal boat accident which occurred in Poole Harbour on the evening of 25 March 1868:

> A clay cutter named Thomas Fry, with his little boy, about six years old, Mary Ann Green, aged sixteen, and her little sister Emily, aged three, left Poole about six o'clock in a canoe, for Middlebere, on the opposite side of the harbour. Nothing was seen of the boat or its occupants until the following morning about nine o'clock when the canoe was found bottom upwards in the Wareham channel, and the dead body of Emily Green floating near it. The bodies of Mary Ann Green and of Thomas Fry were picked up the following day. The little boat was evidently overladen, having on board, besides the four passengers, a sack of seed, three bundles of salt fish and other articles.

"Arne Church" by Alfred Dawson, 1882, from the hill above the church — looking north-east across Arne Farm and Shipstal Point to ships at anchor off Lower Hamworthy and Poole.

CHAPTER IX

Distress And Discontent

BRITAIN HAS never been nearer to anarchy than in 1829 when the year opened with ice and snow, the national economy was ailing, Wellington's once tough regime lay enervated, and everywhere the people were starving. Overseas, the government had other problems and the Insurrection Act was renewed to quell Irish Catholics, eight hundred of whom had marked the anniversary of their defeat at the battle of the Boyne by killing and battering dozens of Protestants in Fermanagh. All over the north of England earnings were counted in pence and workers saw their jobs vanishing before a flood of mechanisation; they looked to an inept government for help and the sole Westminster contribution towards easing distress was an import levy on raw silk. The poorly paid and appallingly housed agricultural labourers of the south had equal reason for their discontent.

The centre of continental Europe seethed in turmoil a year later, with revolution in France followed by international collapse, bringing shudders to the English ruling classes who feared they would be next. In the event, all that came across the Channel was the aged and ejected French monarch who packed his treasures, assembled his entourage, and departed from Cherbourg. The 73-year-old exile, Charles the tenth, arrived in Poole Harbour on Monday, 23 August 1830, aboard the English steamboat *Comet*. His reception at the Ballast Quay, Hamworthy, was better than he deserved and many hats were raised, if only out of polite respect for his age.

The Duke of Wellington, the head of the British government, ordered the Custom House authorities at Poole not to inspect any of the king's baggage. Ten days after his arrival, £500,000 was invested in consols and this was only a fraction of the royal wealth: the king must have fled with considerable loot. Thus a coffer of the French state was emptied into London government stock.

Charles had a following of 120 servants and the whole court went from Poole to Lulworth Castle on the edge of Purbeck where the Roman Catholic Weld family were sympathetic hosts. The guests filled the castle and extra rooms had to be found at

Hethfelton House, four miles to the north and standing on the side of a wild hill above the Holy Stream at East Stoke. At Lulworth, the former king consoled himself by shooting game on the estate preserves and regularly attended mass at the chapel in the castle grounds. He looked out over the sea every day; it was not just any sea but the English Channel with Cherbourg seventy miles distant and beyond the horizon.

Allowing the monarch to set up home on the south coast was seen by the government as provocation against France which was liable to encourage an attempt to land and carry off the young Duke of Bordeaux who was with the king at Lulworth. Diplomatically, Westminster foresaw greater safety and less political embarrassment in moving the entire court to Holyrood at Edinburgh and the admiralty steam packet *Lightning* arrived at Poole for this purpose on 14 October. Six days later, the king sailed to his northern exile.

On leaving Lulworth, there was a gathering in the castle hall when "the English servants knelt to take leave of him" and Charles said "Goodbye, God bless you". Villagers thronged round his carriage and the newspapers tell of their sorrow. Caustic comments were made at the time: that the cause of their unhappiness was the prospect of a speedy fall in the price of butter, eggs and poultry "for whilst the court was at Lulworth, the farmers' wives of the Isle of Purbeck got double, and sometimes treble, prices".

"A revolution in France is a revolution in Europe," was a remark attributed to Napoleon. It came true in 1830 when the revolt spread to Belgium, Italy and the Iberian peninsula, and hastened the debate of parliamentary reform in Britain. Two years later, Corfe Castle and other 'rotten boroughs' were disfranchised as a result of the upheaval in France. The shock of seeing a monarchy, the ultimate in establishment symbols, irreverently overthrown caused much of the opposition on the part of the landed and other vested interests to crumble before the mounting pressure for reform. Resistance to electoral freedom in Britain only scattered unwillingly in the face of a gathering whirlwind and the transition from feudalism to democracy was a victory won on the streets of Paris.

In London, one of the political blunders of 1830 was from the throne in Parliament on 4 February when King George IV spoke of the distress "existing in some parts of the United Kingdom". This statement was regarded as offensive. Lord Stanhope asked in the House of Lords in what parts of the country it was that ministers did not find distress prevailing—the kingdom was in a state of universal distress.

Discontent that was being restrained under a surface veneer of normality started to erupt openly with widespread unrest in the Midlands and North, followed by the riots of the farm labourers in southern England. These outbreaks spread from Kent along the south coast to Dorset where poverty was as extreme as anywhere; for many families existence was barely possible on their wage packet of only eight shillings a week. The southern sky glowed red with the fires on farmland and the death of King George on 26 June came as a welcome respite for the Wellington administration because it served to distract public attention away from empty stomachs.

The waves of discontent reached Purbeck in November when Wareham magistrates met twice daily at the old Town Hall and organised horse patrols to fan out into the countryside and report back on the state of the villages. Only a month after the departure of the dethroned Charles for the safety of Scotland, vigilante measures had been taken by Purbeck landowners. Their posse consisted of a body of horsemen, forty strong, stationed at Wareham with foot guards to protect the town from any mobs.

Says one report: "The Isle of Purbeck was in an excited state for several weeks. The labourers daily became more and more defiant, and by words and actions, as well as by signs and looks, gave evidence that the spirit of rebellion, so prevalent in Hampshire, Wiltshire, Berkshire and Kent, was making its way into the remotest corners of Dorset. One farmstead after another was fired and terror and dismay prevailed everywhere. There was little difficulty in finding out who were the discontented among the labourers, as the discontent was general, but nobody could fix on the right persons the charge of rick burning. At Corfe Castle and Swanage measures were taken to meet by force any attack which might suddenly be made."

One of the Purbeck blazes was at the Voss farm at Bradle, in the valley of the Corfe River between Church Knowle and Kimmeridge, where a large barn and its contents were destroyed on 4 December. Voss was to be unluckier as a second fire took place at Bradle on 20 December and destroyed much of the property saved on the previous occasion. Some landowners attempted to reduce the tension by lowering the rents of farmers, who were asked to pass on the benefit by increasing the wages of their men.

Continued clamour for reform rippled through the politics of the following year and public meetings were held all over the country. Poole was one of the most forceful boroughs supporting the agitation and on 16 March 1831 the town managed to petition William IV. Reformers in east Dorset met at a dinner in Poole and a toast was proposed by Lewis Tregonwell, the builder of a mansion near the sea at Bournemouth, who said that the people of England had long been living under an "odious oligarchy" which would be removed by the reform bill.

The anti-reform government collapsed in April when it was defeated in two divisions—and the encouraging news came to Dorset with the *Magnet* coach, a daily service leaving the Gloucester coffee house, Piccadilly, at 5.45 in the morning.

It is impossible to understand the feelings of the time without looking back at the unfairness of the voting system in the pre-reform days. The borough of Wareham for example had 150 voters in 1830 and Corfe Castle had just forty-four. Yet two members of Parliament were elected by each borough, the rights going back to the year 1302 in the case of Wareham and 1572 at Corfe. Because Wareham, like Corfe, faced disfranchisement under the reform measures, one of its members, John Calcraft, decided to join the two sitting members, Edward Berkeley Portman and Henry Bankes, who were both standing for re-election for the county seat of Dorset in the general election of May 1831. Purbeck's part in the county election dominated the events at Dorchester during the hustings: Calcraft and Portman were the reform candidates and Bankes was the opponent of change, and one man had to lose.

Calcraft was facing his thirteenth election and whilst a member for Wareham he had distinguished himself by his repeated efforts to repeal the salt tax. In 1798 there had been a duty of ten shillings a bushel on salt, and this was increased to fifteen shillings in 1805. During the Napoleonic wars the tax reached as much as £30 per ton and the average retail price of fourpence a pound caused suffering among the poor. Many only survived the winter by living off their pig, and yet when it was killed the cottager had to sell one half to buy the salt needed for curing the other portion. Calcraft urged repeal upon a government that could only see the tax as a means of providing £1,500,000 revenue each year. But in 1823 the duty was reduced to two shillings per bushel.

Two years later a parliamentary committee sat to consider the abolition of the tax and Calcraft called a Purbeck farmer to give first-hand evidence of the hardship it had caused. The farmer was

43-year-old Harry Jenkins from Knitson, a mile away from Cal-craft's home at Rempstone Hall on the other side of the Purbeck ridge, and he came dressed in a long smock, buckskin breeches and gaiters. His appearance brought a touch of humour to the day, but it had a beneficial effect as the tax was removed shortly afterwards, with the result that a block of salt as large as a brick fell in price to a penny.

Calcraft gained political notoriety when he defected from the opposition at the second reading of Lord John Russell's famous reform bill. He enabled the bill to pass with the slenderest possible majority: one. In his new stand for reform, John Calcraft was strongly supported by his friend John Samuel Wanley Sawbridge Erle Drax of Charborough Park, who later earned a reputation as the strangest eccentric of Victorian Dorset, and who was called in 1831 "the ardent reformer of Wareham". Drax's main contribution to the election was on the nomination day when he rode with a number of horsemen to the hustings at the prehistoric fort of Poundbury on a hill just out-side Dorchester. Bankes found it impossible to get a hearing as fights broke out in the crowd of 12,000 and the multitude split into mobs—at the height of the melee a section of the crowd was charged and routed by Drax's farmers. Throughout the day, Calcraft's labourers from Corfe Castle had also enjoyed them-selves.

At the end of the contest Portman had 1,699 votes, his colleague, Calcraft, had 1,542 and Bankes (an MP since 1780) was the loser with 1,176 votes. After the general election the reform bill passed through the House of Commons with a large majority but foundered in the House of Lords where twenty-one bishops were counted among the majority against. Their votes ratified the strongly held conviction that the Anglican Church was a pawn in the hands of the establishment and this truth did the church incalculable harm by alienating the mass of the popu-lation and turned significant numbers against organised religion. In the opinion of last century writers, the vote of the bishops was regarded as a betrayal "and this the country did not soon forgive nor forget".

On 12 September 1831 the news reached Dorset that Calcraft had killed himself the previous morning, a Sunday, at Whitehall Place, his London residence. He had been depressed and confined to the house for nearly two months, but the inquest failed to find any obvious reason for his action. In the light of those times Calcraft was a radical and during the short period between the election and his death he had re-introduced a divorce bill which passed through the Commons. He had lost his old establishment friends when he defected over the reform bill.

The patrons of Wareham had been the Erle and Drax families until 1757 when the Calcraft family bought the Rempstone estate in Purbeck. After that, members of the Calcraft family sat in Parliament for the borough no less than eighteen times. As there were two seats, the second was generally given to a friend, or sold to some wealthy figure who wanted a ticket to the House of Commons. Surprisingly, the country did benefit from this 'rotten borough' because the Calcrafts' lent the seat to some decent humanitarians and in this way Thomas, Lord Denman, an eminent lawyer and opponent of slavery, came to sit for Wareham. His views were ahead of his time and later, when sitting in judgement over a case in 1844, he said: "Trial by jury itself, instead of being a security to persons who are accused, will be a delusion, a mockery, and a snare."

Sir Samuel Romilly also used Wareham as a seat of convenience and was another fighter against slavery and an advocate of law reform. He led protests against the severity and frequency of hanging and for his humanity he incurred the wrath of the bishops who attacked his moves as "dangerous innovations". To his credit, Romilly was not dissuaded and carried on vainly for years trying to persuade Parliament to mitigate the "barbarous laws which were more fit for a nation of savages". The Lords rejected his bill to abolish the death penalty for the crimes of shoplifting goods worth five shillings and stealing items valued at forty shillings from a house. In upholding the old law, the Lords followed the views of the Lord Chief Justice who said in 1810 that his colleagues were "unanimously of the opinion that the expediency of justice and public security requires that there should not be a revision of capital punishment" for stealing goods to the value of five shillings from a shop. In one of his few actual successes against the law-and-order lobby, Romilly was able to remove the death sentence from the necks of soldiers caught begging without a pass! Romilly ended his life as the most moderate politician of the age by cutting his throat with a razor, shortly after being returned to Westminster in 1818. Another leading figure who passed through the Wareham poll was William Gerard Hamilton, an orator in the Irish parliament who left politics for a literary retirement.

Compared with the persons of calibre who served as members for Wareham, the Purbeck borough of Corfe Castle was a lesser and undistinguished seat. Corruption there was complete and contests were unknown: "the patrons divided the honours by each returning a member, and this way got over an infinitude of trouble!". Corfe was owned by the powerful Bankes and Bond families who farcically abused even the system of those times when they went through the motions of holding elections. Hustings were erected, speeches made, beer drunk, and the two candidates duly elected. Tradition demanded that they then responded by solemnly affirming their loyalty to Corfe and their determination "to stick to the place as long as one stone held firm to another in the old castle".

The first reform bill eventually succeeded in becoming law in 1832 and its effect was to totally disfranchise Corfe Castle and to permit Wareham to return only one member. Afterwards, following the Boundary Act, Corfe Castle was included in the borough of Wareham, with new limits extended to include more than fifty square miles. This reform, however, only touched upon the unfairness of representation as even in 1833, when the reconstituted Wareham borough covered the largest area of any in Dorset, it had only 389 voters selected out of a population approaching 6,000.

So many aspects of the nation's problems had touched the edges of Purbeck in those two turbulent years. Poverty was there and in the poor hamlets on the fringes of the south Dorset heath, some help was given by Drax who was cursed by his hard-line fellow landowners for his "most defiant conduct". The arrival of evicted royalty at Lulworth was seen by Wellington as a "bad and mischievous example" to English agitators, but the Purbeck labourers missed the point. A revolution did not erupt across the countryside and an amazing phase in the life of the household of Lulworth Castle ended with Cardinal Weld being tipped as "almost certain" to be elected Pope—but like the reform bill in 1831, he didn't quite make it, and in retrospect it is difficult to concede that he had a chance. Italians were to hold the succession until the 1970s.

Neither did the hopes of reform fully materialise. The Parliamentary boundary changes of 1832 were abused by Drax and John Hales Calcraft, the heir to the Rempstone estates. They had the limits of the borough of Wareham extended far beyond its size as proposed by the Boundary Commissioners. Wareham should, logically, have been extended by the inclusion of the neighbouring out-parishes of St. Mary, St. Martin, Holy Trinity, the chapelry of Arne and a small portion of the parish of Morden.

Instead the ultimate boundary let in an immense tract of land, most of it sparsely populated heath, on which the two "great landed proprietors soon commenced making faggot voters, thereby swamping the independent townspeople".

Its boundaries extended over twenty miles of country from the inland parish of Milborne St. Andrew to the sea at St. Alban's Head. Its size was calculated at 31,560 acres and the population, in 1861, was 6,694. The total number of male occupiers of property in 1866 was only 1,159, about one to every thirty acres. As for voters, they numbered as few as 898. The borough was still rotten.

At every successive election from 1832 until 1865 Drax and Calcraft fought it out "almost alternatively victorious, whilst the townspeople have actually never once been able to present a candidate of their own, independent of these families". The position was not rectified until sometime after Benjamin Disraeli's Reform Act of 1867. Wareham was a "small county" rather than a borough and it was one of the most glaring abuses of the system in the whole of England. The preliminary battle for the 1868 election was fought before a Revising Barrister in the Registration Court. Captain John Hales Montague Calcraft, who followed his father, succeeded in establishing sixty-two claims and objections; whilst Drax managed only twenty-nine. Calcraft actually had Drax himself struck from the list of voters for the borough. Charborough Park lay beyond its limits but Drax claimed to qualify through a "building and land at Fillyholes". This was a "square building of wood with brick foundations" and the examination of Drax became a defence of a qualification for a horse rather than an elector:

BARRISTER: What do you use this building for? DRAX: To put anything in I like. I might put my horse there. BARRISTER: Do you? DRAX: I have not had any necessity; I occupy it so far as I have the key. BARRISTER: For what purpose do you use it? DRAX: I could put my horse there. BARRISTER: Have you done so? DRAX: No, but I might have done so. I don't go and sleep there or dine; but, if out shooting, I might go and lunch there. The BARRISTER said it was all might and could. He did not think the vote could be retained. The Act required that there must be a house, shop, or building upon the land; and it must be a building for some useful purpose. They might erect a pyramid on the land, but that would not be a building within the meaning of the Act. It must have some utility and some real permanence. Now this building was put up for the purpose of making a vote, and not intended for any useful purpose ...

Rev. Nathaniel Bond of Creech Grange was another 'faggot voter': he had registered himself because of certain 'leazes' on

Corfe Common. There was no building attached to them. Richard Sydenham, a Poole publisher, later asked whether it was quite 'professional' on the part of a reverend divine to make that sort of lying claim to try and obtain a vote to which he had no title?

J. H. M. Calcraft died suddenly at Rempstone Hall after winning Wareham by thirteen votes in the election of November 1868. Drax was then given back his old Parliamentary ticket at an election in the following month, where he won the support of the Purbeck families of Eldon, Bond and Bankes, and a majority of sixty-nine over William Montague Calcraft. No rich landowner ruled his voting minions more directly than Drax of the many names. He was called the "Silent MP" and was said to have once spoken in Parliament: when he asked the Speaker if a window might be opened. He held Charborough Park and Holnest Park in Dorset, Olantigh Towers in Kent, and estates in Wiltshire, Yorkshire, Barbados and Wimbledon.

This chapter has, I hope, given sufficient outline of the power politics of our countryside of up to a hundred years ago to show that democracy in this country has roots far shallower than we are usually led to believe.

"Swanage, Isle of Purbeck" by Philip Brannon, 1862.

CHAPTER X

Seaside Swanage

SWANAGE WAS a late developer among the Victorian coastal resorts and had to promote its new found attractions to the full. The foremost propaganda initiative was the publication of "Swanage", a book edited by John Braye, in 1890. This unreliable work praises the achievement of George Burt of Purbeck House who is given credit for transfiguring the town "to such an extent that those who knew it fifteen years ago would scarcely recognise it, were it not for the ancient landmarks".

Unrelieved sedateness and the opinion that Swanage could offer paradise to invalids ripples through the pages of the book. The town laid a determined claim to be an idyllic health resort and bathing machines were far from being all it offered. Enthusiasm for the town's climate was the basic theme: "The range of temperature of Swanage being so small compared with most places, the air being so bracing and dry, and the nearly total absence of fog, frost, and snow should bring the little town to the notice of all seeking a healthy spot, whether to go and settle down indefinitely or during the colder months of the year."

Quietude was another virtue and Swanage differed from the fashionable watering places in lacking "the terrible noise occasioned by German bands or strolling nigger companies". Such nuisances, the writer lamented, had become the pest of not only English resorts but their continental counterparts.

Ventnor was one of the most successful of Victorian resorts and came in for the envy of Swanage. All manner of statistics were thrown against the Isle of Wight town, and a conclusion that hit at Bournemouth for good measure:

> One great disadvantage is that [Ventnor] is overrun with invalids of every description, which is very depressing. Bournemouth, though on the opposite side to Swanage, is in no way so good a residence for invalids. The air is much too relaxing, and after staying there a short time the invalid feels this. There is a want of the tonic air so conspicuous in Swanage. I would also mention the comparative warmness of the Swanage minimum temperature, throughout the year, as compared with Bournemouth, and hence of course the smallness of range at Swanage. Many of the invalids from Bournemouth will probably migrate over to Swanage as time rolls on.

George Burt, John Mowlem's nephew, is the central figure in Swanage history and created the town as it is today. As we have already seen, it was Burt who was the boss of the stone trade and the man who moved operations out from Swanage town. He also started the first steamer service from the pier. And, above all, he built and sold houses to bring people to live at Swanage, which by the 1880s was the fastest-expanding town of its size in Dorset.

Having done all this, he decided to open a police station! Plans for the first police station at Swanage were discussed at Dorset Midsummer Sessions in Shire Hall, Dorchester, during June 1881. Burt had offered to build the station with cells and living quarters for two policemen. The cost would be £600 and Burt proposed leasing the completed building to the county for fifteen years at an annual rent of £24. The Chief Constable, Captain Amyatt E. Amyatt, said he understood Burt also intended erecting a Town Hall close to the proposed police station and this would be available for magisterial purposes. Lord Eldon replied that the scheme to incur expense for a police station at Swanage had come as a surprise to the magistrates of the division. His reported comments were:

> The present arrangement by which prisoners had to be removed from Swanage to Wareham for trial was doubtlessly inconvenient, but he understood Mr Burt was going to construct a railway, and then it would be less inconvenient. (Laughter.) He was not sure the erection of this police station would be a gain. At present no petty sessions were held there, and anybody wanting to get a summons had to go to Wareham. He should like this question postponed until the next sessions in order more definite plans might be proposed.

Replying, T. B. Hanham said he had known Swanage for the previous fifteen years "during which time it has completely changed". The suggested site was central and "there will be a difficulty in delaying the matter. Swanage is a place considerably increasing in value and, to my mind, it is very doubtful if the county will receive this offer again at the same price."

The meeting agreed by one vote not to postpone consideration of Burt's offer. At that time he was working on other ideas as well because in 1881 the building of the Town Hall started on the site of the Drong Cottages in the High Street. The Town Hall was opened in 1883. Although it has only two storeys, it is still a tall building and the striking feature is the stonework of the frontispiece. This was bought by Burt in London: it had been part of the facade of the old Mercers' Hall which had been designed by Edward Jarman after the Great Fire of 1666 and built under the direction of John Oliver.

Among the inscriptions on the walls are "Cheapside 1670" and "Swanage 1882". At the back of the Town Hall is a small rectangular stone building with a stone-slated roof and heavy nail-studded door. The interior is eight feet by ten feet and the single window is small and has an iron grill. This is the Lock-up and a tablet above the doorway reads: "Erected for the Prevention of Vice and Immorality by the friends of Religion and good order AD 1803."

This tiny cell, the local prison, was moved from near the parish church. It was erected originally "on the north side of ye Church Tower" but was moved, when the church was rebuilt, into the south-west corner of St Mary's churchyard. Boys from the quarries would stand above it, at the top of some steps, and bombard the door with stones when a drunk was locked inside.

Burt was a collector of relics for as well as taking from London part of the Mercers' Hall, he carted off lamp standards, cannon posts, columns from Billingsgate Market, two statues from the Royal Exchange, an archway from Grosvenor Square and a (clock-less) gothic clock tower from Southwark that commemorated the Duke of Wellington. Any movable landmarks from the London scene were duly uprooted, dismantled, brought home and put together again at Purbeck House, the extravaganza of second-hand taste that Burt created as his home in 1875, or placed elsewhere across the town. Ten lamp standards on The Parade and Beach Road, for instance, were of cast iron and stamped "Saint George Hanover Square" whilst others proclaimed the "City of London". All over the Durlston estate there are cannon posts standing as bollards or supporting gates. Here is a random selection of their places of origin: "St James Clerkenwell", "St Giles Bloomsbury", "St Anne's Soho", "St Martin's-in-the-fields" and "St James Westminster'.

A monument was raised by John Mowlem to give Swanage a little history. It commemorates an alleged battle between the Saxons and the Danes in Swanage Bay. Sir Frederick Treves started the laugh about it in 1906 when he wrote in "Highways and Byways in Dorset":

> Amongst other litter in the London contractor's yard there would seem to have been some cannon balls. The faithful paviour evidently had some difficulty in working these in for the adornment of his birthplace. Cannon balls suggest battle, but there has been no battle at Swanage. King Alfred, however, is supposed to have defeated the Danes in Swanage Bay in the year of our Lord 877. Naturally enough, the contractor erected a pillar on the Marine Parade to commemorate this proud if dim event, and

placed the cannon balls on top of it. To some these missiles may appear inappropriate, as gunpowder was not invented until more than 400 years after the assumed engagement.

Professor F. M. Stenton in his "Anglo-Saxon England" does not consider there was a battle but says that a Danish fleet, bringing reinforcements to raiders attacking Exeter, "was destroyed by a storm off Swanage". The debate on history and the monument resumed at Swanage urban council's meeting in October 1965 when A. E. R. Gray said the monument was an object of general ridicule. The claim that it commemorated a battle against the Danes in Swanage Bay was historically inaccurate and the three cannon balls surmounting it were likened to a pawnbroker's sign. He said: "The day of monuments has passed. This one should be demolished and sunk to the bottom of the bay."

The discussion concerned the re-siting of the column which stood in the way of development on the promenade. Members decided to spend £200 on moving it, rather than £75 for demolition. So the monument, erected in 1862, still stands though without one of its original four cannon balls. This fell off many years ago and was later washed up near Old Harry Rocks. The only history is in the three remaining cannon balls. These were unexploded thirteen inch Russian shells brought back to Portsmouth in the sides of wooden battleships that had fought the Crimean War in the Black Sea and the Baltic.

John Mowlem erected another monument in 1862, in the High Street, above Court Hill, inscribed to "Albert the Good"—in memory of Prince Albert who visited Swanage in 1849. The top of this obelisk was removed forty years ago and its base was demolished after a dispute in 1971.

Burt's monuments were less controversial and the largest he left at Swanage is Durlston Castle, a palatial French riviera-style villa set on the cliffs to the south of the town and surrounded by innumerable tablets of stone inscribed with statistics. There is also a forty-ton globe, ten feet in diameter, carved in Portland stone with continents, oceans and rivers. It was made in sections at Mowlem's Greenwich works. Lest visitors should get the carving urge themselves, an inscription nearby if for them: "Persons wishing to write their names will please do so on this stone only". "The king of Swanage," Thomas Hardy would call Burt.

Life at Swanage improved somewhat in 1884 when water was extracted for the first time from the base of the chalk downs at Ulwell and pumped into a reservoir at four hundred feet on the

side of Ballard Down. Burt marked this achievement by re-
erecting a stone gas-lamp pillar from the Mansion House in London on the hilltop above the waterworks in 1892. This Cornish
marble obelisk was pulled down to deprive the Luftwaffe of a
landmark in 1940 and re-erected (minus one section) by the Royal
Engineers in 1973.

Much Swanage history, thankfully, is still in the great outdoors.
I had to search the archives for years, however, for George Lewingdon's "Swanage Song" of circa 1880, which carries the compulsory
dedication to George Burt. Swanage's late twentieth century
pressman, George Willey, congratulated me on finding "the only
copy in captivity" and I put it into "Old Swanage"; as that is going
out of print I'll insert it at the back of this book. Further research
was triggered by an earlier correspondent for the Western Gazette
who had reported in April 1869:

> An Artillery Corps has been formed here. Fifty-five members were
> sworn in on Monday, and afterwards marched to Herston and
> back. Mr J. Pope is Hon. Secretary to the corps. Lord Eldon and
> Mr G. Burt have granted leases of the ground necessary for a
> battery and for carbine practice.

In 1968 I published an old photograph of the gun battery on
Peveril Point and this led to a Purbeck diver, Bob Campbell of
West Drive at Swanage, writing to let me know of his discovery
of six inch diameter cannon balls weighing 26 lb. as well as a
few four inch balls of 5 lb. on the floor of Swanage Bay. Before
the artillery guns were stationed on the Point, there had been an
earlier battery fashioned in the shape of a ship's gun deck and
with a flagstaff. Two or three of its guns came from the wreck
of the *Halsewell* and this battery seems to have been abandoned
after a landslip in the middle of the last century. Campbell wrote
in "Waterspout", the Bournemouth subaqua journal:

> A recent revelation was a photograph published in the first issue
> of the magazine DORSET. This showed two cannons at Peveril Point
> which were used by the Dorset Artillery volunteers. The presence
> of the clock tower and the old pier in the background dates the
> photograph between 1867 and 1897. The guns were mounted on
> large wheeled carriages and kept at the drill hall in Swanage, being
> dragged out to the Point with much local excitement for practice
> shots. They remained in use until the turn of the century. The
> calibre of the guns is not quoted but I recently came across some
> drawings of cannon which showed a thirty-two pounder gun to
> have a bore of 6.4 inches. This ties in with the size of ball
> found. . . . I had the good fortune to talk to an old hand who had
> fired these guns in his youth and he confirmed that the target, a
> barrel, was moored on Tanville Ledge.

CHAPTER XI

Communications And Inoculations

COMMUNICATIONS ARE necessarily a subject that has a place in the majority of these chapters. Turnpike roads, horse-drawn tramways, the postal service, early Swanage steamers, and the arrival of the railway in the town are all mentioned at various stages of this book. Other transport projects were contemplated but never constructed, like the proposed extension of the Poole tram system in 1904 to run over the mouth of Poole Harbour and across Purbeck to Swanage. An earlier, and minor, railway project that was never proceeded with was authorised in 1859 when the old pier was built at Swanage. A mineral line, called the Swanage Pier Railway, was scheduled to run westwards from the pier through the town quarries and as far as the newer quarries at Langton Matravers. Only a short distance of tramway, between the pier and the stone bankers at Swanage, was ever built.

The purpose of this chapter is principally to note some of the more interesting survivals from the early road system in Purbeck. There is a certain lack of continuity in this section but there does not seem any point in detailing every old road in Purbeck as they are all amply covered by Professor Ronald Good's "Old Roads of Dorset".

Two of the oldest ferry services in Dorset connected the Purbeck countryside with the port of Poole. The service for Swanage and Studland ran from Redhorn Quay on the west side of the South Haven Peninsula. This quay has the remains of bankers of stone that show it was once, like Ower, used by the Purbeck stone trade. Other stones, found in the mud of the harbour shore and especially near Goathorn, include granite boulders. These do not have local origins but were brought as ballast by ships that entered Poole Harbour to collect stone, marble and clay. The Corfe Castle ferry service to Poole operated from Wytch Passage. A tarred county road still leads to Wytch and a short track continues to the water's edge. Wytch is known to have been a harbour crossing point as thirteen people drowned when a market boat returning from Poole sank in the mud off Brownsea on 9 March 1759. Wytch Passage is still marked by the timbers of a decaying boathouse that lie in a reed bed next to a rusting winch.

A two-storey, eighteenth century, stone cottage with a thatched roof stands beside the marshes and is occupied by tenants of the Rempstone estate. Their view of the waters across to Hamworthy was previously watched by professional eyes as the building was once the home of the Poole harbourmaster.

Less than a mile from Wytch is Sharford Bridge. This is the clue to a lost road. It is about the remotest bridge in Dorset and is also among the most unusual, being a narrow stone packhorse bridge with two rough arches that span the Corfe River. To Thomas Gerard, 'river' seemed an exaggerated description—"the brooke or river, choose you which." The present bridge was built, probably, around 1700 but 'Sharford Bridge' is named as such on a map of the sixteenth century. The name is obviously much earlier and indicates that originally it was simply a ford. *Shard* was a dialect word in Purbeck for a 'gap' and it was usually pronounced as *shar*. To Good, Sharford Bridge was the most interesting of the few packhorse bridges in Dorset and of importance "because it is emphatically marked on the earliest county maps" before roads were even shown. There is a curious duplication of virtually identical placenames in east Dorset: three miles north of Wareham was a Sherford Bridge and under a mile away a farmstead called Slepe. The only other occurrence of Slepe in Dorset is the farmstead north of Sharford Bridge in Purbeck. The early maps point to this packhorse bridge having been built as part of an old road from Stoborough to Swanage that avoided passing through Corfe Castle. The castle was not only liable to be politically involved but was the equivalent of a Purbeck police station.

This alternative route into eastern Purbeck is perpetuated by the tarred road at Nutcrack Lane, Stoborough, and then forked right near Ridge to run across Slepe Heath. It skirted Hartland Moor and crossed the straight cart track that ran from Middlebere to Norden. On the heath the track is open and sandy but towards the Corfe River it is a hedged road with the remains of rough paving. After crossing the river by Sharford Bridge the road ran over Wytch Heath to Thrasher's Lane and Rollington Farm where the farm track that rises through a pass between Challow Hill and Rollington Hill is a county road. The direct way to Swanage originally ran through Bushey and over the Great Heath to the gap in the hills at Ulwell: its passage through Rempstone estate is now lost and it is more practicable to look at the southward extension of the road that leads over the hill to the vale of southern Purbeck.

Descending to Sandy Hill Lane, this old road connected with the concentration of rough lanes, many of them waterlogged hollows, that were interwoven and spread across the whole of the clay soils of the vale. One led south to Little Woolgarston, Jenkin's Barn, Woodyhyde, Afflington and Worth Matravers. This, at the now demolished Jenkin's Barn, crossed the former Northvalley Road that ran from Corfe Castle to Swanage. The Northvalley Road has largely vanished and little of it is even preserved by the present system of public rights of way. It left Corfe Castle from the south end of West Street and ran across Corfe Common to Patchfield House, Jenkin's Barn, Harman's Cross, just south of Rickett's Copse, and to New Barn. From there it went to Windmill Knap and the north corner of Marsh Copse, and along the sunken way that follows the edge of the wood to Burnham's Lane. From there it branched right, along Washpond Lane for a short distance, and turned off through the brickworks to another cutting that virtually carried a stream throughout the winter. This was Eel Pond Lane and it led to Prospect Farm and the edge of Swanage but the whole of its length has since been filled in and eradicated as a highway; its course is even confused by the pattern of later field boundaries. The road from Prospect Farm is now Victoria Avenue and it joined Northbrook Road for the last few yards to Court Road and the centre of Swanage. Northvalley Road has disappeared to the extent that the middle part of its course can only be found by following the deep ditches and thick hedgerows beside the Byle Brook, and the stream that flows towards Swanage on the other side of the watershed.

Another completely mediaeval lost road linked the quarrying settlements of the northern slope of the limestone hills and is called the Valley Road where it is taken over by the A351 between Three Acre Lane and Crack Lane at Langton Matravers. It continued westward from the sharp bend in the present main road, beside Talbot's Wood, and went through Wilkswood, Quarr, Dunshay, Woodyhyde Cottages, Afflington, Scowles Gate, Lynch and into Corfe Castle.

Two other Purbeck roads have been in use since prehistory. One is the east end of the Dorset coastal ridgeway and runs along the entire length of the chalk hills from Ballard Down to a point between Lawford Sheard Gate and Flower's Barrow. There a road from Worbarrow cuts across the hill and the ancient trackway drops down into East Lulworth, where it is covered by a modern tarred surface, and climbs on to the downs again at Burngate, West Down Farm, Dagger's Gate and onwards to the west.

A length of the ridgeway's next section used to be known as the Roman Road or "gypsy track" and as Warren Road where it neared the headland of White Nose.

The Purbeck ridgeway is part of one of the great ancient roads of prehistoric Wessex—a high and dry route that is still largely straight and clear, and easy to follow, as it has been for well over two thousand years. Another really old trackway ran along the north shoulder of the limestone hills from Egliston to Smedmore Hill and then along the scarp of the inland headland of Swyre Head, above Encombe and south of Kingston, to join what is now the straight section of the B3069 to Acton and Langton Matravers. The southern coastal belt was later linked to Swanage by the Priest's Way that led from Cowlease at the High Street, to Belle Vue Farm, Verney Farm, South Barn, north of Spyway Barn, south of Blacklands, to Eastington Farm and into Worth Matravers. A loop then turned northward to Renscombe Farm, Hill Bottom, and Kingston; for all this part of its length it is today an unclassified county road maintainable at public expense.

Near the western boundary of Purbeck is an unusual concentration of old roads that cannot logically be explained. Broadmoor Farm, on the heath northwest of Creech Grange, is shown by Good as the meeting place for more than six roads. Today the farm is ruined and served by none. But even before the army ranges were extended in 1943 its communications had dropped to a single track that connected with the county road from Creech to Povington. The ruined Broadmoor Farm is a nineteenth century house but its battered sides show signs of earlier cob and stone walling. Good found no reason for its importance apart from the fact it offered a firm crossing of the small stream that runs from Grange to Hurst Mill.

One of the major points of entry into Purbeck was at Holmebridge where a stone bridge was standing in the 1620s and had probably stood for much longer. The main route into Purbeck ran through East Holme, across Holme Heath and to Broadmoor Farm where it linked with other roads that radiated to Stoborough, Hurst Mill, West Holme, Coombe Keynes, Povington and Steeple.

As for the road over the South Bridge at Wareham and across the heath to Corfe Castle, traces of its mediaeval predecessor can be seen as a straight, furze covered hollow crossing the skyline just west of the curve of the present road at the hill beyond Stoborough. There are similar relics of former traffic lanes all across Purbeck. One of them, the forbidden path from Arish

Mell to White Gate Lodge at East Lulworth, is among the most appealing of the walks from the past. It is now inside the barbed wire of the army ranges but previously followed the course of a road that ran inland from the beautiful natural anchorage of Arish Mell to the old village of East Lulworth which lay around the parish church until the castle was built. It passed Sea Vale Farm, the site of New Barn, and beside chalkpits on the edge of the appropriately named Old Marl Plantation. It was of no modern use, but as with many of the lost roads of the rest of Purbeck, it offered an unobtrusive way into the quietest of coastal countryside.

An understanding of the former inaccessibility of Purbeck is important as a background for the study of its history. Many of the strangest English superstitions survived longest among the countrymen of areas such as Purbeck. Folk medicine was also practised but it was not always just a baseless extension of witch-craft charms. This brings us to the second subject discussed in this chapter: inoculations against smallpox were part of the folk medicine of many parts of the country long before Dr. Edward Jenner scientifically advocated a system of immunisation. One of the pioneers was Benjamin Jesty of Downshay who in 1774, at Yetminster, experimented with his family. They did not catch smallpox but Jesty was far from being the first to find an effective cure and, years before him in a west Dorset vale, children used to call on a strange figure in a farmhouse who treated them against the disease. A Gloucestershire milkmaid said: "I shall never have the smallpox for I have had cowpox. I shall never have an ugly, pock-marked face."

It was reported to the House of Commons that Jenner "found the vaccine matter first in the west of England". There is a wide-spread story in Purbeck that Jenner travelled in Dorset during the 1770s and heard that a farmer called Jesty had protected his family from all forms of smallpox then raging through the countryside. Dr. Jenner investigated the matter and found that Jesty had taken pus from a pimple on the teats of a cow's udder and transferred it to his wife, two sons and seven daughters, by scratching the skin on their arms and rubbing serum into their blood. Jenner is said to have recognised that the Purbeck family had been vaccinated against the fever by giving themselves a milder form of the disease contained in the cowpox. The know-ledge later enabled him to protect the nobility from one of the most dangerous diseases of the time; a profitable task.

Jenner is remembered in Dorset as the plagiariser of a Purbeck farmer's theory. This is not entirely true as Jenner was only in his twenties when he gave up a promising London career as a physician to experiment in the cure of disease at his home village in Gloucestershire. His work on smallpox was held up for more than twenty years before he decided to put the idea to the test by inoculating the arm of eight-year-old James Phipps with pus from a milkmaid's cowpox sore. Six weeks later the boy was inoculated with pus from a smallpox sore but showed no reaction. When in 1798 he came to publishing his results, Jenner had to do so at his own expense, and faced the critical disbelief of doctors. He had to campaign for the acceptance of the cure and the long lapse of time since his reputed visit to Purbeck shows he made no attempt to capitalise out of any discovery. In fact, he was far too slow and careful, and wasted years pondering over the knowledge. Vaccination was widely used in 1800 and onwards but did not become a necessity of national life until 162,000 died in the epidemic at the start of the 1870s.

Jesty lived at Downshay Farm and was buried at Worth Matravers where his headstone can be seen. He did receive some belated recognition as he was invited to the Vaccine Pock Institution in London in 1805. There his son Robert "willingly submitted publicly to inoculation for the smallpox in the most vigorous manner". Benjamin Jesty said he decided to inoculate his family in 1774 because it was an accepted country belief that those who caught cowpox would not later have smallpox and he had heard this saying since he was a boy. The immunisation was said to have been performed with a knitting needle. The doctors gave Jesty a signed testimonial of their respect and had his picture painted. History has since paid him less tribute than he deserved.

Sharford Bridge repaired

Hindsight I brought the deteriorating condition of Sharford Bridge (see page 99) to the attention of Dorset County Council and workmen carried out repairs in 1972.

CHAPTER XII

Prehistoric And Roman

HAVING TRACED the history of the more obvious aspects of Purbeck's past—industries, the influence of the sea, recent social and political life, and the development of Swanage—it is time to look deeper into more distant times. Between 6000 and 5000 BC, when the Isle of Wight broke away from the mainland, Britain had left the ice age and was completing the process of parting company with continental Europe. The land was then sparsely inhabited by bands of hunters who gathered food on the coast, by rivers, and across heathland. Deer and other wild animals were an important part of their diet.

Purbeck has one definitely Mesolithic site, and its survival is amazing because of the set of circumstances leading to the preservation of the relics of these early weapon-making men. A spring at Blashenwell Farm, which gave the place part of its name, gushes clear water from a rocky hole at a point where the northern edge of the limestone hills meets the Wealden clay of the Purbeck vale. This water is impregnated with calcium carbonate and has filled a depression in the nearby land, immediately west of the county road that leads to Blashenwell Farm, with a tufaceous deposit eight feet deep and spreading across twenty acres. The tufa has covered and preserved a site of Mesolithic habitation complete with its rubbish—and this is unique.

Its importance was first realised by geologist Clement Reid who wrote in 1896 of the Blashenwell deposit as an "ethnological storehouse". In 1959, bones from the tufa about four feet below present ground level were taken from the Dorset County Museum and given a radiocarbon testing. This provided a date of 4490 BC plus or minus 150 years. Correction of the radiocarbon chronological sequence, carried out by botanists studying the tree rings of the bristlecone pine in California, suggests that this and all dates before 2000 BC are inaccurate. The precise differential has yet to be decided but it was considered in 1970 that such dates should be set back up to seven hundred years. Therefore current scientific opinion gives the Blashenwell site a place in the time scale at around 5190 BC.

Mesolithic waste found under the tufa has included the bones of pigs, deer and ox, charcoal, land molluscs, and abundant flint debris. The finding together of few flint implements but hundreds of flint flakes, and a sharpening device picked up in the vicinity, shows that tools were cut at the site. Blashenwell may be more than a simple settlement and instead the centre of an industry producing worked flints. Only a small area of the tufa has been excavated but it is probable that eventual exploration will show the Mesolithic habitation covered several acres.

Changes in scenery came about 4500 BC as a warmer, drier climate spread across Britain. Forests shrank into valleys and large areas of the chalk scarplands, bitten by the westerly wind, became grassland. Man helped the changes by clearing small areas by tree felling. Neolithic man made small scale plantings of emmer wheat and a little barley—the first attempt at agriculture on Britain's soil. Across the downs moved small semi-nomadic bands of people, including settlers who landed on the south coast from France and the Low Countries.

Extreme reverence for the dead played a vital part in the religion of the Neolithic peoples. Tremendous energy was exerted by these small communities to raise great monuments to their dead. When sufficient bodies had accumulated, an elongated mound was built over the remains—the long barrow. One survives in Purbeck, on Nine Barrow Down, and is the earliest earthwork in the island. It is about 112 feet long and forty feet wide but is on the south shoulder of the chalk ridge and cannot easily be seen. It really only shows up in silhouette from the slope and is a poor example of its kind. A second mound on Stonehill Down at East Creech is transitional in shape, between a long barrow and a round barrow. It stands nine feet high and is rounded in profile but the ditches at the side are characteristic of a long barrow. Only excavation can show its origin.

About 2500 BC barrow architecture changed from the mass-graves of the long barrows to the smaller round barrows covering a single body. This was the culture of the Beaker Folk, so named from their burial urns, who were invaders from the Rhine. These settlers also changed the cereal ratio to almost entirely barley and little wheat. New methods of weapon making developed on the continent and took England into the Bronze Age.

Farming spread and populations increased in a climate which continued warmer and drier than it is today. The downlands of Wessex attracted the warrior aristocracy of Ireland, Brittany and northern Europe who created the first great political and social organisation in these isles. The principal barrow cemetery of this culture in Purbeck is that on Nine Barrow Down. Other concentrations of population lay across the arid and acid soils of the Great Heath. Whatever its poorness, the land was easily cleared and it supported scattered populations, although life was richer on the chalk downland. The Bronze Age cemetery which is the easiest to visit in Purbeck comprises eight round barrows and straddles the bracken-covered ridge that runs from west to east across the centre of Corfe Common. This land still has full commoners' rights and the straggling line of barrows are part of a piece of the landscape that has not changed in centuries. The largest of the mounds is fifty-five feet in diameter and about eight feet high.

Of Dorset's total of about 2,250 surviving round barrows around 150 are in Purbeck. Here I can mention only a manageable selection, and to do so I will describe those that have been given popular names. Often, they are the more prominent of the mounds and the most interesting. Almost all are of the common 'bowl' form of barrow but this is a mere archaeological technicality as the others have only slightly modified shapes and all belong to the same period of prehistoric time.

Three Lords' Barrow is just a low mound placed on a heathland knoll but it serves as the meeting point of four parishes—East Holme, Arne, Church Knowle and Steeple. A piece of old church window has been planted in the top of the three foot high mound as a boundary stone. It came probably from the priory church at East Holme, a cell of Montacute Abbey founded in the twelfth century, that was pulled down in 1746.

Two Purbeck barrows have names associating them with kings. King Barrow is in a clump near the Warren Wood at Studland and King's Barrow is in a wooded garden at Bog Lane, Stoborough. The latter mound stood twelve feet high but was reduced to half this for road-making materials in 1767. The Gentleman's Magazine reported the opening of the mound in the best of the early accounts of barrow digging that came from Purbeck:

> The barrow was composed of strata, or layers of turf, in some of which the heath was not perished. In the centre at the bottom, even with the surface of the ground, in the natural soil of sand, was found a very large hollow trunk of an oak. . . . In the cavity were found as many bones, unburnt, black and soft, as might be contained in a quarter of a peck; viz. a bone of an arm, two thigh-bones, two blade-bones, the head of the humerus, part of the pelvis, and several ribs. These last would lap round the finger. There were no remains of the skull. . . . All had been wrapped up in a large covering, composed of several skins, some as thin as parchment, others much thicker, especially where the hair

remained, which shewed they were deer skins. They were in general black but not rotten; neatly sewed together; and there were many small slips, whose seams or stitches were scarce two inches asunder. As the labourers expected to find money, these were pulled out with much eagerness, and so torn that the shape of the whole could not be discovered.

This wrapper seemed to have passed several times round the body, and in some parts adhered to the trunk. In the middle of it the bones were compressed flat in a lump, and cemented together by a glutinous matter, perhaps the moisture of the body. On unfolding the wrapper, a disagreeable smell was perceived, such as is usual at the first opening of a vault. A piece of what was imagined to be gold lace, four inches long, two and half broad, was stuck on the inside of the wrapper, very black, and much decayed. Bits of wire plainly appeared in it. There were no fragments of iron or brass, whence one might have concluded that any arms or armour were deposited here.

Near one end of the coffin, which had been hollowed from an oak tree, was a small cup which had probably held food or drink for the after-life. Coffins hewn from tree-trunks are unusual in barrows. Another Purbeck barrow that has yielded its secrets is the Afflington Barrow, a six foot high mound on the Kingston limestone plateau, above Coombe Bottom. It was opened last century and the main burial was apparently a crouched skeleton in a stone grave. A shale ring and widespread signs that a cremation had taken place on the spot were also found beneath the mound. Though the barrow has been dated between 1500 and 1250 BC, it was opened up apparently in Roman times and used as a burial place for nine bodies in two rows of graves. Some were stone-lined and one was covered by a shale slab. All the skeletons lay extended and parallel in the upper part of the mound with their heads towards the southwest.

Afflington Barrow takes its name from the mediaeval settlement that existed to the north: other barrow names express the character of their topography. The two Water Barrows and Ferny Barrows, another pair, lie on the southwest Purbeck border. The largest of the Water Barrows is nearly ten feet high and surrounded by a deep-cut ditch that is now twelve feet wide and two feet six inches deep. It is water-filled in winter, and hence the name.

Ferny Barrows actually are bracken covered and Thorn Barrow, a large ten foot high mound at Povington, was overgrown by heathland vegetation until it was destroyed by the army in 1971. Drinking Barrow on the Grange Heath takes its name from a nearby ditch that is much younger than the barrow itself and was cut before the planting of a now abandoned copse. On the east side of Purbeck there is Fishing Barrow standing nine feet above the Dean Hill golf course with its top scalped and flattened for a tee. The name is another that comes from a well-marked ditch water-logged in winter.

Nearby is a Thorny Barrow but this has been virtually eaten by a sandpit. All these barrows with topographical names are prominent mounds in the southern sector of the Great Heath beneath the wall of the Purbeck Hills. Because they are on the edge of Saxon settlement area, man had the opportunity to notice their features and give names. Numerous other barrows scattered across the uninviting remoteness of the heath are without names and seldom noticed even today.

Barrows sometimes have 'number' names (for example, in the Purbeck area, Three Barrows, Five Barrows, Seven Barrows and Nine Barrow Down) but never was an 'even' number chosen. Often the numbering in barrow names is inaccurate.

Seven Barrows are a line of eight burial mounds running along a low ridge between Northport and Cold Harbour on the north-west side of Wareham. Five Barrows are just inside Purbeck and lie in comparable positions on a very similar piece of landscape. There are actually six magnificently preserved barrows and they were raised in a straight line on a rise in the heathland midway between the Heath Gate and West Holme Heath on the road across the army ranges from East Lulworth to Holmebridge. A nearby milestone used to read "London 117, Lulworth 2" and the slight hill rises from Povington Heath a mile west of Hurst Mill and overlooks the undergrowth that hides Luckford Lake.

Three Barrows are, for once, three in number, though badly damaged, standing on a hill opposite Halfway Inn in the middle of the Great Heath that spreads from Stoborough to Corfe Castle. Nine Barrow Down, the largest of the barrow groups with a popular name derived from numbers, actually has seventeen round barrows and is by far the most impressive of the prehistoric cemeteries in Purbeck. Additionally, there is an earlier long barrow, around which the round mounds were placed. The name is not so wildly out of place as only nine of the barrows are over two feet high.

All the larger barrows are set in a line running for about eight hundred feet along the summit of the Purbeck ridge at a point six hundred feet above sea level and with extensive views across the Great Heath, Poole Harbour, and northward to the hills of Cranborne Chase and central Dorset. The Swanage vale, and lime-stone hills, and the sea are overlooked from the other side. At the centre of the group is a mound nearly a hundred feet in diameter and ten feet high surrounded by a ditch that is still four feet deep. All the other barrows are much smaller and most have had their centres explored by the early barrow diggers but no record exists of the results.

Local tradition says that the mounds on Nine Barrow Down are the graves of nine kings killed in battle. Most of the popular tales about barrows link them with soldiers and battles. This is not unexpected as 3,500 years is too long for folk memory and country people thought the mounds had to cover bodies other than the peaceful dead—otherwise they would have gone with everyone else into a churchyard—and violence was the best explanation. All barrows are king-sized mounds.

The Nine Barrow Down group is well preserved under grass and clumps of furze. Further east, above the Ulwell gap through the chalk hills, are a couple of more overgrown mounds. These have local names—the Giant's Grave and Giant's Trencher. There is some doubt whether they are in fact barrows as J. H. Austen dug them in the last century and found nothing. Empty barrows have been excavated elsewhere in Dorset and raise the possibility of cenotaphs.

Contemporary with the round barrows are circles of standing stones. Purbeck's stone circle at Rempstone lies below the northern slope of Nine Barrow Down but it, and the monolith at Hurpston, are discussed in the next chapter as science has only spread a cloud of doubtfulness and it is difficult to place them in accurate perspective. The possibility of a second Purbeck stone circle, also below the northern shoulder of the hills, was raised by Charles Warne who in his "Ancient Dorset" (1872) said one stood "within living memory between East Lulworth and Povington, but not a vestige of it remains". His informant, J. F. Pennie, said the stones were taken away by a farmer named Bower and used by him for gateposts and a bridge over a stream.

No later information has been forthcoming, but on examination of maps I was surprised to find at a point midway between East Lulworth and Whiteway the name of Rempstone Gate. It is where the old county road crosses the East Lulworth and Tyneham parish boundary. This is the only occurrence of the name *Rempstone* in Purbeck apart from at Rempstone itself. The Rempstone Gate area has no less than ten round barrows within a short distance and nearby, beside the present road to Whiteway Hill, is Bower's Coppice preserving the name of the farmer's family.

The fact that both the Rempstone place names are connected with stone circles is sufficient to discredit the accepted but unproven view that Rempstone at Corfe took its name not from the stones but a family that settled in Purbeck. Any notion that the name was transferred from Rempstone to Povington by one of Dorset's fanciful antiquaries can be discounted as Rempstone Gate was so called during the nineteenth century, if not earlier, and the circle at Rempstone itself was not even noted by archaeologists until 1908. I am sure that both placenames are derived independently from the existence of stone circles but have found it impossible to uncover any suitable root word to explain the *remp* element. There is only the French word *remplissage* for 'padding, irrelevant matter in a book'. Irrelevant stones? Certainly, for scientists have still to clarify their thoughts on the purpose of megalithic monuments, but my words only add to the conjecture. More about stone circles later, but now the greatest prehistoric legacy of western Purbeck, the massive Flower's Barrow that overlooks East Lulworth and was built when whom-soever had erected the stone circles had lain in their graves for more than a thousand years.

There is only one hill-fort inside Purbeck but it is a masterpiece of Iron Age expertise. Flower's Barrow takes full advantage of the sheer 565 foot high chalk cliff above Worbarrow Bay and no defences would have been necessary along its southern side. The fort encloses only the modest area of four acres but it is likely that half as much again has fallen over the cliff edge, or "gone off to sea" as the Purbeck fishermen would say.

On the east, north and west there are two double banks with ditches. The inner rampart stands thirty feet higher than its ditch in places. The distances between the two lines of defence are wider at the west and east. The reason for this is an enlightening revelation into the ways of war in the century before the Roman invasion of AD 43. The ramparts were planned with care and the strategy of the layout based entirely on the needs of slingstone warfare. The aim was to keep an advantage of height over distance constantly with the defenders, so that the outer rampart was always within firing range of the inner defences. Should attackers have breached the outer rampart they would have been unable to fire forward from there to the inner defences as the fortification maintained an advantage of height that gave longer slinging power to the home side.

Therefore the two ramparts are close together on the northern side, where there is a deep slope, but staggered on the east and west flanks where an almost even ground surface could only be utilised by the introduction of a wide and open gap between the ramparts. This distance, coupled with the essential factor of an increased height of the inner rampart over the outer one, maintained the advantage for the defenders. Today the inner rampart on the east side of the fort stands six feet higher than the outer bank.

As for the weapons themselves, small-scale excavations in 1939 revealed several slingstones. These were the standard form of defence in the complex fortifications of the Durotriges in the years leading up to the Roman invasion. On the domestic side, the excavators explored a grain storage pit that had later been filled with refuse. Other undulations on the hilltop are probably the sites of huts. The original entrance is on the east where the fall of the hill presents a passage overlooked by the outer rampart as the only easy approach. Both ramparts are slightly inturned to protect the double gateways.

Whatever tribal conflicts Flower's Barrow may have seen, there can be little doubt as to its end. A clue was given by a nineteenth century author, J. F. Pennie, who wrote in his "Tale of a Modern Genius" that "a shepherd boy, while tending his flock on this hill, discovered lying just beneath the surface of the inner rampart a perfect skeleton of great stature (7 feet 9 inches in height). It was placed with the head to the west; the skull not lying in line with the rest of the bones, but being found in an upright position, led to the conjecture that the warrior to whom it belonged had been decapitated. It was very perfect and the teeth beautifully white." Skeletons elongate as the joints open.

Because of its strength, Flower's Barrow was probably one of the twenty or more *oppida* (hill-forts) stormed by Vespasian's Second Legion (Augusta) in the campaign to subjugate the West following AD 43 and the successful Roman landings in Kent. The position of that skeleton on a rampart suggests it was hurriedly buried after a battle in which the fort had fallen. He may have been killed by Roman arms and covered as the victors slighted the fort's defences at the point of the last stand. Vespasian later became Emperor and as a commander he did not lack ruthlessness: the defenders of the Dorset forts of Maiden Castle and Spetisbury Rings were massacred after their resistance had been overwhelmed and a couple of bodies have been found with lethal javelin-heads embedded in vertebrae and skull.

Flower's Barrow is an example of prehistoric engineering on a gigantic scale but a much more widespread though less obvious legacy from the Iron Age are the systems of Celtic fields that can be found across Purbeck. About thirty acres of small squarish fields lie on the slopes immediately northwest and northeast of Flower's Barrow itself. Other contemporary field boundaries spread across fifty acres eastward along the Purbeck ridge at Whiteway Hill and Povington Hill where a series of parallel banks runs down the hillsides. These fields are on the chalk but other soils were also used and seventy acres of sand on the Wealden beds immediately east of Corfe Common were farmed at Sandy-hills. An outlying block of two acres of Celtic fields lies at the centre of Corfe Common and is much better preserved. Southward on the limestone uplands there are forty acres of fields at Encombe Obelisk and another area east of the chapel on St. Alban's Head and linked by lynchets at Pier Bottom with an associated field system on Emmetts Hill. The St. Alban's Head complex amounts to sixty acres in all.

The well preserved contour strip lynchets to the east above Winspit are some of the finest agricultural survivals that can be seen in Britain. These do not date back to prehistory but are the strip fields of the mediaeval open field system of the manor of Worth Matravers. The lynchets are in superb condition on the slopes of West Man and East Man but the whole system covers another two hundred acres as well.

On the other hand, a further ancient field system in the Purbeck quarrylands was farmed in the Iron Age and lies across twenty acres at Mount Misery, Langton Matravers. The banks are in poor condition and were badly damaged by mediaeval activity and quarrying. Thirty-four further acres of Celtic fields lie on the Purbeck ridge at Challow Hill to the east of Corfe Castle. Various blocks of similar fields are in various stages of disappearing from Ballard Down. The best preserved group used to be a twelve acre block of small square enclosures on the northern slope of the down. Some of the lynchets were eight feet high and a remnant of a much more extensive complex of prehistoric fields: all have now been destroyed by modern ploughing.

The origin of these field systems was in the Iron Age but they did not fall out of use when the Romans came. Peace in Purbeck brought the development of the marble, shale and pottery industries and the continuance and growth of Celtic settlements and field systems. These native farms later gave Purbeck a high density of settlement in Romano-British times. Although the sour soils of the heath were virtually completely ignored, the limestone uplands were exploited intensively at Smedmore Hill and

Kingston Down. South of Kingston a flat-topped hill stands four hundred feet above Chapman's Pool, isolated from the downs on either side by the deep-cut valley of Hill Bottom to the southeast and a coombe towards Westhill Wood. The lines of the banks of ancient field boundaries can be seen across 150 acres and the slight depressions of four hut circles have also survived. A narrow entrance can be detected on one—facing east and away from the driving rain. Trackways run between the fields and the slighter outlines of further fields continue down the west side of the spur. Water was readily available in both valleys and there are several springs.

Evidence of minor occupation in the Roman period has been found from about fifty sites across Purbeck but the remains of only four large Roman buildings have so far been uncovered. All are in the region of the mixed soils between the chalk and the heath within half a mile of the northern slope of the Purbeck ridge.

A tessellated pavement and other substantial remains of a Roman villa, including a Tuscan column, were found on the edge of the claypits at East Creech in 1869 and 1888. Norden Clay Works has revealed several traces of Roman sites including a "fine collection of Roman pottery" taken by the third Earl of Eldon about 1882 and since lost. A floor with stone paving and some fourth century pottery have been found near the Wareham-Corfe road and a chalk and limestone paved floor was nearby. Another layer of stone blocks may have been part of the surface of a road. As three Kimmeridge shale plaques have been found together with two carved shale table legs this indicates that one of the major workshops for the manufacture of quality articles in the shale industry was at Norden. The associated buildings were of a far higher standard than those usually found near shale workings and suggest something more important than the average labourers' huts.

In 1961 and 1967 two mosaic pavements were discovered in a field to the north of Brinscombe Farm and digging revealed the walls of buildings. This was another villa and pieces of roof tile, flue brick, tesserae of chalk and sandstone, and potsherds were scattered over the site when I was there after the first excavations. The third substantial group of Roman buildings in Purbeck spreads across a considerable area, at least 1,600 square yards, in the eastern part of the wood on Woodhouse Hill at Studland. Foundations of heathstone and flint up to three feet thick were uncovered in the 1950s and they probably supported cob walls. The site had a long life and was most likely still occupied in the early fourth century.

Archaeologists consider that these buildings, except that at Norden, were almost certainly farms with Celtic owners. They also come to the conclusion, doubtful in my view, that the farms existed solely for pasture lands. But the positions at the foot of the downs suggest that arable farming was also important. The soils between the Bagshot beds of the heath and the chalk of the hills would have offered ideal opportunities for mixed farming. The London clay soil, immediately adjoining which the buildings are situated, was described by a University of Reading and Dorset County Council investigation into the problems of land improvement, published in 1931: "In former times good crops of wheat were grown on it, but the tenacious character of the soil and difficulty in obtaining a good tilth have resulted, as elsewhere, in much land being laid down to permanent pasture. It generally only supports poor crops of grass with little clover." About the Reading beds, immediately below the chalk ridge, the report becomes enthusiastic: "Excellent land is found where the Reading beds join and mix with the chalk."

Both these comments amount to higher praise than other Purbeck soils were given and, as the Roman farmers had to accept the land in its natural state, it seems inconceivable that the farmsteads were sited for any reason other than the general suitability of the nearby ground.

A baffling question for archaeologists has been the location of the Roman road that must have run from the industrial centres in Purbeck to the tribal capital at Dorchester. No trace of it remains. The answer is that the development of Purbeck industries came after the building of the main Roman road system: the raising of great long causeways across the land was done for military purposes mainly at the time of the occupation. The initial system divided the conquered territories on the south coast by a succession of military front lines. These roads were divisions rather than highways and there is evidence that many led nowhere and later attracted only insignificant settlement.

G. B. Berry's revealing article in The Times of 26 August 1967 outlined the mathematical precision of Vespasian's campaign. Berry plotted grid lines of Roman advance, from a master section between Chichester and Silchester, with roads pushed inland from the coast at stages westward. Such roads ran north from the water at Portsmouth Harbour, the Solent, Hamworthy and Weymouth. Beer Head, at the southwest end of the Fosse Way frontier, marked the western limit of Vespasian's advance.

The recent discovery of the largest Roman fortress in southern England under the Stour meadows near Wimborne is strong new evidence supporting Berry's theory as the site of the fort lies precisely on one of his conjectural lines of Roman advance. The fort was built at the time of the occupation.

Trunk roads radiating from London were constructed a little later. Other routes, such as that to link the industrial centre of Purbeck to its tribal town, were made as they were needed. These did not have to be elaborate. They were simply flat metalled tracks without any agger to act as a demarcation and no flanking ditches. That is why no trace remains of the Roman road from Dorchester to Purbeck: there was no earthwork in the first place and a mere surface can be highly elusive after two millennia.

We have, however, been left some very clear pointers. Roman burials occur in a line for more than half a mile from the south-east corner of old Dorchester. They must have been placed alongside a road, and that could only have led to Purbeck. More burials have been uncovered by this unrecognised road than beside any of the four known Roman approach roads that enter the town. That is hardly surprising as Purbeck was the only important industrial area of Roman Dorset.

Roman buildings beside the Copper Bridge

Hindsight The location of another set of Roman buildings (see page 113) was discovered in the mid-1970s on the west side of the Copper Bridge which carries a public bridleway over the Corfe River, from Bucknowle to the northern edge of Corfe Common. This site is a quarter of a mile south-east from Glebe House, which is beside the road from Corfe to Church Knowle.

CHAPTER XIII

Mysteries And Burials

THE FOREMOST mystery is Purbeck itself. No one has yet found sufficient evidence to explain the name. It is definitely an old word, and is first written as *Purbicinga* in the year 948, and then as *Purbic* in many mediaeval documents. Various etymologists have suggested it derives from OE *pur* 'a bittern' and another word *becca* 'a pick-axe or mattock'. There might, Swedish expert Anton Fägersten suggested, have been another OE word, *becc,* meaning 'a point or headland' but he was unable to prove anything.

All the evidence is shaky and, more damning, supports only tenuous and unconvincing ideas. It was left to W. J. Arkell to put forward an obvious explanation in 1940. He thought that 'beck' might be derived from the Old English word *baec* meaning 'ridge'. There could be no more appropriate single word to describe the dominating feature of the Purbeck landscape, the hogs-back of the chalk spine that runs across the island.

Even that, however, is impossible to prove from the extensive list of recorded names for Purbeck. No feasible explanation was forthcoming from Arkell for the first element either. It is difficult to see that the name of Purbeck can ever be proved beyond all doubt and the hope of a reasoned hypothesis is slight.

For historians, there is a mystery about which the name alone is not in doubt. Newton, a placename at the foot of the Goathorn Peninsula, is all that marks the intention of King Edward I to create a new town and port on the southern shore of Poole Harbour. The site today is deserted but even the survival of the name is aggravating as it suggests that something was actually built there. Otherwise there is no reason for the name to have survived as an unnecessary label for nothing. All that I have managed to find are the low ruins of a collapsed stone building, apparently a church, beside a track from Greenland. This, however, has not been noticed by the investigators of the Royal Commission on Historical Monuments so it is doubtful whether it can be the foundations of a mediaeval building.

House footings and other settlement remains lie in a shallow valley, among numerous oaks, a short distance west of the Goathorn Railway at the south end of the peninsula. Fresh water passes along a ditch beside the house. Another structure is marked by clayey banks and the Royal Commission has dated an oak tree standing there as being 350 years old. As the likely date for these is the seventeenth century, no connection can be proved between this collection of remains and Edward I's new town. Yet Newton is named and shown by a symbol to be a settlement on a map of 1597, so there is the suggestion that something was built at an earlier stage.

All that can be proved is the existence of an entry in a document of 1286 that reads as follows:

> Appointment of Richard de Bosco . . . to lay out, with sufficient streets and lanes and adequate sites for a market and church and plots for merchants and others, a new town with a harbour in a place called Gotowre super Mare, in the parish of Stodland [Studland] and on the king's land . . . the lands and tenements of which said new town the king is prepared to commit to merchants and others willing to take them and to enfeoff them thereof for building and dwelling purposes.

It was almost certainly the silt of the harbour reaches, and the fact that Newton would have been an entreport to an inaccessible district cut off from the mainland of Dorset, that killed the scheme at an early stage. But it is still possible that some building was done and these remains may one day be discovered.

A problem of another kind is for archaeologists and lies not far away. On the heath west of the sand dunes on the South Haven Peninsula, concentrated in the area between Redhorn Quay and Jerry's Point, are no less than seventy-one circles with single banks about a foot high and around twenty feet across. Overall diameters of the circles vary between forty-five feet and 150 feet. Another six lie to the south between Brand's Ford and Greenland. The enclosed surfaces, though slightly dished, are almost flat. Some of the banks have narrow gaps and the Royal Commission observes:

> Many held rainwater for short periods, displaying a wet bog flora; others are heath-covered. One or two circles with relatively deep-cut interiors may have been ponds but the function of the others is quite unknown and their date only fixed between the Iron Age and c. AD 1700. The northern group are associated with thirteen low sandy mounds but these have also defied explanation. In the centre of the peninsula is a straight line of five regularly placed stones, originally standing upright, with a sixth N.W. of the N. end of the line.

Another set of inexplicable circles are southwest of Squirrel Cottage at East Holme. They now number about fifty but more than twice as many were noted in 1860. J. H. Austen described them and observed that trees planted on them "were of much larger size than those upon level ground". He dug into many of them and found burned furze. Two were excavated in the 1960s and Professor Dimbleby of the Commonwealth Forestry Institute examined pollen samples. The mounds contained raw humus buried "not later than mediaeval times and not earlier than the Iron Age". Nothing was found to indicate their date and the only other relevant fact is that one appears to overlap the edge of a Bronze Age round barrow. Two other barrows lie on the gravel knoll.

Stone circles provide endless mystery for prehistorians and, as Purbeck has one, that can be discussed next. It is the remains of a simple ring of standing stones, all unhewn and with no carvings, in a wood beside the Corfe to Studland road at Rempstone. It has taken the advance of the computer to prove that Europe's most famous monument of big stones, Stonehenge, was a fantastically complex observatory for calculating in advance the coming positions of the sun and moon. All that was being started before the Mycenaean civilisation of Greece had even begun.

Rempstone is nothing in comparison but it was also built by the first bronze-using peoples of Britain. But because it is a damaged circle, its geometry can never be fully explained, and all archaeologists will do is provide their stock explanation for all stone circles: "Built around 2000 BC in the Bronze Age for some unknown religious reason."

I always held a certain fondness for Rempstone as it used to be: only a few feet from the road but concealed in a dense wood. When I was first there, four stones were standing about four feet high, another four large stones had fallen, and a few smaller ones were hidden in the undergrowth. They formed a perfect half-circle eighty feet in diameter; a half-circle because it was sliced years ago by a bank and ditch, its southern area being almost totally cleared and the rocks piled irreverently together a short distance to the east. Where these originally stood, I took careful steps across a bog, purple with vetch flowering in August.

The wild wood was felled in 1966 and the stones opened to view from the road, though protected by barbed wire from picnickers, the undergrowth tidied and young trees planted. You can see the stones; but the magic and mystery as sunlight dappled a pagan shrine, dank and forgotten in the tangled underwood of bramble, hazel and ivy, is gone.

Some added uncertainty came for archaeologists in 1957 when

an avenue of smaller stones was ploughed up about half a mile to the west and found to be pointing roughly towards Rempstone. Twenty-three stones, about 2 feet 6 inches long, were uncovered in the field immediately south of the main road and west of the track that leads from Rempstone Farm up Brinscombe Hill. Purbeck archaeologist J. B. Calkin knew of no former boundary that might have run across the field and considered that the arrangement of the stones showed "a deliberate layout in two parallel lines three yards apart with stones set up at five yard intervals".

These stones may have been part of some ceremonial way or sight-line connected with Rempstone, though one fanciful suggestion was that the rocks for the circle itself were hauled along the avenue from Rollington Hill, whose name might preserve a memory of the event. This theory can be immediately discounted as Rollington is part of the Purbeck chalk ridge that runs southward of Rempstone. The stones of both the circle and the avenue are a hard gritstone russet-brown in colour: the iron-impregnated sandstone of the Bagshot beds which underlie the Great Heath to the north. The Agglestone and Puckstone and other natural boulders near Studland are of the same stone. These outcrops are the eroded remains of a layer of rock that once covered the softer sands and clays of the heath. The remnants now lie on steep sided hillocks between shallow valleys filled with peat.

The Agglestone, the greatest of these rocks, led in its time to a stream of folk tales. The name itself has roots in the supernatural and probably means *hagolstan,* the Old English word for 'hailstone', suggesting that it was thought to have fallen from the sky. Puckstone obviously gets its name from *puca* meaning 'goblin'. Charles Warne, a nineteenth century antiquary, wrote of the Agglestone:

> The country people say of it that his Satanic majesty (who is often a very important personage in these capricious freaks) was one day sitting on the Needles Rock, Isle of Wight, whence, espying Corfe Castle in the distance, he took the cap from his head and threw it across the sea, with the intent of demolishing that structure. But it would appear that he had over-estimated his powers of jactation, for the missile fell short of its mark; and there it stands to this day on Studland Heath, a monument of disappointed malice, a wonder to the peasantry, and a theme of antiquarian conjecture.

The conjecture ended long ago when geologists explained that the Agglestone was in no way mysterious and had not been taken to Studland Heath by a glacier, the devil, prehistoric man or anything else. It has therefore ceased to be eligible for discussion in this chapter, but the connection with Rempstone makes its inclusion here seem suitable. It was a single great stone about sixteen feet high, twice that in diameter, and weighing about four hundred tons. It became a natural wonder of Purbeck because of its anvil-shape and grand position on a sandy hill overlooking Studland Bay and Poole Harbour. These words are in the past tense because the stone took a tumble in 1970 and collapsed on to its side.

Another boulder, and this time it is still a mystery stone, stands in the valley of the Corfe River southeast of Steeple. It is an upright limestone monolith over seven feet tall on the bank of a small stream and on the west edge of a narrow coppice. It is called the Harpstone and this is assumed by romantic writers to mean the 'harp player's stone'.

The farmhouse of Hurpston, an eighteenth century building, lies roofless and ruinous to the east. Surrounding it are the remains of earlier desertion, the mediaeval settlement of the place called *Harpera* or *Herpere* in the Domesday Book. Those names omit any mention of 'stone' and it is open to doubt whether this was dropped from the name by accident or, alternatively, was not added to the original name until later. If it could be proved that the 'stone' part of the name was older (it occurs first as Herpston in 1340) this would be evidence of the antiquity of the Harpstone. Instead we are left with nothing except a single standing stone with a date that might be anything from prehistoric to Saxon.

Its position in a damp valley would count against it being prehistoric were this anywhere but Purbeck. As the position of the Rempstone stone circle is highly unusual, in that it lies below a six hundred foot down instead of on top of it, this argument does not count. The obvious answer there is that the stones of the circle are from the heath and the effort needed to drag them to the top of Nine Barrow Down would have been phenomenal. In any event, the circle at Rempstone was in easy distance of the Bronze Age populations of both the downs and the heath.

Probably the Harpstone is also from the Bronze Age although this suggests prehistoric penetration of the woodlands of the Corfe River at an early time. It has certainly stood there long enough to be deeply grooved by weathering. Standing stones are common on the western moorlands but rare in Dorset. The ready availability of stone explains why Purbeck is the most eastward part of the south coast to have a prehistoric stone circle. As the megalithic know-how and inclination was present in the island it is an appealing thought that the monolith might have been raised near the Corfe River as a tribute to the water deity.

If so, the remains of those responsible lie less than seven hundred yards away in the Bronze Age burial ground at the west end of Smedmore Hill. This was cut into by quarrying operations in 1929 and two skeletons blasted out of the ground. The cremated bones of a young child were found by two picnickers in August 1952. Earlier, in 1944, an American bulldozer smashed into two stone cists in another part of the quarry but the woman and child it revealed were probably Romano-British.

On the other side of Purbeck in January 1951 a grave-digger at Studland parish church uncovered the top of a stone cist and found inside a skull detached from the body with the lower jaw placed behind the head. J. B. Calkin excavated the grave and found the cist had a stone floor with sides, ends and covers of Purbeck marble slabs. A Kimmeridge shale spindle-whorl was near the pelvis and cockle shells seemed to have been scattered around the feet. Professor John Cameron wrote in his medical report that the remains were of a woman probably in her thirties. Calkin commented "it is reasonable to suppose that we are here dealing with a case of decapitation. The position of the lower jaw indicates almost certainly that it too had been severed from the head. The removal of the head was clearly not due to the shortness of the cist. There would have been over three inches to spare had the head been in place".

The burial was dated Romano-British but the excavator recalled that Rev. J. H. Austen had found bodies trussed up before burial when he dug into prehistoric barrows on the Purbeck ridge during the last century. One crouched skeleton also had its lower jaw lying behind the head. Calkin himself had excavated a woman from a third century grave at Kimmeridge and found her buried with her head placed at her feet and, again, the lower jaw detached.

Calkin was the foremost twentieth century investigator of ancient life in Purbeck. He gave his findings on the Studland lady in the "Proceedings" of the Dorset Natural History and Archaeological Society for 1952, adding the opinion:

These primitive rites seem to suggest that the Bronze Age inhabitants of the Isle of Purbeck had a very lively fear of being haunted by the dead, and accordingly took practical measures to prevent them from walking and talking. The mutilation practices recently revealed at Studland and Kimmeridge would indicate that this belief was still prevalent in the third century AD. Indeed the practice of burying criminals at the crossroads and driving a stake through their chest, a custom which survived until a few centuries ago, is evidently an example of the same superstition.

He later added in his book "Ancient Purbeck" that it was highly unlikely the woman had been executed because the cist was so carefully constructed with marble that had been quarried and brought to the site. She had also been respectfully provided with a spindle-whorl and some food. He considered an answer was that these women had spoken too freely and the ceremonial beheading was to prevent them continuing to do so in the afterlife. The spindle-whorls were to keep them occupied. Calkin added that the Silent Woman, an inn at Cold Harbour near Wareham, had a sign showing a woman carrying her head in her arms. As other decapitated women have been found in graves in north Dorset and elsewhere in southern England, the practice—for whatever reason—seems to have been widespread. Scientific excavations on Roman burial grounds in the future may provide evidence of similarities between decapitated bodies and uphold, or disprove, the view that they were simply gossips who had died young with arthritis or some other complaint that had made them particularly surly in their last years.

Ritual mutilation of the dead, I might add, continued in Britain during this century until the belated abolition of the detestable practice of capital punishment. The bodies of murderers who had been hanged at Pentonville and other prisons were placed in coffins drilled with holes. Quicklime was packed around each body and hosepipes directed at the perforated casket as it was lowered into a sodden pit in the prison graveyard. Corpses and coffins were to be eaten away and no grave in the body-dump was marked. So was the theory. In fact lime acts as a preserver.

Other barbaric practices have been longer past. One Purbeck incident has been forgotten but a reminder is preserved in a couple of place names: high on the ridge between Creech and East Lulworth is a spot known as Maiden's Grave Gate on the site of an ancient crossroads at the boundary between Tyneham and Steeple parishes. There stands a windswept old oak known as the Coffin Tree. It is so called because the shapes of two small coffins, a few inches across, are cut into the trunk. The second appears to have been carved as the first became obliterated.

The names of the gate and the tree, together with the symbols, preserve the memory of a girl who killed herself probably in the late eighteenth century and was deprived of Christian burial: she was deposited instead, as law and custom demanded, at night by the highway at a crossroads, as far as possible from the village church — preferably, as here, on the parish boundary — and with a stake driven through her heart to prevent the appearance of a ghost. But who she was, we shall probably never know.

A later instance of a suicide's burial, after 1823 when the law had banned stakings or other mutilation, was that of John Ball, landlord of the old Ship Inn at Langton Matravers. This building is now a cottage nestling beside the three-storey inn which replaced it on the summit of Steps Hill in 1884. R. J. Saville documented John Ball's case in the seventeenth issue of "Dorset, the county magazine".

John Ball and his wife, Mary Holmes Ball, were incompatible and had parted. On the night of 18 December 1878 they came together again for Christmas. After closing-time they had their last row. Mary ran back to her mother's home and John followed with a shotgun. She was barely behind the cottage door as it was hit by a blast of shot. John went back to the inn and shot himself in the public room.

Rev. Lester Lester, rector of Langton, wrote to a local newspaper:

> The body of John Ball, late of the Ship Inn, Langton, was buried like a dog at 9.30 p.m. on 22 December. For charity's sake we must protest against this! It is time for even Purbeck juries to know that the sentiment of our times is dead against such verdicts as *felo-de-se*. He wanted his wife to come and live with him. She felt that she could not. Life then appeared so black to him that he shot himself. If he was sane, why be so cruel to survivors, so uncourteous to a poor dead man; seeing that to him prayers could mean nothing, and even a suicide's burial nothing, while to them the touching service might have been of vital importance. We do hope this verdict will be the last of its kind in our neighbourhood.

The burial had taken place in a field at night so that relatives could not know the spot or mark the grave. Lester started a letter writing campaign against *felo-de-se* ('felon of himself') which was applied to a person who killed himself, either deliberately or accidentally, whilst committing a felony. This was "the crime of suicide" and it was society's retribution on the body of the dead. The rector's letters supported a winning cause as the existing law was repealed by Parliament in Acts of 1880 and 1882. Suicides were afterwards buried in a churchyard as if they had died normally. Another Langton suicide who died before the law reform was Tom Burnham who was buried beside an old oak tree at an old crossroads near Godlingston. Burnham hanged himself but his name, at least, has persisted with the tree named Tom Burnham's Oak and standing beside Burnham's Lane.

CHAPTER XIV

Corfe Castle

IN THE words of the foremost authority in the land, the Royal Commission on Historical Monuments: "Corfe Castle visually and historically is one of the most notable castles in England". Despite its ruination and subsequent decay it remains, to quote the same source, "one of the most important buildings in the country".

Corfe Castle was a grand and noble achievement of mediaeval military architecture which figured less in English history than its size would suggest. Its inaccessibility gave it other roles in the background of the times; as an impregnable storehouse for treasure, regalia and political prisoners. It was a great fortress and a state prison by 1106. John Hutchins, Dorset's county historian, wrote that "its structure is so strong, the ascent of the hill on all sides but the south so steep, and the walls so massy and thick, that it must have been one of the most impregnable fortresses in the kingdom before the invention of artillery".

History, for Corfe, might have ended so differently. It was on May Day in 1643 that a troop of 'republican' horsemen entered Purbeck. They, like Thomas Gerard in the 1620s, knew that the mayor of Corfe "by an olde custome, hath free power everie yeare on May Day to hunt, course, kill and carrie awaye such stags as maye bee founde in the westerne woodes; to which sporte diverse gentlemen for their recreation resorte". The troop chose their day well and the island gentry were duly gathered together for their customary staghunt. Only Lady Bankes stood between the visitors and the castle but she became suspicious and closed the castle gates. With a handful of royalists, she held the fortress against allcomers as Corfe was unsuccessfully besieged while the lines of war flowed across the open English countryside, with great battles at Marston Moor and Naseby Field and minor movements and skirmishes that touched Dorset less than many counties. Corfe held out until the first hour of 27 February 1646 when an officer of the garrison, Lieutenant-Colonel Thomas Pittman, conspired with the besiegers and allowed a disguised body of 'republicans' to enter under royalist colours. My label of 'republicans' is technically inaccurate but justified by Cromwell's later realism when he regarded Charles I, the divider of our kingdom, as "an accursed thing". Pittman is depicted as a traitor by the authors of older works on Dorset history but he in fact only ended what had already become a futile and tiresome exercise. Corfe was making a valid stand as long as it deployed some 'republican' forces, but when those were no longer even needed by their own side, the heroism of the defenders had no purpose. Sieges like that at Corfe had become purely local diversions and these royalist last-stands were being systematically eliminated. Luckily for England, the creation of the New Model Army early in 1645 had been the means of bringing the war to a close. Endless fighting was destroying the basis of the country's economic life and breaking up both families and communities. From all the confusion of the spring of 1645 came the decisive Parliamentary victory at Naseby on 14 June and the inescapable conclusion that the English Civil War was now won and lost. That Corfe Castle would become part of the losses became irreversible with Sir Thomas Fairfax's easy expedition into Somerset in July 1645 when the last hope of a royalist stand in the West faded before his cavalry at Langport and Bridgwater.

Dorset had been largely in Parliamentary hands throughout the war and by 1646 the only royalist garrisons in the county were holed-up at Corfe Castle and Portland Castle. In January Corfe was again put under siege; there had been other attacks since that May Day and constant, if less direct, pressure for surrender. A fortress of the strength of Corfe would have played a full part in the war if it lay in the Midlands but Purbeck, in the strategy of an inland war, was simply a backwater on the Channel coast. Bristol fell to Fairfax in the previous September and he proceeded to clear up the royalist remnants in Devon and Cornwall. The king's colours had gone from the West and there was no possibility of an organised attempt to rescue Corfe from its last siege; the only chance of reinforcements came from stray bands of retreating royalists who found refuge at the castle.

These were the circumstances of the plight of Corfe Castle at the time when Pittman talked with the other side. The outcome was that he told Colonel Henry Anketell, governor of the castle, that he could go into Somerset and privately raise a hundred more royalists for the castle's defence. He offered to leave under a truce arranged for the exchange of a prisoner. The hundred men were secretly marched from the Parliamentary garrison at Weymouth to Lulworth Castle, where some more troopers were found, and Pittman led them into the sally-port at the northeast corner of the castle where they were welcomed by Anketell. But he may have become suspicious as he refused to let more than fifty enter the castle, saying he could not deploy any more; Pittman protested that the governor was endangering the men's lives. The fifty men were dispersed to the Keep, a tower on the walls, and two platforms. They had entered at about two o'clock in the morning; after dawn, when the Parliamentary siege force attacked from the outside, the loyal gunners in the castle were caught between crossfire. The castle surrendered at eight o'clock on the morning of 27 February 1646 after a siege that had lasted forty-eight days and enforced isolation that had lasted nearly three years. There were 140 prisoners taken but no vengeful actions on the part of the victors. That was reserved for the castle itself. The official end for the fortress, a penalty on masonry and grandeur, was a decision taken on 4 March 1646 when the House of Commons ordered its demolition and the subsequent operation took several months. Only its sheer strength prevented total destruction and Corfe survives as the greatest rugged pile in the country and the most massive of the lasting monuments to the struggles of the English Civil War. Battlefields have been grassed over for three centuries but Corfe still stands spectacularly, helped a little by repairs that have been carried out since the government came to its aid in 1958.

The history of Corfe had started in Saxon times and the place was forever associated with the assassination of a seventeen-year-old king. Young Edward was the eldest son of Edgar and the natural heir to the throne which he took on his father's death in July 975. On 15 April 978 he was hunting in Purbeck and called at the *domus* where his stepmother, Elfthryth, and her son Ethelred were living. As he was mounting his horse to leave, Edward was knifed in the back. In the words of William of Malmesbury: "The Kinge, findeing himselfe hurt, sett spurs to his horse, thinking to recover his companie; but the wounde being deepe, and fainting through the losse of much blood, he felle from his horse, which dragged him by one stirrop, untill he was left dead at Corfe gate."

Professor F. M. Stenton, the authority on Anglo-Saxon England, says that the "circumstances of abominable treachery" shocked men who were ready to tolerate any crime of open violence. He adds: "So far as can be seen the murder was planned and carried out by Ethelred's household men in order that their young master might become king. There is nothing to support the allegation, which first appeared in writing more than a century later, that Queen Elfthryth had plotted her stepson's death."

Edward had been unpopular among the nobles, and for violent outbursts of rage that shook his own household, but the assassination removed all prestige from the crown and elevated the victim to the position of saint and martyr. Edward, according to the Anglo-Saxon Chronicle, was buried at Wareham with no royal honours.

Legend perpetuated the story in the minds of the Purbeck peasantry. In 1908, Wilkinson Sherren recorded the traditions in his book "The Wessex of Romance". Men from the castle found the king bruised and dead:

> . . . and conveyed him to a mean house, where lived a blind woman, who, it is said, awakened at midnight with restored eyesight, the house being radiant with light. Hearing of this marvel, Elfrida [Elfthryth] had the body removed and concealed in a well in a marshy place, where the year following it was found by some devout person, the spot being discovered to them by the illumination of a pillar of fire. Ever after the well yielded pure and sweet water, good for the healing of the infirm, being known as St. Edward's Fountain. The corpse was removed to the church of St. Mary, Wareham; three years afterwards it was found to be in an uncorrupted condition, when it was removed to Shaftesbury.

St. Edward's Fountain, a clear trickle issuing from the east edge of the castle hill close to the Byle Brook, was said to have had healing properties especially powerful in the treatment of failing sight. Despite the wealth of tales, the exact spot where Edward was killed is unknown, but there are a few clues.

In the West Bailey of Corfe Castle are some herring-bone walling and windows surviving from the Old Hall of the time of William the Conqueror. This building was on the site of an earlier building which excavation in 1950 showed to be Saxon. Little was found but it is likely that this was the position of the royal house where Edward was murdered. The Southwest Gatehouse, two hundred feet away, was known as Edward's Gate to Corfe villagers who said it had been built on the spot where the murder took place.

Today, Edward's remains may even be on public display in a glass case at the ruins of Shaftesbury Abbey. In January 1931 a small lead box was found ten inches below the ground and jammed into a recess at the base of an abbey wall. The box was apparently hidden at the dissolution and contained ancient bones, the remains of the skeleton of a youth. These relics were obviously highly regarded at the nunnery and may well be Edward's bones.

Corfe's role as a fortress started with the coming of the Normans. The potential of the hill, which rises precipitously over 150 feet above the streams that lie at its foot, was realised immediately.

Such evidence as exists points to the eighty feet high Keep having been standing in the year 1100 and, even if it is slightly later, it is still one of the earliest mediaeval fortresses in Britain and its style was ahead of its time. It is built upon and otherwise surrounded by an earlier, eleventh century, wall that was about nine feet thick and stood nearly thirty feet high on the outside.

The stronghold was of sufficient strength in 1139 to withstand a siege by Stephen, the last king of the house of Normandy. Baldwin de Redvers, first Earl of Devon, remained safely inside. It was a period of complete anarchy when "every lord of a castle acted as king in his own domain". In the words of a contemporary chronicler: "When traitors perceived that he [the king] was a mild man, and soft and good . . . every powerful man made his castles, and held them again him." King Stephen did, apparently, leave something substantial at Corfe as he is thought to have been responsible for the ring-and-bailey earthwork known as The Rings, four hundred yards southwest of the castle. These overgrown remains can only be those of a siege castle that Stephen built to marshal his troops in a secure position overlooking the town and blocking an approach road from the west. The bailey is now largely ploughed out but it seems to have been deliberately designed to take advantage of the sloping ground so that activities there could be less easily observed from the castle heights. The Rings was later utilised by the 'republican' forces of another Civil War and may have held a camp and artillery emplacement. Because of this it was called Cromwell's Battery in the last century.

By 1212 Corfe had become one of King John's fortified depôts for holding state treasures. Money taken from church estates was put into custody at Corfe and in 1213 about fifty thousand marks were stored in the keep prior to the French campaigns. John also liked living at Corfe and hunting in Purbeck and his royal state rooms are now a mass of shapeless ruins and rubble to the east of the Keep.

Fortification of the West Bailey and the building of its three towers was achieved between 1201 and 1204. Most of the ruined curtain walling surviving in the Outer Bailey, and all its towers, were built later in the thirteenth century. The first version of these fortifications was started about 1212 to replace the original palisades and survives at the Second, Third and Fourth Towers and the walls between them. Improvements in the latter half of the century replaced some other parts of these stone defences with the First Tower, Southwest Gatehouse, Plunkenet Tower, Horseshoe Tower, Outer Gatehouse and Outer Bridge. Minor changes to small sections of walls and the building of a tower immediately southeast of the King's Hall followed in the fourteenth century. Only minor work was carried out in the final phase of the castle's life which ended with its destruction.

Earlier in its history, Corfe Castle had also held out against authority. In the time of King John it was a dungeon for Savaric de Mauléon. He was a baron from Poitou, a county on the edge of Aquitaine, a province claimed both by England and France. Savaric led a hundred men in an uprising that took the castle of Mirebeau in Vienne in 1202 and resulted in John's mother, Queen Eleanor, being locked in the keep there. Eleanor was able to smuggle a message to John who marched from Le Mans and took Vienne by surprise with his Flemish mercenaries. Savaric was taken across the Channel and "put into the tower" at Corfe "where there was never food nor drink". Corfe Castle was then a state prison as well as one of John's favourite residences. Conditions were appalling for his twenty-five prisoners from Aquitaine and most of them starved to death.

Savaric was luckier. He is said to have made his guards drunk and then knocked them on the head; he released some of his followers and they took possession of the "maistre-forterece" which John had then to make plans to storm. But intervention by Hubert Gautier, Archbishop of Canterbury, made this unnecessary and Savaric was allowed back to France under an order dated 20 August 1203. He remained in captivity but was released a year later on agreeing to serve the king and providing hostages. The British treasury gave him two hundred marks and he embarked on a dangerous career. He fought, plundered, intrigued, governed and became a troubadour: he became one of the famous men of his age.

In 1204, when John's French troubles culminated in the loss of Normandy, he completed the strengthening of the West Bailey at Corfe. The great ditch was dug three years later as an internal defence between the vulnerable Outer Bailey and the strongly fortified Keep and West Bailey. John then made plans for provincial castle treasuries and Corfe became an important storehouse. After 1208, £1,000 profit from the church estates was taken 'into custody' at Corfe, and in 1213 50,000 marks were transferred to the Keep from Bristol—a part-payment for the coming war against France. The following year Henry Esturmy was commanded to come to Corfe with all the carts he could muster to take the king's treasure to Portsmouth.

The longest memory to linger from John's associations with Corfe concerns Peter de Pomfret, an astrologer, who predicted the king's reign would end on Ascension Day, 23 May 1213. He was wrong. Peter had meanwhile been held at Corfe to wait and see, and with the passing of Ascension Day he was tied to the tails of horses and dragged along the streets of Wareham. His end came at a gallows on the Saxon town wall flanking the northwest edge of Wareham. One high section of the old wall, opposite where Streche Road runs today, is still known as the Bloody Bank.

Purbeck has other and less direct links with the monarchy. Not only was it the scene of the death of Edward the Martyr but it has connections with two later royal murders. Sir John Maltravers, a knight of the shire of Dorset, took part in the killing of Edward II, homosexual king of England. Maltravers had been forced to flee the country after the defeat of Lancaster at the battle of Boroughbridge in 1322. He returned in 1327 to conspire with Edward's wife, Isabella (the daughter of Philip IV of France), to imprison the king. Isabella had a lover, Roger Mortimer, and the trio wanted freedom and power. Maltravers and his brother-in-law Thomas, Lord Berkeley, deposed the monarch and were paid a hundred shillings a day for holding him at Berkeley Castle in Gloucestershire. The brother seems to have been less determined than Maltravers who, with William Gurney, appears to have murdered Edward in September 1327 while Berkeley was away from his castle. The outcome was that Mortimer and Isabella, now the Queen Mother, ruled the country in the name of the late King's son, Edward III, who was only 15 years old.

Ian McQueen, who has investigated the Dorset links with Maltravers, wrote in the "Transactions of the Monumental Brass Society" for 1966 that Sir John was given the task of inducing the dead king's brother Edmund, Earl of Kent, to plot against the new regime and provide an excuse for his disposal. This Maltravers achieved by lying to Edmund that Edward was still alive and held at Corfe Castle. It appears that Edward was transferred to Corfe for a short time during his imprisonment and elaborate pretences, including an impersonation at a dinner party, were maintained after he had been removed. Edmund fell into the trap and schemed for his brother's escape. He was beheaded.

Maltravers was rewarded by a writ of summons to Parliament

as a baron, and appointed constable of Corfe Castle. But his gains were short-lived as Mortimer was overthrown and "he fled abroad once more and in his absence was sentenced by Parliament to be drawn, hanged and beheaded as a traitor for compassing in the death of the Earl of Kent". Eventually, in 1345, he was allowed to return to England though it was not until the age of nearly seventy that he returned to an estate at Lytchett near Poole where he died peacefully in his own home in 1364. There in the church of St. Mary his brass lies on the floor of the north aisle. The village was known as *Luchet Mautravers* in 1291 and, today, as Lytchett Matravers, it still preserves the family name. Likewise do Worth Matravers and Langton Matravers in Purbeck.

As constable of Corfe Castle, Maltravers was the controller of one of the favourite hunting grounds of the mediaeval English kings. The island was variously known as Purbeck Chase, Warren, or Forest. The editors of Hutchin's "History of Dorset" observed: "To the uninclosed heath which stretches away from the range of chalk hills to the northern boundary of the island, the term forest is almost as appropriate as it is to the Black Mount Forest in Scotland, where neither tree nor bush are to be seen." King John is said to have subjected the island "to the forest laws, but it was found that it ought only to have been a hare warren. The popular idea of a forest is an uninclosed and uncultivated district thickly covered or interspersed with trees, but this could never within the reach of history have been the condition of the Isle of Purbeck." Generally, it was called "the king's warren" but whatever its designation, the island was a royal hunting ground and it provided sport and deer for the palaces from 1212 to 1615, when James I was the last king to hunt in Purbeck. As many historical documents make mention of "the king's warren" as they do to "the king's marble" in the island.

The deer of Purbeck were more important than its people and no killing was allowed for sport, food or protection of crops. It was entirely a royal game preserve. No inhabitant was allowed even to build a stone wall, hedge or bank "above the assay": higher than a doe and fawn could leap. Any wood cutting could only be done with the consent of the king's warrener and whatever decent timber grew in Purbeck belonged to the constable of Corfe who used it for castle repairs. All falcons nesting in the island were the king's property, as were all 'royal fish' caught on the coast: porpoise, sturgeon and grampus.

Thomas Bond described other restrictions to a meeting of Victorian antiquarians: "It was contrary to the island law for any man to take or hunt any rabbit, hare, fox or pheasant with dogs, net or a ferret within the warren without licence of the warrener; and no man was permitted to keep, carry or lead loose any dogs or curs, in the heath or elsewhere, to the disturbance of the game, or to drive them out of their pastures. Even the building of new houses in the heath or elsewhere was prohibited without a licence from the constable."

Apparently the interference went further and probably explains the insular outlook of the old quarrymen: "No islander was allowed to marry his daughter out of the island without licence from the constable or other officer of the Castle of Corfe . . . it is quite natural therefore that in a district where the liberties of the freeholder were straitened by such despotic rules and customs, the proud mediaeval baron refused to take up his residence, and thus it is that we find the gentry of the island, though rather numerous in proportion to the extent of the territory, yet neither wealthy, nor exercising much influence beyond the limits of their own remote and secluded district. Even such influence as they possessed at home was sometimes exercised for evil rather than for good, and they seem to have entertained a low sense of the moral responsibility which attached to their social position, so far as it called upon them to set a good example to their humbler neighbours of obedience to the law."

An attempt was made in 1224 to challenge the forest laws in Purbeck but Henry III resisted it and issued orders forbidding anyone to "hunt the king's game in the warren of Corfe". He continued to use Purbeck and in the following year ordered Ralph Gernun, the constable of Corfe, to hunt with his hounds and take forty bucks "to be salted and retained" until the king wanted them. The only concession Henry made towards relaxing the restrictions was to exempt the inhabitants of the royal forests from having the ball cut from the forefeet of their dogs to prevent them chasing the king's game.

Numerous trials and disputes resulted from the various laws. The deer needed protection: in 1323 Robert Hardle was indicted for poaching deer and hitting the sub-constable of Corfe with a barbed arrow. Hardle took refuge in the church at Church Knowle and escaped. Edward III complained in 1341 that much of the once abundant game in Purbeck had been destroyed. By 1401 the forest law had crumbled further and a licence was granted by Henry IV for the destruction of the "deer and all manner of wild animals except hares and rabbits in his warren of Purbeck, being so increased that they cause great annoyance to the inhabitants in eating their corn, and destroying their meadows and pasture".

The strict forest laws were abandoned a couple of centuries before the great castle met its end. But there is a postscript to this chapter: Corfe Castle had one last resident after the fortress was demolished. A rector of Corfe set up home in the South Tower and inserted a fireplace, cupboard and window. He slept in the North Tower on the opposite side of the West Bailey. John Wesley visited the castle in 1774 and wrote in his "Journal": "Some time since the proprietor fitted up some rooms in the Mural Tower [South Tower] on the southwest and laid out a little garden, commanding a large prospect, pleasant beyond description. The rooms were fitted up and occupied for many years by the rector of Corfe. . . ."

"Corfe Castle from Knowle Hill" by Philip Brannon, 1862.
It is no longer quite this picturesque. West Mill, in the near distance, was demolished early in the twentieth century, though the eighteenth century bridge has survived.

CHAPTER XV

Dinosaurs

SEVENTY MILLION years ago when the world's vegetation was cycads and ferns there was a single group of animals that dominated the earth—the dinosaurs. These great cold-blooded reptiles were on land, in the skies (pterosaurs) and on the oceans (ichthyosaurs and mosasaurs). Then came a disaster. Everything was destroyed; plants and reptiles and all, except for a few token survivals from whole ways of life. The great dinosaurs, however, left no descendants. The amazing and unaccountable fact is that they disappeared together, simultaneously, the world over.

Carl Dunbar wrote in "Historic Geology" that "it is difficult to account for the simultaneous extinction of great tribes of animals so diverse in relationships and in habitats of life." Disease is no answer as a virus has never wiped out an entire species from everywhere in the world, and the catastrophe that removed the dinosaurs destroyed not one but hundreds of species of both animals and plants. Evolution is no answer as its rules call for gradual change. Edwin H. Colbert, another dinosaur expert, wrote: "The great extinction that wiped out all the dinosaurs, large and small, in all parts of the world, and at the same time brought to an end various other lines of reptilian evolution, was one of the outstanding events in the history of the earth . . . it was an event that has defied all attempts at a satisfactory explanation."

Whatever caused the destruction also allowed the preservation of seventy unhatched dinosaur eggs on the plains of the Gobi Desert where they were picked up by astounded explorers in 1922. Most were filled with sand but some had traces of embryonic bone. Others have since been found elsewhere in the world and show various stages of embryonic development. Something stopped all dinosaur eggs, however near they were to breaking open, from actually hatching. In the same way, something preserved the trunks of cycad trees petrified on a shelf above the sea to the east of Lulworth Cove. This Fossil Forest is one of the textbook sights of British geology.

In Purbeck, the limestone hills have revealed more sets of fossilised dinosaur footprints than any other area of Britain. It is likely, from the evidence of large numbers of bones washed up by the sea, that a graveyard of dinosaurs lies somewhere off-shore in the northern part of Swanage Bay.

The first strange fact about the footprints was, as their historian J. B. Delair noted in 1962, that "the vast majority . . . came from the *roach bed*" of the Purbeck quarrylands. Until 1965 it was not proved that any tracks had been found from any other of the Purbeck beds. The roach is also known as the *pink bed* and varies considerably in thickness, even in adjacent quarries. The bed lies only a few feet below the ground surface and is "unmistakably fissured both horizontally and vertically". The footprints, observed Delair, occur mainly along horizontal fissures.

These fissures are almost certainly mud cracks caused by the same heat that baked the last impressions of the reptiles into stone for posterity. Other clues suggest that the dinosaurs were in shallow water that was just deep enough to prevent their tails dragging through the mud and sand. Some lines of prints start off as firm impressions, showing the animal was not supported by water, but then become less distinct as water moved up its body.

In all cases where sufficient of the prints have been uncovered they show action. There is no evidence that any of the dinosaurs were merely standing and eating. All were on the move, some on the run, and others made sudden changes in direction. An individual called *Purbeckopus pentactylus* left six inch long prints in an old quarry west of Acton. Two imprints have survived from those found in 1936 and one faces away from its partner at a ninety degree angle. Another set of prints has been found placed in an almost complete circle on the rock bed. Delair also recorded the discovery in a quarry between Worth Matravers and Acton of footprints "pointing in all directions in and around the margins of a pronounced bowl-like depression in the strata".

A comparison exists with the Connecticut valley of New England. To quote Colbert: "Most of the tracks and trackways show us dinosaurs on the move, either walking or running. Some of them show that their makers came to sudden stops; some of them slipped in the mud."

Dozens of tracks have been found in Purbeck but only a handful remnants have been saved and most of these are now partly obliterated by the weather. A fine set of double tracks was exposed at Herston in 1961 when E. W. Suttle reopened an old quarry in the area known as Mutton Hole. There were twenty-six separate footprints and another line of tracks was found in the following year. These attracted more scientific attention and were said to have probably been made by a megalosaurus but no move was made to have them preserved. In 1963 the British Museum (Natural History) decided to intervene and excavated a further seventy-foot undamaged section at Mutton Hole to find more tracks. Other prints, of tridactyls, were found in quarries at Queensground, Langton Matravers, between 1963 and 1965. One discovery was notable in coming not from the roach but the freestone bed that lies about four feet below. This was the first confirmed discovery of reptile tracks from any layer of stone other than the roach. The comparative absence of the dinosaur traces from other layers of stone shows how they lived and died for millions of years but rarely under conditions that were suitable for fossilisation. Circumstances were far different at the end.

This end came for the dinosaurs as a sudden catastrophe. They appear to have been killed by a sudden rise in temperature and carried by torrents of water to swampy hollows and gullies where their bodies accumulated in hundreds and were covered with mud from the land by the surge of water. All the dinosaur bones were buried rapidly as they survive in a condition too perfect to be accounted for by gradual accumulation. The temperature change also killed all the embryos in their eggs.

What caused the simultaneous extinction of the dinosaurs? The only plausible theory so far advanced is that an asteroid collided with the earth and fragmented to shower tektites across land and sea with the effect of a few dozen hydrogen bombs scattered across the globe. This happened on a small scale in Siberia's Tunguska forest in 1908 when twenty-five miles of trees were flattened on either side of a crater caused by a meteorite that crashed through the earth's atmosphere. Significantly a fire storm was created of the sort that accompanies atomic explosions and devastated German cities during the terror-bombing at the close of the last war.

This cosmic accident theory has been tentatively supported, though in another context, by the scientific commentator Robert Ardrey. He writes in his book "The Social Contract" that in 1963 the chairman of Canada's defence research board, Robert Uffen, presented the hypothesis "that these periods of reversal when life was exposed to cosmic blast could have been times of rapid mutation, appearance of new species, extinction of old. Many such unexplained periods exist in the evolutionary record. No satisfactory explanation has ever been advanced for the sudden die-off of reptiles at the end of the Cretaceous".

The hypothesis would account for heat, radiation, and a simultaneous fluctuation in water level all over the world. The earth's magnetic poles would also have been reversed. After the catastrophe, mammals ruled the world and no traces of dinosaurs are found in later rocks. Yet neither are there any fossils to explain the sequence of intermediaries between the reptiles and their successors, the mammals. Clearly, the mammals did not come about through gradual evolution, but erupted suddenly as a result of some dramatic interruption to the order of the world. That Purbeck holds the clues to the truth is apparent from the reptilian evidence and also from the fact that one of the earliest mammal beds in the country is on the cliffs at Durlston Bay where scattered remains of marsupials have been found. They show the start of the advanced stages of mammal development that have led to ourselves; but what created the marsupials? The answer is either a cosmic accident or divine intervention.

Hindsight   It has almost become a scientific truth that it was an asteroid that ended the domination of the earth by the dinosaurs which had lasted 140 million years (see page 136). Continental drift, with the subduction of the undersea tectonic plates, is the explanation of what happened to the hole in the north-western Pacific that was caused 65 million years ago when an asteroid plunged into the planet. Its crater had gone back into the melting-pot.

The energy created by that impact, which had a piston-effect on the atmosphere, was of the order of a thousand billion times the power of the Hiroshima atom-bomb − it has been quantified at somewhere around 20,000,000,000,000,000 tons of TNT.

Steam, dust and firestorms did the damage, blocking sunlight from the planet and triggering an ice-age. Traces of this contamination, containing twenty to thirty times more iridium and osmium than would be expected from a normal earth-event, have been found all across the globe. Plant life in Europe and on the eastern seaboard of North America survived largely intact but a vast loss of flora species occurred in a wide belt of the northern hemisphere stretching from the Russian Urals to the American Rockies.

Plants, in the main, had seeds by which to survive as a species but for animals the effects were devastating. The rotting of the vegetation caused the deaths of the herbivores and soon there was no prey for the predators to eat. The disaster was global and caused the extinction of all animals on earth that weighed more than 25 kilograms. In a matter of weeks all the dinosaurs were dead.

CHAPTER XVI

Wildlife

BRITAIN'S TWO rarest reptiles are found in comparatively large numbers on the Great Heath of Purbeck. They are the sand lizard and smooth snake. It is partially thanks to these two animals that the government's conservation agencies stepped in and created a 429-acre national nature reserve on Studland Heath. This not only helps protect the wildlife but it preserves at least a corner of the Great Heath in its natural state and holds at bay the threat from the west. There, between Newton and Middlebere, the scientific advances of the twentieth century have allowed modern man to carve plantations and farmlands from the arid wastes of a vast wild region. Snakes and lizards gave the impetus to a rearguard action before the advancement reached Little Sea and the sand dunes of Studland.

The sand lizard (*Lacerta agilis agilis*) is restricted in this country to the dry sandy heathlands of the south and coastal sand dunes in the north. It is brighter and more spotted than the common lizard and the males are particularly beautiful in spring. Sand lizards are often found living in colonies and frequently spend the hottest parts of summer days in abandoned tunnels left by small mammals. The number of sand lizards in Purbeck is difficult to estimate but it is common on most heather-covered areas of the heath.

The smooth snake (*Coronella austriaca*) often has its numbers underestimated. Rare in Britain as a whole, it is reasonably plentiful across the pockets of natural heathland that remain in Purbeck. This snake is harmless and differs from the adder in a number of ways. Its body is more slender and the tail longer than that of the adder; its head is smaller and a pattern of spots, sometimes joining to form cross-bars, contrasts with the familiar zigzag marking of the adder. The smooth snake can be brown, greyish or even reddish in colour. Despite these differences, all snakes are persecuted by man, and a large number of smooth snakes are killed on sight in Purbeck every year. Even this has had less effect on distribution than the elimination of suitable territory by the encroachment of conifer plantations and the recent drive to put virgin heathland under the plough for crops and pasture. In

1959 the Nature Conservancy captured, marked and released ten smooth snakes in Purbeck as a "pilot experiment" to study movements, habitat, hibernation areas and other facets of their lives. While the snake has been able to hold more than an enclave in Purbeck, it has been systematically eliminated by development from its former habitats of Bournemouth, Poole and Ferndown. The first specimen known to have been captured in Britain was caught by Frederick Bond on Parley Heath in June 1853 and put in a bottle. He recognised it as something new but omitted to make an identification. The first official British record was made by Dr. J. E. Gray of the British Museum in 1859 when he examined a snake that had been caught "near the flagstaff" at Bournemouth. In 1880 a naturalist looked back on the abundance of smooth snakes before the building of Bournemouth:

At that time Bournemouth was a very small village, surrounded by large expanses of moorland, intersected with marshy valleys and a famous hunting ground for naturalists. At that time *Coronella* was extraordinarily abundant. During the very hot summer of 1868 the snakes were seen literally in scores and great numbers were killed. Since then, however, their numbers have gradually decreased and, most of the wild moor having disappeared before the advance of civilisation, they are not now met with in places where they formerly abounded. The favourite haunt of the *Coronella* is a dry sandy hillside, overgrown with short heath and gorse and coarse grass, sloping down to a marshy valley where water is at all times available. There on some bare patch of sand the snake lies loosely coiled and basks in the sun, and there it can, when thirsty, get water. During the heat of the day it frequently comes down to some pool to drink.

It is commonly stated that smooth snakes and sand lizards are found together because one is the favourite prey of the other. This is no valid explanation for distribution. Smooth snakes are also found in areas where there are no sand lizards to eat. Instead they live there on common lizards and slow worms. The sole reason that brings the species together is that they share a need for the same sandy habitats. So too does the natterjack toad and this cohabits in several areas with smooth snakes and sand lizards. Neither eats the natterjack. The smooth snake cannot even manage a full-grown sand lizard but is able to eat a large common lizard in a matter of minutes. The interrelationship of the smooth snake, sand lizard and natterjack toad is in no way explained by such tastes but comes about because, in our climate at least, sandy soils offer the only suitable conditions for the survival of each species.

The natterjack toad (*Bufo calamita*) is another present (or past) Purbeck species. It is a small and colourful little animal with a yellow stripe running down its back and a skin that shines when wet. I kept four for several years in a large box of sand in my bedroom where they burrowed happily. They croaked frequently and loudly. The toads occur locally in England, mainly on coastal sand dunes but also on the Surrey heaths and the sandier fringes of the New Forest. They have been found in east Dorset and Purbeck; but whether there are still a few Dorset colonies is doubtful. I am inclined to think that it remains present in isolated pockets as I know only too well how a number of individuals can disappear in a mound of sand and not show themselves for days. Most likely the toad is unobserved rather than non-existent.

One group was recorded from somewhere in the Poole and Wareham region in 1843. The colony must have been natterjack rather than common toads as an observer, W. Thompson, wrote in the Zoologist that they were a new species of toad "which I believe to be distinct and not yet described". Common toads, on the other hand, have been well known for centuries so he could hardly have been thinking of them. Furthermore, the burrowing habits he described are precisely those of the natterjack. The natterjack digs with its fore-legs and like a terrier throws the soil backwards. Common toads are not habitual diggers, are much slower, and edge their back feet into the ground.

Thompson's colony of natterjacks travelled across two miles of heath in March from a sandpit where they had hibernated to an expanse of water where they spawned. The annual journey was accompanied by a mass-slaughter as rats and birds found easy prey. A second migration, from the heath to the sandpit for hibernation, took place in the autumn. These journeys were noted for ten years but came to an end when Thompson cut a dyke across their path and let in the sea water. He wrote:

> On looking into a pit one day in the early part of November, I was surprised to see a number of toads and a vast quantity of loose sand in motion. On turning it over with a spade I found numbers of toads working themselves further into it. The sand in its natural bed is replete with a thin laminae of hardened sand. I observed several of the larger toads climbing the perpendicular side of the sandpit by clinging to these laminae by their claws, some to a height of three feet from the bottom. When they found two laminae sufficiently wide to suit their purpose they proceeded to rake out the soft sand with one hand while they held on with the other, relieving themselves by changing hands; in this way they soon effected a lodgement and then rapidly worked out of sight, turning the sand they excavated behind them and thus burying themselves to a depth

of eighteen inches from the face. In the spring they came out, leaving their holes open, which were taken possession of by the sand martins. Being obliged to abandon their summer quarters in consequence of the obstruction by the canal, they located themselves in two pools, both subject to drying up, within two hundred yards of their winter quarters, which they still frequent.

An extensive search on the South Haven Peninsula in 1934 failed to reveal any natterjacks. Yet there are numerous ideal habitats across the Great Heath and although no reports have been made it is still possible that these little toads may turn up again. All of Britain's commoner reptiles and amphibians occur in Purbeck with the adder by far the most plentiful. It is found all across the Great Heath and in limestone country as well. Grass snakes occur widely, but especially in the pasture lands of the vale between the chalk ridge and the southern hills, an area that also supports a population of common frogs. Common toads are more widespread and all three British newts have been found in Purbeck with the attractive little palmate (*Triturus helveticus*) the commonest.

Yet for all this comparative abundance of reptiles and amphibians they are the most neglected class of animals in Purbeck. The birds are the most obvious and closely watched branch of its wildlife. Each belt of scenery has its separate soils, vegetation and a specialised section of bird life of its own. Sea birds are the most dramatic and easily noticed of all Purbeck's flora and fauna. This rocky coast is for many birds the eastward extremity of their range along the mainland of the south coast. Puffins still occur in Purbeck to some degree although they decreased through the 1960s and there may now be only ten pairs. I have seen them in recent years at Winspit. The decline is blamed on the increasing effects of polluted plankton and the large numbers of puffins killed each year for food and feathers in northern Atlantic waters. Against this decline in one species, there is the success story from another. The fulmar has spread its range outwards from Iceland in the last two centuries. The first fulmars to be recorded in Britain were on Foula in the Shetland Isles in 1878. Fulmars were first noticed regularly in Purbeck towards the end of the 1950s and are now established in a colony on the limestone crags of Gad Cliff at Tyneham. This is only one movement in the rapid spread of the fulmar along Britain's coast and its establishment of numerous breeding grounds in the last ten years.

Kittiwakes are another gain. Old colonies of this oceanic gull increased in size and one of many new breeding sites lies in Purbeck. Two nests were found on Durlston Head in 1956. The prospecting was successful and this is now the haunt of the kittiwake and fifty nests were counted in 1967. The number had risen in 1969 to 111 nests. By 1980 it would exceed 300 pairs.

Guillemots are still a much commoner bird westward along the limestone cliff-faces: but their numbers are falling fast. The total numbers in Purbeck are assessed at around six hundred but a decrease has taken place over a number of years and is generally blamed on pollution of the sea. Another auk, the razorbill, has always been less abundant than the guillemot and probably numbered a hundred birds in 1967. Then came the crunch. The strength of a razorbill colony elsewhere in Britain was reported to have dropped from 659 pairs in 1968 to only 189 pairs in 1969. Such losses meant that the Purbeck colony could be on the verge of extinction. When the local figures were produced they showed deserted nesting places and a gloomy tally, taken in May, of only three pairs between St. Alban's Head and Durlston Head. There is no hope of a recovery while the Channel makes news with frequent oil spillage, stricken tankers and colliding freighters.

The shag, on the other hand, also numbered about a hundred birds in Purbeck in 1967 but has maintained its small population. This again is a bird of the limestone rocks and it is often found sharing cliffs with the cormorant. These birds are similar looking but do not appear to compete for nest sites as the cormorants take the higher ledges and the shags the lower ones. This demarcation between the species can be seen from the cliff-top at West Man. Whereas the shag tends to go seawards for food, the cormorant often turns inland to the spacious waters of Poole Harbour. Each evening, dozens of individuals can be seen flying south from the harbour and many head for Gad Cliff, a nesting site for two hundred birds and the highest single concentration of the cormorant in Purbeck. Most of the cliffs to the east also have their colonies. An isolated group, away from the limestone cliffs, breeds on Old Harry Rocks.

The limestone region even has a colony of cliff-nesting house martins, breeding as they did before the introduction of buildings. By far the commonest of the sea birds breeding in Purbeck is the herring gull: it has over a thousand nests in the island each year.

This concentration of sea birds along the southern shore in summer is matched only by the winter invasion of Poole Harbour by large flocks of ducks and geese. One small area in particular maintains considerable interest throughout the year. Little Sea is a large freshwater lagoon lying between heathland and sand dunes on the South Haven Peninsula. It is one of the few semi-natural lakes in the south of England and, like the snakes and lizards, one of the reasons for the creation of the Studland national nature reserve.

There is a guidebook fallacy (doubtfully ascribed to an old Studland legend) that it was into this expanse of water that King Arthur's sword was cast as he lay dying. No amount of folklore research could make that one come true: Little Sea was formed in comparatively recent history. Maps of the sixteenth century show the South Haven Peninsula as a very narrow spit of land, now the part that carries the ferry road, at least as narrow as Sandbanks is today. Since that time, however, the sea currents have brought along a succession of Bournemouth beaches and deposited them on the southern side of the entrance to Poole Harbour and down as far as Redend Point. Gradually an arm of the sea became landlocked but in the 1840s it was still connected to the sea at high tide by a passage that opened to the northeast. This entrance is now blocked but a second, smaller, lake to the east of Little Sea is a fragment of the channel and a marsh that extends to Shell Bay shows its former course. Modern maps detail the same trend of sand accumulation and this was shown strikingly by the local Ordnance Survey sheet (six inches to the mile) published in 1963. The section of beach east of Little Sea had been partly surveyed in 1954 and the remainder was revised in 1959. At the meeting point of the two survey dates the map shows the high water mark to have jumped fifty yards out to sea in only five years.

Parts of the former channel carry reed-beds and there are impenetrable thickets of sallow on some swamps. Immediately east of Little Sea are some sand dunes created about 1800 and now colonised by heather and furze. Then comes a later area of dunes covered with marram and Lyme grasses and merging with heaps of blown sand that spread nearest the beach. Pygmy and common shrews are abundant in the dunes and harvest mice are found in smaller numbers.

Beside Little Sea the bog bean, marsh cinquefoil and yellow flag flower in spring and the small quillwort is there but less common. The bog beside the water is brightened in summer by the yellow flowers of the bog asphodel and the varying conditions suit virtually every species of aquatic and wetland plant. Eels in Little Sea itself attract cormorants and an occasional otter, and the visiting herons from Brownsea fish probably for the palmate newt, the only amphibian that is seen in any numbers. As for the area of the old peninsula, the spit of heathland on which the ferry road was built, this has not only the smooth snake and sand lizard but the four other British reptiles (adder, grass snake, common lizard and slow worm) as well. The meadow pipit is the commonest bird and the linnet, stonechat and wren are plentiful.

Little Sea in winter has large flocks of mallard, teal, wigeon and pochard, and smaller numbers of tufted duck, pintail, shoveler, coot and Bewick's swan. There are a few pairs of dabchick nesting at Little Sea each summer and these are the only grebes to breed in Purbeck. The water rail's Purbeck population is also based on Little Sea and about ten pairs breed there in most years. Regular visitors to Little Sea include garganey, gadwall, goldeneye, long-tailed duck, goosander, common scoter, scaup, mute swan, whooper swan and reed warbler. The redpoll breeds in clumps of silver birch on the adjoining heath.

The coastline of the South Haven Peninsula is the best region for seeing the waders and other shore birds of Poole Harbour and the sandy beaches of Shell Bay. The bird population fluctuates in species and numbers throughout the year and even differs markedly between the changing shorelines of Shell Bay, the harbour entrance and Bramble Bush Bay. Birds commonly seen include oystercatcher, curlew, ringed plover, grey plover, redshank, turnstone, sanderling, common tern, arctic tern, roseate tern, little tern and sandwich tern.

Brand's Bay lies to the west of the peninsula and in winter has flocks of shelduck, eider, black-tailed godwit, wigeon, black-necked grebe and Brent goose. The shelduck have been counted in numbers up to a thousand strong and many stay to breed beside the harbour shore.

Westward along the fringes of Poole Harbour is Arne Heath with its nature reserve run by the Royal Society for the Protection of Birds as Britain's last hope if the Dartford warbler, one of our rarest breeding birds, is to be saved from extinction. This purple-breasted warbler stays in Britain throughout the year and its refusal to migrate has led to severe reduction of its numbers in cold winters. The Reader's Digest "Book of British Birds" states: "At the beginning of the last century Dartford warblers bred widely throughout southern England; and they were still found in most counties south of the Thames just before the Second World War. Then came a succession of hard winters. The worst, 1962-3, cut down the entire British population to a mere ten pairs. By 1966 this population had doubled itself, all but six pairs being in Dorset. The bird is still one of the half-dozen British species in the most danger of extinction."

The Arne reserve was established on land held under a lease and is intended to counteract an added difficulty faced by the bird. Many wild areas of furze where it formerly bred in Purbeck have been cleared and Arne is the largest area where a suitable habitat remains. Work has been done to reduce vegetation unsuitable to the Dartford warbler (although, like rhododendron, attractive to us) and replace it with furze. H. G. Alexander, a former vice-president of the British Ornithologists' Union who lives at Swanage, saw the decimation of the warbler and its subsequent attempts to rebuild a population: "Before the severe winter of 1962-63 it was generally distributed on the heaths near Poole Harbour. It is, however, a resident species and suffers severely in prolonged cold or from heavy snowfalls. Very few were noted in the summer of 1963 but by 1968 some recovery had been achieved. Unfortunately, each year some of its former haunts are brought under the plough, so its position as a British breeding bird, with headquarters in Purbeck, is very precarious."

The extent of the recovery was shown by a further count in 1969 when thirty-eight pairs were located and a further seven unattached males. The population was still considered to be at danger level and far from strong enough to withstand a new winter setback. Although the winter of 1969-70 was in many ways hard it does not seem to have done real harm and that of 1970-71 came as a relief for both ornithologists and birds.

But this story of precarious survival from hard winters is nothing new. J. C. Mansel-Pleydell wrote in 1888 that the severe winter of 1880-81 was believed to have exterminated the species. Some survivors were later seen but he considered these probably succumbed "to the severity of the past winter of 1886-87, and it is doubtful whether we shall any longer see our heaths enlivened by this active little bird."

He was however wrong, as Eustace Bankes noted in 1908: "Specimens have been seen of late years by thoroughly reliable ornithologists at Poole, Sandbanks, on the Purbeck heaths and also near Wareham. A few of these have been recorded. The species has therefore managed to avoid extermination, although it was reduced almost to vanishing point by the above mentioned winters, and more recently by that of early 1895."

As the Dartford warbler continues its recovery, so too do the birds of prey. Like much in the survival business, their fortunes are based on geography. Purbeck's land is unsuitable for extensive fields of barley and wheat and the only wide area of cornfields lies on the chalky hillside to the south of Studland. The heath has diminished in extent but it has been replaced by a wider selection of habitats that include pine woods, poor grasslands, and indifferent clearings for cereals. Pasture land for dairying, and some pigs and poultry, continues to be the basis of agriculture on the clay soils of the vale between the chalk and the limestone hills. Even the plateau of southern Purbeck is only partially under corn and its large, flat fields give way to deep-cut coombes towards the coast. There some wild gullies lead into the coastal scenery and the area supports cattle and sheep rather than crops.

This is sufficient variety of land use to appeal to any bird of prey. The comparative smallness of arable farming has also been significant as most parts of Purbeck escaped the intensive use of insecticides, herbicides and other toxic chemicals during the 1950s. This, more than any other of man's advances, decimated the population of preying birds in the lowlands of England to a scattering of remnants and for a time it ended the residence of the peregrine falcon in the island. For as long as anyone could remember they had nested at Blacker's Hole and near Parson's Barn but now only stray individuals are spotted around Swanage. By 1971, however, the peregrine was breeding again inside the Lulworth and East Holme gunnery ranges.

The buzzard and kestrel did not disappear from Purbeck and continued to breed in the island. They are now present in plentiful numbers and Purbeck has a higher population density of both species than any other part of east Dorset. Sightings of the hobby are made almost every year in western Purbeck and up to six at a time have been seen flying across the heath at Povington. It is now a resident breeding bird in the quieter and wilder parts of the Lulworth army ranges and is also occasionally seen taking dragonflies at Little Sea. Honey buzzards frequently drift into Purbeck during September when their continental migration is at its peak. The merlin often appears in Purbeck during winter months. The hen harrier is also occasionally sighted but throughout the year and sometimes in pairs. Marsh harriers too are seen on the southern fringes of Poole Harbour in the spring and summer. Ospreys usually turn up in autumn, on passage, but occasionally stop off for several days to fish in Poole Harbour.

The present is even brighter for the largest member of the crow family, the raven, which currently has four pairs in Purbeck and maintains its traditional territory above Parson's Barn near Old Harry Rocks. J. C. Mansel-Pleydell wrote in his "Birds of Dorsetshire" in 1888:

The raven is another bird which has become nearly extinct through persistent persecution. Fifty years ago it used to breed in the cliffs of St. Alban's Head and Gadcliff; several were often seen together soaring over the cliffs above Kimmeridge, with their ominous croak. . . . A pair of these birds showed much precautionary skill in stealing the eggs of seafowl from the perpendicular cliffs of Ballard Down, near Swanage. While one stood as sentinel on a commanding eminence, the other swooped below, and after taking an egg, returned with it in its bill to its companion; both then flew off out of sight and after a short interval returned to repeat the same tactics. This was observed several times in one afternoon.

Another crow, the chough, has failed to survive in Purbeck. Until about 1850 it used to occur in scattered colonies along the limestone shore and nested in crevices on the cliffs. Five were trapped near Swanage in the summer of 1885 and the bird was also found about that time at Seacombe and Studland as well. The last known Purbeck sighting was in 1925 but it is not only here that the chough has disappeared. It was once common on the Cornish coast but no longer breeds there and the nearest surviving colonies are in Wales.

The chough has become a rare bird. Rarities often turn up in Purbeck, but it is unnecessary for me to document those of recent years as all have been carefully recorded and are in print in several sources. The arrival of rare birds brings out the 'tick-hunting' ornithologists whose only aim is to add another species to the tally they have seen. Such a pursuit has little to do with ornithology, makes no contribution to our knowledge of the habitat or behaviour of birds, and usually frightens off the subject. When a wallcreeper arrived at Winspit in November 1969 it was the first seen in Britain since 1938. Obviously its coming was a complete accident and hardly heralded anything new in the distribution of birds.

Ornithologists came to Purbeck in their hundreds and sat in lines on exposed positions with their binoculars trained on other sets of ornithologists who maintained a continual movement between positions. No one found the wallcreeper on that crowded Sunday when I watched sea birds from the cliffs towards St. Alban's Head. Not one of the multitude of bird-watchers bothered to join me in looking at the sea birds. They were only interested in glimpsing that wallcreeper once and then leaving. One ornithologist departed with a broken leg and I do not even know if he gathered the coveted 'tick' for his list. The crowd made sufficient disturbance to drive virtually all birds from the area and the wallcreeper likewise departed. But it put up with all the attention for some months and left in April 1970. As one lady observed: "That bird could write a book."

Eustace Bankes of Norden House, Corfe Castle, went in for 'tick-hunting' at the end of the last century but his notes are worth mentioning as they have not been published and were made at a time when little was known about the distribution of birds. He did attempt more than just 'ticks' and noted, where he could, whether the rarer birds had actually attempted to breed in Purbeck or been found in unusual circumstances.

The rough-legged buzzard has not been seen in Purbeck for years but on 28 March 1908 Bankes saw one ("identified by a clear sight of the white basal part of the tail") on Middlebere Heath and from reports he had received he was sure that one or two individuals had been "haunting that and the neighbouring heaths for the previous four months".

Another irregular visitor to Purbeck, mainly in the spring, is the golden oriole. It occasionally breeds in Britain and Bankes collected evidence that it had done so at Rempstone:

A male bird was seen several times by myself and others at Corfe Castle, 1-4 May 1889. It has also been seen at Rempstone; and I am quite certain from exact details given me by Miss L. Marston that a pair nested and reared their brood in the shrubbery at Rempstone House in or about 1892. A pair nested in a deodar cedar on the lawn there in 1893 where I saw the finished nest. It was unluckily deserted, without laying, owing to frequent disturbance by the gardeners who were unaware of the existence of the nest until too late.

The hawfinch is one of the rarest of our native birds that would be expected to breed in Purbeck. It is secretive and a bird census carried out in 1965 failed to reveal any. H. G. Alexander observes: "Possibly a pair or two nest in Purbeck but this species is only very rarely recorded." Bankes had a little better luck but he found no nests: "One hawfinch was picked up dead at Corfe Castle rectory during the great snowstorm of 19 January 1881. Another, which had been crippled by old shot wounds, was caught in the rectory garden on 16 November 1896. Seen, though only very occasionally, in the garden at Norden House."

One of the most exotic birds to reach these shores is the hoopoe and it crosses the Channel as a vagrant in April and May. Every year there are newspaper reports from south Dorset and its sighting is as much of a local journalistic institution as mention of the arrival of the cuckoo. Bankes records: "Two were shot in the grounds at Corfe Castle rectory about the year 1847: one was seen in the same place on 23 August 1888, and another seen many times on 7 April 1893. One was shot at Creech Grange in April 1888. Another was seen on Wytch Heath on 15 April 1890 by A. E. Bankes. It has also been observed at Encombe by Lord Eldon. An individual was watched at Norden on 25 April 1901. Another was seen on Povington Heath on 6 May 1903 by Captain Maurice Portman."

A rarer visitor is the nutcracker from northern Europe. The most recent sighting in Purbeck was at Encombe in September 1968. Bankes refers to one that was shot at Swanage on 14 July 1884: "It is in the collection of N. White, a stone merchant, whose garden it frequented for about three days before being killed by John Stainer."

Flying mammals also have a stronghold in Purbeck. Because of the hiding and hibernation places offered by the quarry shafts and coastal workings, Purbeck has the widest range of species of bats in southern England and some of the densest populations. Care has to be taken in writing of these localities as most of the abandoned shafts have been at least partially blocked by dumped rubbish and the hibernating bats are especially vulnerable to vandalism. One malicious person could kill an entire population of hundreds of sleeping bats in less than an hour. As an example of the other hazard, a colony of the mouse-eared bat was discovered in a Purbeck quarry in 1956 but the entrance was then bulldozed and the bats disappeared. It was only the second record for the whole country but the bat has been seen in Dorset since.

No less than seventeen species of bat have been found in the cliff quarries at Winspit and these groups are being protected by naturalists. In the Swanage quarries in the 1940s, Bernard Gooch explored many lanes that have since been filled. He found that badgers, foxes and rabbits also used the deep shafts and measured a constant underground temperature of 50°F, only lessened where air could circulate from one shaft to another, and the bats preferred the lower temperatures for hibernation. Gooch was told that bats spent the winter underground even when quarrymen were cutting stone in neighbouring galleries. The rare Bechstein's bat was first discovered in Purbeck in 1947 and during the cold winter of that year, five hibernating Serotine bats were also found, the first time this common bat had been recorded from caves or mines in the British Isles. Gooch found the greater horseshoe to be the commonest bat underground. In some quarry lanes he was surprised to find no bats on any visit, "these neglected or deserted lanes had one feature in common—rough, untidy quarry walls. The latter are generally neatly made of relatively large blocks of stone, or they may consist of solid rock, both of which the bats use, as well as the ceiling, when looking for somewhere to hang. Has this avoidance of lanes with rough, or rubbly, walls anything to do perhaps with the bats' echo-location requirements? Emitting a series of ultra-sonic squeaks as they fly along these pitch-dark lanes, they receive perhaps confusing or disconcerting echoes . . . then naturally they might prefer to hang up in lanes where echo-location proves easiest. These rough lanes afford ample footholds and bats evidently fly along them."

Leonard Tatchell, a Purbeck naturalist, was driven into a cave at Winspit by heavy rain. He found himself in a quarry that had not been worked for many years: "After getting accustomed to the semi-darkness I began to explore and, looking up I saw about a score of the common horseshoe bat, and going further in found that the roof of this working was teeming with hundreds of the creatures, and the odour was not pleasant. I amused myself by throwing up small stones and got many of them flying."

As for other wild animals, it has always been the fox, badger and otter that are large enough to receive popular attention in the countryside. The cruel pursuit of badger digging, the vilest of Britain's blood sports, still continues in Purbeck with tongs that are supplied by a Somerset firm. So, occasionally, does otter hunting and this is one of the few areas of the country that still has an otter population to be hunted. The huntsmen dress in green and carry long poles, and are helped by dogs to cause maximum disturbance on the riverside in an attempt to dislodge the otter from its breeding haunts. A recent hunt violated the quietest and remotest reaches of the Corfe River in the region near Wytch Heath. This damaging encroachment of one of the last retreats of a virtually exterminated animal brought the hunt in contact with a formidable opponent. He is Richard Ryder, a psychologist, who gave the 1970 hunt a rough start. His campaign has some weight as he is a member of the Rempstone family that owns much of the eastern Purbeck heath.

Deer are now the animals most frequently seen by walkers in Purbeck. On the western fringe of the island, in the belt of woods on the other side of Luckford Lake, all three species of deer that are resident in Dorset can be found together. They are the fallow, roe and sika.

Fallow deer in the woods immediately west of Purbeck comprise a small herd of about thirty and are the descendants of those released from the park at Lulworth Castle during the First World War. Fallow deer are known to have been in the royal hunting ground of Purbeck before 1257 but by the nineteenth century they had disappeared. The deer park at Lulworth was the last in the Purbeck area. Unfortunately the wild herd has been decimated in recent years, mainly by the guns of farmers, and its survival is now doubtful.

The history in southern England of the other two species of deer started in both cases in Dorset. Sika, an Asian deer, were introduced to Brownsea Island in 1896 and continued there until the last war. From the start this strong animal had no trouble in swimming the calm waters of Poole Harbour to the Purbeck mainland. They now live in moderate numbers along the harbour shore and across the heathland as far as the chalk ridge. An occasional stag swims out to visit one of the harbour islands, but never do they cross the hills to establish a population in southern Purbeck. The wild herd found improved conditions after 1948 when work was in progress on creating the Purbeck Forest across the heath between Rempstone and the harbour. This block of conifer stands now supports about sixty sika deer and would have far more but for regular culling.

Other sika escaped from a deer park at Hyde House on the Piddle and established themselves in Wareham Forest, on the heath towards Bere Regis, after the first trees were planted in the 1920s. By 1950, and despite some ruthless killing, the sika population was thriving and it has remained the largest herd of this species of deer anywhere in England. Today there are four hundred sika in Wareham Forest and others have spread west along the Frome valley.

The third species of deer, the ubiquitous roe, has reached the sheltered woods of the vale between Tyneham and Swanage. It is also present in breeding groups in the conifer plantations and heathland scrub north of the hills as well as in the deciduous woods on the north flank of the Purbeck ridge itself. Roe appear all across Dorset in all habitats—heathland, scrub, coverts, coppices, deciduous woods and pine forests. These deer have lost their shyness and can often be seen grazing openly in pastures beside their woods even in the middle of the day. The story of this deer in southern England again started in Dorset. They were reintroduced at Milton Abbey in the year 1800 and have since expanded across all Dorset and much further. They are now, according to Morley Penistan of the Forestry Commission, absent only in Cornwall, Worcester and Hereford. Dorset, because of the introduction of the roe and sika and the survival of fallow deer in

Cranborne Chase, is one of the few English counties that has held populations of wild deer continuously since prehistoric times.

Deer are usually seen as the result of accidental encounters whilst on cross-country walks. All wildlife in Purbeck has its followers and surveys of the extent of Purbeck's use by naturalists shows that most come to watch birds and the South Haven Peninsula is the most visited part of the island. There too is a bonus, the chance of discovering an unusual phenomenon—the elusive 'singing sands'. Between Shell Bay and Studland, just above highwater mark, visitors have occasionally trodden musical notes. Miss M. S. Homer wrote in 1930: "There was no doubt about it; as the foot stepped on the sand, there was a distinct note, and on striking the sand with a stick, a resonant musical sound." Kathleen Green was shown the sands by Studland children in 1918: "One patch of these sands lay about four hundred yards north from the point where the lane from the Coastguard Station leads to the beach. They gave a high pitched note . . . midway between the lane and the remains of an old wreck, the coarser sand under the sand dunes gave a low pitch, the finer sand on the sea side of the patch, a higher note." In the 1920s, S. E. Clarke was asked: "Have you ever heard the whistling sands?" He recalled that "each footstep produced a swishing or whistling sound at a high-pitched note". A guide book of 1890 stated that these sands were composed of rounded, polished grains mostly of quartz, occurring "in a narrow zone varying from twelve to fifteen yards between blown sand and the high-water mark". To the south of the great beach, at Redend Point, a fifty foot cliff marks the limit of Studland's open sands. Here the cliff itself provides sands of a wide variety of colours, as does the corresponding part of the Isle of Wight; the chalk ridge was a continuous deposit from Old Harry Rocks to The Needles before the sea broke through and created Poole Bay. Alum Bay sand is one of the oldest of holiday souvenirs and similar bottles were sold at Studland up to half a century ago.

One of the rarest seaside finds of the century came in the autumn of 1954 when the jelly-fish *Physalia physalis,* called the 'Portuguese Man-of-war', was blown in from mid-Atlantic in vast numbers. It is exceptional for them to be found anywhere in Britain except occasionally Cornwall and South Wales but in 1954 they came up the Channel in October and November and dozens were washed up in Purbeck at Kimmeridge, Chapman's Pool, Winspit and Studland Bay. The only previously recorded sighting for Dorset, at Lyme Regis, was as long before as 1840.

As for the later batch, they were even stranded on the sands at Bournemouth and I remember seeing one of the purplish-blue bladder-shaped, masses with its heaps of long tentacles armed with stinging cells that are both vicious and numerous. That dull and rainy year of 1954 was also when myxomatosis arrived in Dorset. Out at sea, the easiest noticed life is the porpoise. Large schools of several dozen can be seen swimming and turning in the choppy water off St. Alban's Head. Individuals used to follow the steamers between Swanage and Bournemouth. Now the headland of St. Alban's, the southern tip of Purbeck, is the best vantage point for watching the mammals of the sea, common dolphin and bull-nosed dolphin included.

Auk numbers crash

Hindsight Auk numbers have slumped in Purbeck, and the rest of south-western England, over the past fifty years (see page 142). In 1932 there were more than three thousand guillemot nests in Purbeck but by 1948 this had been reduced to five hundred pairs. The decline continued, down to two hundred and fifty pairs in 1962. Razorbills and puffins shared the decline, with the puffins down to seventeen pairs by 1975. Razorbill numbers crashed from 189 pairs in 1969 to a handful of nests. During this time the numbers of herring, black-back and greater black-back gulls increased all along the coast as these adaptable birds exploited the niche created by the huge wastage of human food that was finding its way to municipal tips. By the mid 1950s the herring gull was the commonest of the sea birds breeding in Purbeck. It exceeded a thousand nests in the 1960s, from a fraction of that number in earlier decades, and by 1980 this had soared to three thousand or worse.

Otter hunting banned

Hindsight Richard Ryder (see page 150) went on to coin the term "specieism" and to become chairman of the Royal Society for the Prevention of Cruelty to Animals. He can look back on the abolition of otter hunting as one of the successes of his combative years.

CHAPTER XVII

Landscape Cameos

HARTLAND MOOR lies where the Middlebere Heath dips towards the harbour-side at Slepe: an area of marshy damp and cold peat in a flat plain at about the thirty-foot contour. A narrow byway known as Soldiers Road turns off the main Wareham road, towards the harbour, opposite the thatched Halfway Inn. Hartland Moor is on the right as this unfenced heathland road approaches the Purbeck power line that takes electricity from Wareham to Swanage. This wide bog drains ineffectually towards Slepe where a single farm stands on harder ground rising northward from a stream.

The area remains a virginal wilderness, unreached by the modern forest of Rempstone, Newton and Wytch, and leaving both development and a few green fields away on the Wareham road at Stoborough Green. Hartland Moor is still a giant sponge, soaking up rains from the sandy hills surrounding it on the Great Heath. Underlying seams of ball clay prevent normal drainage.

Because it is a unique area with a cross-section of all types of heathland vegetation, 640 acres of Hartland Moor are officially protected as a national nature reserve. Its main interest are the tracts of the rare Dorset heath *Erica ciliaris* which is a major component of the vegetation on the damper heathland soils of Purbeck, but a plant unknown elsewhere in Britain except for a few isolated locations in Devon and Cornwall. It is a bell heather with rosy-purple flowers that appear in late summer when the moor is relatively dry. The pitcher-shaped bells are large and come in threes, on spikes coming from central stalks, and continue far into the autumn. The plants grow nine to twelve inches high but straggle to become a shrub two or three feet wide. It is, despite this untidyness, the most attractive of our wild heathers.

Handsome and distinctive, *E. ciliaris* is a plant native to Britain. It can be useful in gardens, as one of the best heaths for planting under azaleas, though it does best in a moist acid soil. *E. ciliaris* is found wild in south western Ireland and seems to have been checked in the great ice age. It is widespread only in the distant Pyrenees and is distinguished by having ovate, hairy leaves tinted grey-green, and set closely together in whorls of three on slender branches. Another plant growing on the damper parts of the heath and in bogs is the marsh gentian (*Gentiana pneumonanthe*) which produces brilliant blue flowers in early autumn. Hartland Moor is one of the Purbeck bogs where sundews can be easily found. These insectivorous plants catch their prey on spoon-shaped leaves that are sticky with gland-tipped hairs. A juice is produced by the leaves and the insects are absorbed as food for the plant. All three British species of sundew (*Drosera rotundifolia, D. anglica* and *D. longifolia*) occur on boggy heaths in Purbeck.

Another national nature reserve lies on the harbour shore in the northern part of the Big Wood at Arne. It is only nine acres but encloses a remarkable natural damp woodland. In fact, it is one of the few places in the country where a transition from salt marsh to woodland of birch, pine and oak can be seen. The whole of the Big Wood has been voluntarily excluded from the mining rights held by English China Clays at Arne.

Generally, Purbeck's countryside has received the highest official praise. The entire island is scheduled as an area of outstanding natural beauty and virtually all of its shores, except at Swanage, were designated as a coastal preservation belt in 1966. The Nature Conservancy reported on Purbeck's ecological merits in 1968:

> The east Purbeck heaths including Brownsea Island and the adjoining marshlands are of outstanding importance. Floristically, the richest areas are those where there is a steep gradient of conditions, for example on the sand dune peninsula at Studland, and in the southeast part of the area known as The Moors, near Ridge. At the latter site, for example, there grow some 260 species of flowering plants, among them twenty-one rare or locally distributed species. Studland Heath may well support over six hundred species. In southern Purbeck important sites lie on the chalk and limestone cliffs.

Purbeck is one of the last strongholds of the wild orchids. Several species of orchid, the most beautiful of our wild flowers, are found in some abundance on the chalk ridge and the limestone hills. One of these is the early spider orchid (*Ophrys sphegodes*). It has always been restricted to the warmer south of England and may well be virtually extinct except for its colonies on the Purbeck limestone. This orchid flowers usually from the last week of April and into May, with spikes of purple, yellow and brown flowers, having a circular lip giving the spider resemblance. The plant grows best near the sea and at Winspit has established itself in the disturbed ground of the quarry shelf among the ruins of wartime buildings on the edge of the cliff.

Even the uncommon bee orchid (*Ophrys apifera*), the most attractive flowering plant in the British Isles, can be found in small numbers in a few Purbeck locations. This orchid flowers in June and is self-pollinating which tends to produce and perpetuate abnormalities. One of these, a white-flowered type, occurs in the northern part of its range and an example was reported from Swanage in 1926.

Another of the rarer orchids found in Purbeck is the yellow-flowered species *Hammarbya paludosa* which grows in cushions of bog-moss and is difficult either to approach or spot. Called the bog orchid, it is limited to the acid soils of the Great Heath and occurs in saturated hollows where there is much sphagnum moss. The plant has no roots as such but depends on fine hairs that lie on the moss and are hosts to fungal infection. Young plants are rapidly infected with fungus and would be unable to obtain sufficient nitrogenous or carbohydrate food on their own. The orchid is highly specialised in other ways and produces seed to float on the water that covers the bogs in winter so that it not only spreads but remains within the restricted marshland habitat.

The early purple orchid (*Orchis mascula*) is reasonably common across Purbeck and one particularly attractive colony grows on a grassy bank beside Thrasher's Lane to the south of Wytch Heath. This orchid flowers in May with deep-purple spikes and has a variety of Dorset dialect names from different parts of the county. The flowers are known variously as *regals, granfer-griggles, granfer-grigglesticks* and (in Purbeck) *giddyganders*.

Another of the distinct geographical regions of Purbeck is the chalk ridge. The line of the Purbeck Hills is twelve miles from cliff to cliff: it runs virtually west-east with a shallow curve towards the north, and is broken only by gaps at Corfe Castle and Ulwell. The ridge is consistently half a mile wide, a hog's back of chalk flowing smoothly between the 350 and 650 feet contours. It is a perfect and miniature example of a type of scenery and stays in a more natural state than most of the English downlands as its scarps are too steep for ploughing. There are four thousand acres of grassy slopes with fields and downs on top, but nowhere a building.

The hilly belt is so narrow that there was never need for even a single lonely barn away from the valley farms. There is seldom even a tree at the top of the scarps but, as the hills fall away north, the slopes gather woods for an intermittent belt eight miles long. The extremes of east and west are West Creech and God-lingston Hill, after which the sea and winds count against forestry. Conditions are also unsuitable along the entire southern side of the hills where the single clump of trees is an ageing and decaying Alms Grove at the road entrance to Tyneham valley. The southern slope of the ridge, with its continuous covering of turf, is the main habitat of one of Britain's rarest butterflies, the small brown Lulworth skipper (*Thymelicus acteon*).

Yet man in former times did live on the hills. He left his dead crouched under burial mounds on Ballard Cliff, Nine Barrow Down and Stonehill Down. Along the ridgeway from Stonehill is another construction, also outliving its purpose and equally un-visited. It is known as Bond's Folly and was the foible of a member of that family, Denis, who in about 1740 gave a fillip to the stone industry by having Purbeck masons erect a structure on the edge of the hill overshadowing his home. When seen from the road at Creech Grange, it appears like a castle uprooted from Transylvania, and spirited to above the topmost trees of the Great Wood, its battlements etched against the clouds: for fairies indeed—just a single wall, thick and tall, castellated, adorned with pinnacles and having a round-headed arch as its centrepiece. From that vantage, the Grange is at the bottom of a view that rises outwards across the heath and harbour to the distance beyond. The arch was not Denis Bond's only folly. He was elected to the House of Commons as the member for Poole in 1725 and was subsequently expelled, by the House itself, for having "fraudulently and clandestinely" contracted to undersell the Derwentwater estates.

At the far west of these hills, where the turf yields to a cliff dipping instantly—almost vertically through 550 feet—are the double ramparts of a prehistoric fort, Flower's Barrow. Equally obsolescent are two wartime pillboxes poised above the Swanage valley on the south shoulder of Nine Barrow Down, where con-crete was poured into the hill to take guns that watched incon-spicuously without breaking the skyline. East of them, above the Ulwell Gap on the landward side of Ballard Down, lies the toppled stone of an obelisk built, not particularly well, by an inhabitant of Swanage in thankfulness for that day in 1884 when purified water was taken from below these hills.

Adjoining the ridge at Stonehill Down is Creech Barrow which appears as an offshoot of the Purbeck ridge. Creech Barrow always looks to be a mysterious hill. It is not hard to imagine it as the cone of an extinct volcano, still smouldering on summer afternoons when a thick fog creeps from the sea and follows the Purbeck ridge. I have read in a guidebook that its 634 feet are the handiwork of prehistoric man—which would raise its stature to that of the largest man-made hill in the world! In fact, its whole mass is simply a part of the Purbeck heath, thrust upward from the rest by a natural convulsion of the ground in ancient times that folded it to the height of the adjoining chalk ridge. The stuff of Creech Barrow is the gravel, sands and clay of the Great Heath; clays that here lie submerged and twisted under the conical heap of the hill. The only subtle difference is that fossils found between some greenish clays and marl show there is also an outlier of freshwater limestone from the Bembridge beds of the Isle of Wight. The usual mineral deposit of ball clay lies further beneath the great hill: it has not been abandoned by man but is followed by a drift mine that was opened in the 1940s. Its entrance is beside the lane junction where a footpath starts for the top of the hill. And up there, prehistoric man *did* leave a mark—the lower of the twin peaks of Creech Barrow carries the shape of a barrow, an outline confused by the shifting of sand and a thick covering of bracken. This fern gives colour to the whole hill: the entire mass is treeless and completely conquered by bracken which gives a virile green in summer and dies brown when the frosts come. The other historical clue on Creech Barrow is a scattering of stones on its summit, said by legend to mark the site of a hunting lodge built by King John, which is confirmed by John Speed's map of 1610. A similar tradition is attached to Windmill Knap near Godlingston, where a rangers' lodge was standing in 1618.

In the limestone belt of southern Purbeck the drystone walls are one of the most noticeable features. Again it is a treeless landscape, and often a hedgeless one as well. These are the only examples of drystone walls that can be seen in east Dorset. Their architecture is interesting: the custom was to lay the bed-joints at an angle of forty-five degrees rather than on the horizontal. This prevented sheep from finding a foothold and jumping the walls. Ivy has covered many of the old walls for centuries, first forcing the stones into disarray and then holding the whole mis-shapen mass together.

As much a part of the landscape of Purbeck as anything are its own distinctive buildings. The use of Purbeck stone is largely restricted to the limestone country and the village of Corfe Castle. Even on the edge of the quarrylands, at Kimmeridge and on the other side of the ridge at Studland, stone rubble was used for cottage walls but stone slates are absent. There thatch of wheat straw predominates as in the whole of east Dorset outside the Purbeck quarrying areas.

Before mentioning some of the notable domestic buildings I will deal briefly with the churches as these are the earliest structures that survive. The oldest is the parish church of St. Nicholas at Studland which was built shortly before the Norman Conquest and has a chancel, central tower and nave. The latter was rebuilt in the twelfth century and other alterations followed. The Royal Commission on Historical Monuments commented: "The church is an interesting example of mid-twelfth century elaboration of a comparatively simple pre-Conquest church. The building has a solid robustness of character which is impressive." On a mound at Studland, beside a turning leading to the church, is the base of the only mediaeval cross that has survived in Purbeck. It is a circular block of heathstone four feet in diameter and two feet high with a socket hole (two feet square around a circular depression a foot deep) that would have held the shaft. The cross is at the junction of Water Lane with four other roads and the village stocks stood nearby until about 1850. As if this was not sufficient indication of the age of the settlement, the largest bell at Studland church is stamped "C.P. 1065" and has the inscription, "Draw nigh to God." It shows fire-cracks and is obviously old but it has been suggested that the middle two digits of the date were transposed in the casting.

Another old parish church is that at Worth Matravers with a nave and tower built about 1100. The square stone chapel with a single window on St. Alban's Head was likewise erected in the twelfth century and is appealing as it is both unusual and little changed. Pieces of work from that century also remain in the churches of Steeple and Kimmeridge. That at Church Knowle is mostly of the early thirteenth century. St. Mary's church at Swanage has a few fragments of thirteenth century date but the only part of mediaeval design to survive is in the lower part of the tower and dates from the fourteenth century. At Tyneham, where there is no tower and just the sheer beauty of simplicity, the north transept and part of the nave have thirteenth century walls. The church of St. Nicholas at Arne was a single-unit chancel of the same date. Langton Matravers has a tower that survives from the fifteenth century. The church at Corfe Castle is Purbeck's biggest disappointment as so much of age would be expected to remain in the church where the marblers worshipped. Instead there is only a fifteenth century tower and the rest of the building was pulled to pieces and rebuilt in 1860.

Domestic architecture—the manor houses, farms and cottages—seems to offer so much more; if only because from them you expect so little. Barnston Farm at Church Knowle, for example, is a former manor house and one of the earliest inhabited buildings in Purbeck with a hall and solar wing of the late thirteenth century, and the remainder of the building has changed little since the 1500s. Scoles Farm, at a meeting place of old roads in the valley south of Corfe Common, is a fine piece of seventeenth century building that also incorporates parts of a small hall-house of about 1300. One original wall was rebuilt and has a series of beeboles under stone arches. Beehives were not introduced into Britain until 1862 and before that a straw skep was used instead. Recesses were built into walls to protect them from the weather; and these are called bee-boles. They are mainly found in the wetter parts of the country and appear to have been constructed from the fifteenth century onwards.

Godlingston Manor at Swanage has work of various periods up to the present and this includes a rounded tower of about the year 1300 which is preserved at the west end of a long frontage. Its exterior walls are no less than ten feet thick and this probably accounts for its survival—and also more or less proves that it had a defensive purpose. Some walls of the original manor of that time remain intact and show that the tower was an integral off-shoot of a substantial rectangular building. The fine state of the preservation of Godlingston is the more remarkable because, in 1867, it was threatened with demolition. Thomas Bond wrote: "I lament to add that these interesting remains have been permitted to fall into a sad state of dilapidation, and it is now contemplated to sweep them all away, to make room for a brand new farm house, fit for the requirements of the agricultural magnates of the present day, who have wants unknown to the Purbeck gentry of times gone by. Such destruction will be deplored by every one who has any regard for mediaeval architecture, or even for what is merely picturesque."

Godlingston is still with us, but instead the end has come for the home of a branch of Bond's own family. He said about Tyneham House: "In size and importance, as well as in solidity of masonry and general appearance, this house ranks far before any other ancient mansion now remaining in the Isle of Purbeck, though its aspect has been sadly marred externally by the introduction of sash windows on the ground floor which, however they may add to the comfort and convenience of the occupiers, are highly disfiguring to a building of this character."

Tyneham House is now a ruin that can only deteriorate further as it is totally abandoned and crumbles within the overshoot area of the Lulworth army ranges. The main section of the building, the east side, was built in 1583 and demolished in 1968. Some of its architectural features were removed to other Dorset houses but that is little compensation. At the back of the main building are the derelict remains of a fourteenth century hall with great oak beams and elaborate timber trusses supporting the roof. The hall was built by the Russel family and altered somewhat by Henry Williams in 1567. He added the great open fireplace that stands in its eastern room. The Bonds arrived in 1583 and expanded the house to the north and east.

The Tyneham valley was evacuated for a battle training area a few days before Christmas in 1943. In December 1947 a government command white paper (No. 7278) stated:

> In the case of some of the proposed training areas particularly Stamford and the Purbeck tank gunnery school it has been, or may be represented, that pledges were given that persons required to leave their homes would be allowed to return at the end of the war. The Government accept that pledges of this kind were given or understood to be given, and it will not therefore be necessary to press the point at any public inquiry; at the same time for reasons given in earlier paragraphs, areas for practical training must be provided and it follows that if an area in respect of which a pledge was given were surrendered and a new area taken up; one result would be the eviction of residents in the new area for the benefit of those originally displaced.

That sealed the fate of Tyneham House. The Government freely admitted that promises of the land's return "at the end of the emergency" had been given. But Britain's extended firing ranges were part of the War Office's gains from the Second World War and it was not going to give them away. A public inquiry was duly held in 1948 and upheld "the national interest". Much of the modern history of the Tyneham affair is given in a booklet which I edited, "The Fight for Tyneham", and I will not repeat any of that here. The scandal of Tyneham House, however, has been generally neglected and some explanation is justified as its loss is the greatest single blow that the historical heritage of Purbeck has suffered during this century. The sequence of events is clearly set out in the following previously unpublished letter. It was signed by J. M. Melhuish of the Ministry of Public Buildings and Works and sent to the Wareham area planning office of the Dorset County Council on 19 January 1968. The facts are apparently correct apart from the statement about the Bonds who have denied complicity in the affair:

Under the planning clearance of 1949 which followed the Government decision, the War Department were required to provide all practicable safeguards for the house, but having regard to its siting and the impossibility of employing a caretaker, the consequent risk of damage (particularly to roofs) by lead thieves; the impracticability of keeping the rooms aired and dry; and the structural deterioration which was bound to result in such circumstances, to say nothing of the risk of direct hits by shells, the Ministry came to the conclusion there was nothing they could satisfactorily do to maintain the building.

After discussions with the War Department which continued at intervals from 1949 to 1951 it was reluctantly concluded that it was simply not practicable to envisage the permanent preservation of the house as a historic building to which the public might eventually be admitted, that there were insuperable difficulties of access for maintenance purposes, and that in the circumstances expenditure of public funds on the building would not be justified. The Ministry therefore resigned themselves to the survival of the house in a survey record only, and to its final abandonment, although the War Department were requested to explore, with its owners, the possibility of preserving, away from the site, some of the woodwork fittings.

This decision was prompted solely by the conditions in force because of the War Department occupation, and not to any undervaluing of the house. Such fittings as could be salvaged and were worth preserving were, in fact, removed and placed on display in the Dorset County Museum.

There, the matter rested for the next fourteen years.

In 1965 it was reported to the Ancient Monuments Board for England that the Elizabethan part of the house had collapsed internally, following the loss of its roof, but that the 14th century wing (which, it had been found, had been substantially modified in the 16th century, although retaining much original work) was still relatively intact. It was decided that the Ministry should be asked to make further enquiries, and in particular to report the cost of a temporary roof, and shoring, with a view to preserving the building for a limited period—say ten years—by which time a change in defence policy might have made more permanent consolidation or transfer to another site feasible.

The report by the Ministry's architect and inspector for the area showed that the main block of the house seemed to be somewhat less severely damaged than had been feared, since the roof had not wholly collapsed, and the Southwest Wing, containing the earliest work, although in a deplorable condition, partly collapsed internally, sodden, and covered with ferns and creepers, at least retained one bay of its timbered roof and its supports from ground level upwards, most of which appeared to be original. Damage was due to natural causes and had not been caused by shell fire.

A detailed estimate of the cost of preserving the building from further deterioration which included such things as clearance of vegetation and debris, formation of drainage ditches to take away rainwater, erection of a temporary roof and other coverings, closing up of door and window openings, and strutting where required, amounted to the substantial sum of £8,000—£2,500 for the South-west Wing; £300 for the East Porch, and £5,200 for the main house.

With the exception of a few odd days when access was possible it was only feasible to carry out such work during two brief periods of the year when the ranges are not in use—three weeks in August, and two in December. The condition of the building was such, however, that it was considered that if action was not taken very soon to preserve the more perishable part of the work, all would be lost except the masonry shell.

In these circumstances, it was felt that there were formidable difficulties in the way of preserving the building, and the Board eventually decided that salvage of the building as a whole would be an impossibility, and that the best that could be done was to allow certain features of the building which were capable of being dismantled and erected elsewhere to be removed from the site. This has been done and Mr. Robert Cooke, MP, and Lord Southborough, with the agreement of the Ministry of Defence and the former owners, the Bond family, have taken such features as the Elizabethan porch, a door-arch at the rear of the building, ashlar facing stones to the front of the house, window frames, windows and facing moulds, roofing tiles, coping stones, water tabling plinth and paving stones, crest from front door etc., for incorporation in their own historic houses of Athelhampton and Bingham's Melcombe.

With the greatest regret, the rest of the fabric has had to be abandoned. The Ministry of Housing and Local Government, on whose list the house appears, are aware of the position.

The village of Tyneham was one of the good things of the past that died in this century. Whatever its future, the old Tyneham has gone for ever and would anyway have changed since 1943. It cannot be resurrected though the scenery can. Other lesser buildings of the seventeenth century and later were also destroyed during the last decade. The large nineteenth century rectory was burned down in 1966. The schoolhouse still has long rows of empty pegs but is derelict. Tyneham Farm was a ruined shell until its recent demolition; Jack Miller's Sea Cottage is virtually nothing now; Worbarrow's other old cottages and the former coastguard station are nearly down to their foundations; houses at South Egliston are battered; the seventeenth century house and barn at Lutton are decaying. Only a couple of farmsteads have a partial reprieve because they are used by farmers who turn cattle, ponies and sheep on to the rough grazing of the ranges.

The remains of one of the early telephone kiosks, a white concrete affair, stand outside the Post Office where Wilson Coombes erected it in the 1920s. He faced a tirade of abuse from the rector who resented the innovation. This would long ago have been replaced by a red metal box had peace returned to the valley.

Everything at Tyneham except the armoured cars belongs completely to the past. It is history that has died and even the story of the life of its final ruler is as much a cameo of that past as the deserted cottages. He was a representative of England's landed gentry and an upholder of its empire.

Ralph Bond was the last man to own Tyneham. He left with his tenants in 1943; an ironic departure as he formed the Tyneham home guard to defend the village from invasion and became its platoon commander. After the war he lived at Moigne Combe, near Moreton railway station, and died in 1952.

Born during the exceptionally cold winter of 1880, Bond went through Eton and into the colonial service for a long term in Sudan. There in 1913 he shot a Dorcas gazelle with a head of world record size. Later he became an expert naturalist, gave a giraffe to London Zoo, and retired to study the smaller fauna of Dorset.

In Sudan, Bond lived with his pets and servants, including faithful Said who came to him as a small boy and remained throughout his career. Bond married more than twenty years after he left school and as the last squire of Tyneham he left a memory of a kindly old man doing his best to protect his tenants from officialdom but accepting his own fate without bitterness. An administrator to the last, he succeeded his cousin, John Bond of Creech Grange, as chairman of Wareham bench which he left through deafness in his declining years when the ruination of Tyneham "hurt him terribly".

An attraction of the landscape of the part of Tyneham parish south of the ridge was its 'gwyles'. This is a Dorset dialect word given to wooded glens, through which flow small streams, near the coast. Inside the army ranges are Tyneham Gwyle, Lutton Gwyle and Egliston Gwyle. These secluded woods are decaying and in their present state the stench of the ground covering of wild garlic is overpowering. The origin of the word 'gwyle' has yet to be properly explained but Purbeck is the area where the word is most plentiful, with other 'gwyle' names at Encombe, Bucknowle and Rempstone.

For all that has been lost in the destruction of Tyneham, and despite the more widespread disappearance of heathland cottages, Purbeck's catalogue of survivals remains immense. Even the spoliation of old Swanage has not lessened the contribution that living history makes to the landscape. There is still a staggering total of four hundred historic buildings standing in Purbeck.

This includes the noticeable and the secreted. One of the latter is my favourite, but I cannot explain why as it would be modest enough apart from its situation. Scotland Farm is the single superb building on the architectural wastelands of the Great Heath. It stands on the edge of the New Mills Heath and was built by William Whefer with large blocks of ashlar. The stone is thought to have come from Corfe Castle and a dated slab in the walls gives 1665—twenty years after the destruction of the castle. Stone slates cover the roof and it is a solid single building with attics, stone-mullioned windows, two ashlar chimney stacks and a stone porch.

Probably the appeal of such old buildings in the Purbeck landscape is that there is little modernity to detract. Nowhere in the countryside is there an appalling mass of straggling estates mixed up with the fields. The only new community that has come into existence during the twentieth century is the collection of seventy houses at Harman's Cross in the southern vale. There alone it can be said there was not a single building at the end of the last century. All the development has occurred in ribbon fashion across seven fields along the A351 although, luckily, the sudden kink in the line of the road at Harman's Cross was straightened before it became entrenched in bricks and mortar.

This is the only instance of the creation of an entirely new community in Purbeck—without even the nucleus of a single existing building—and it is a typically spreading example of wasteful rambling development across acres of land with only the main road to give it direction and no features of either man or the landscape to hold it in check.

Another new settlement is Stoborough Green but this is hardly a separate community. It is only a projection of its parent village but is entirely modern as the only old building in the area lies derelict below Hyde Hill. This may be one of the casualties, a pair of eighteenth century cottages with thatch that has sunk through the roof and cob walls that have cracked and split. They may not vanish, however, as there is now a plan for restoration.

Harman's Cross and Stoborough Green are the exceptions as Purbeck otherwise continues to grow inside its ancient framework. It is this continuity of history into modern life that has prevented the Tyneham shambles causing more widespread disruption.

Purbeck's unique landscape has even received some active

Government protection. In 1971 the Environment Secretary intervened to prevent planning permission being granted for a scheme that would have increased the number of houses at Corfe Castle by nearly thirty per cent. It was one of those few cases in which a local authority loses a planning appeal. Significantly, the entire scheme to build forty-five houses and bungalows in the neck of land separating West Street from East Street had already been approved by the local planning authority. It was only 'called in' for examination by the Ministry after objections were made by villagers at Corfe. The result was a classic example of the man from Whitehall stopping a local council from fouling one of the prettiest backyards in Britain. Such vetoes have wide implications as they increase the uneasiness of architects and conservationists that the shaping of the land of this highly populated country should not remain the hobby of shopkeeper councillors.

What the Corfe project lacked entirely was the aesthetic approach. Objectors said it was totally out of step with Corfe's character and the inspector who held a public inquiry at Wareham in July 1970 found that the part of the proposal for private houses was out of scale with the village and also socially unacceptable as it would not have alleviated the position of young families seeking accommodation. On the other hand, the Wareham and Purbeck rural council's plan for twenty-five old people's bungalows would have released under-occupied council houses for young couples. But the bungalows were to be built too far from the heart of the village and its activities to be satisfactory to the old. The inspector suggested instead that the homes for the elderly could be fully integrated with the village if they were placed on the site of the old slaughterhouse.

The scheme had another proposal that wholly disregarded the historical appearance of Corfe: the inspector's most sweeping observations were reserved for the planned demolition of the old stone wall beside West Street. It preserves the present feeling of intimacy and cohesion in the former main street of the village. To replace it with asphalt, as intended, would have given the street a suburban appearance and, in the inspector's words, been "utterly incongruous".

Man's control of the landscape is in every way decisive for today's lives but eventually it is nature that decides the course of things. Changes are taking place on the coast as they have always done: new land is being deposited beside Studland Bay while only a mile southeast the same sea is on the offensive and the water has left fragments of the cliff standing offshore. These are

Old Harry Rocks and The Pinnacles, and all are sea-stacks that have been detached from the parent cliff. Old Harry used to be accompanied by a slim wife until she had an accident in a gale of 1896 that also destroyed the old chain-pier at Brighton. The grave of Old Harry's Wife is now marked by a patch of stones covered with seaweed. The main cliff as well is showing signs of the relentless action of the sea and there is St. Lucas Leap, a gap where the water is making new stacks to replace Old Harry, together with a natural arch and Parson's Barn. This is a great cavern eaten out of the chalk and was actually used as a smugglers' cave; it is a huge example of the genuine thing. There is humour in these names. Parson's Barn, for instance, took its name because there is a proverbial saying in Dorset that no barn is more accommodating than a parson's, and the vast space in that lofty cave offered the ultimate in barns. St. Lucas Leap has its saintly name borrowed from, believe it or not, a pedigree greyhound that is said to have dropped over the cliff there whilst coursing a hare! As for Old Harry, well that was the devil himself (going under a pseudonym) and the land on the clifftop opposite is called Old Nick's Ground. The detached piece of cliff standing beyond where St. Lucas leapt is known as No Man's Land and is densely populated with nesting sea-birds. Finally, as the cockney said when he stood on the cliff edge at the end of the last century: "There's Old 'Arry, but where's 'Arriet?"

In fact, the future of the whole of Purbeck will be decided by the sea. There are two pointers existing in the wide tidal estuary of Poole Harbour, to the north, and the double-bay effect of Worbarrow Bay and Arish Mell in the southwest. There the sea is breaking through the chalk ridge at its lowest and weakest point along the entire length of the formation between Old Harry and Weymouth. The barrier of the harder Purbeck limestone and marble has already been bypassed at Worbarrow Tout where a cone-shaped hillock thrusts into the sea with slanting ledges and great blocks of white gypsum. Westward the sea spreads across a mile-and-a-half to Mupe Rocks and inland a huge curve is broken in the middle by the development of another, miniature, bay at Arish Mell. Any sinkage of the land would give the sea an entrance to first the lower regions of the chalk and then the heart of the Great Heath, and through Luckford Lake towards Poole Harbour. It all sounds futuristic but C. P. Chatwin's official geological survey of the area looked at the prospect with thinly veiled enthusiasm: "If the chalk were breached, say, near Worbarrow Bay, and a subsidence took place, the sea would soon convert the peninsula [of Purbeck] into a true island, comparable with the Isle of Wight."

For all the apparent imminence of that statement, nature is providing other changes that could have results far nearer our own lifetimes. Climatically, we are facing less comfortable conditions and if the present rate of atmospheric cooling continues, in 1990 it will be impossible for an icebreaker of the size of the *Manhattan* to clear the Northwest Passage through the Arctic; and should the present trend carry on for two hundred years then the world will be in its second great ice age. With scientific predictions like that, it is futile even to think about the prospect of how long before the sea manages to make it truly Purbeck Island. Other worries will long before have eclipsed the geological calculations.

Out of the freezer, into the greenhouse

Hindsight It is frightening how quickly global concerns swing into total reverse. When I wrote the above text (here on page 168) I was relaying predictions from issues of New Scientist and The Times science reports. Now, in the same sources, there are features pointing out the implications of an overall warming of the planet. Temperatures generally, as an average for Earth as a whole, were higher in the first half of 1988 than at any time since records began. The talk now is of the "greenhouse effect" triggered by atmospheric pollution.

"Branksea Island, Poole Harbour" by Philip Brannon, 1862.

CHAPTER XVIII

Offshore Islands

THE ISLANDS of Poole Harbour are historically and politically a part of Purbeck. Although the largest, Brownsea Island, has had far more connections with the port of Poole, it was a part of the manor of Studland at the time of Domesday Book and is today within the area of Wareham and Purbeck rural council. The other smaller islands—Long Island, Round Island, Furzey Island and Green Island—all remain in Purbeck and the present administrative boundary of the island runs as far north as the middle of the Main Channel, the deep water only three hundred yards off Hamworthy.

The indented shore of Poole Harbour measures about fifty-two miles at high water and the shoreline is a mixture of gravel, sand and mud. Tides produce a double high-water and there is a tidal range of over six feet at spring tides; this falls to little more than two feet at neap tides. The importance of Poole Harbour for wildfowl was shown to be on an international scale in 1954 when work started on the draining of the Oostflevoland Polder in Holland. The wildfowl population there dropped by around 750,000 birds during the following winters and a Dorset planning department report shows that "correspondingly the winter figure for wildfowl in Poole Harbour increased enormously". The roosting areas are provided by 1,057 acres of *Spartina* marsh, mainly on the Purbeck shore, and this entire coastal belt has been designated a "site of special scientific interest" by the Nature Conservancy.

Fish caught in the harbour include bass, mullet, plaice and flounder. Trawling is done in the channels where there is a depth of more than a fathom and *set* nets are sometimes positioned off Shipstal Point, in Blood Alley (south of Brownsea) and at Middlebere. Flat-bottom punts are used in shallow water by fishermen and wildfowlers. Shooting is done on an extensive scale and the wildfowlers use a houseboat, moored in Ower Bay, as a store. There were forty gunning punts in the harbour in the 1890s, as well as more than twenty professional wildfowlers, and the number of gunmen has since been maintained. The Dorset planning report states that "on a peak winter day there may be as many as sixty guns around the harbour tideline".

169

The harbour fisheries also provide cockles, winkles and oysters. Prawns have now recovered from severe losses in the hard winter of 1962-63. Winkles are found mainly around Green Island, Furzey Island and in Brand's Bay. The oyster beds are in South Deep, the middle section of the Wytch Channel, and in the lower Wareham Channel off Hamworthy. These beds are owned by the Crown Estates and leased to the Southern Sea Fisheries Committee who sublet to oyster farmers. The Poole Oyster Company has put down stock from Brittany near Goathorn. The prawns are trawled in the South Deep and are also found off the wall of the Brownsea Island lagoon.

Sewage is a threat to the waterlife of the harbour. There are a number of outfalls on the northern shore, including sewage from Lytchett and Upton, and eventually the bulk of Poole's sewage will go into Holes Bay. The Frome river is still diluted by sufficiently pure water but it carries effluents into the harbour from Dorchester, Wool, the Atomic Energy Establishment, Bovington Camp and Wareham. In danger are the trout and the salmon and all other water and plant life of this rich 'chalky' river. Schemes to dump increasing volumes of sewage into the harbour have continued throughout this century and even the empty and unpopulated Purbeck shore is now affected. Effluent has been discharged into Brand's Bay since a sewage works was completed at Studland in the 1960s.

One recent use of the harbour, since passed into history, was as a flying boat base. Salterns Pier at Poole was used from 1939 until after the Second World War by Imperial Airways (later British Overseas Airways) and Coastal Command. Two Sunderland flying boats were moored off Patchin's Point, Arne, until 1958 when they were grounded on the beach at Lower Hamworthy. One lay stranded like a dead whale and I clambered into its gutted fuselage and through to the ripped-out instrument panels in the cockpit. Four of the Sunderland Mark III flying boats (technically known as Sandringham Mark IVs) were broken up for scrap on that beach in March 1959. They were named Penzance, Pembroke, Portsea and Perth. Another, named Hailsham, ended its life in a different way when it crashed and sank off Poole on 4 March 1946.

History is sometimes raised from the harbour waters. In August 1964 a dredger of the Poole Harbour Commissioners was at work in Brownsea Roads, off the island, and brought up a large block of sodden oak. This was twenty-three feet long and it turned out to be a dugout canoe with the stern virtually intact. A second part was located by divers in the harbour silt and recovered to complete the boat, measuring thirty-three feet from bow to stern, which was placed in a purpose-built tank of fresh water at Scaplen's Court, a museum in Poole. It was later gradually dried off before being finally treated with a polyethylene glycol preservative. The canoe is a monoxylon, a boat made from a single piece of timber, with two strengthened transverse ribs carved out of the floor. A groove in the stern shows that a 'stern-board' was used as a rudder. The boat was made about 300 BC in the Iron Age and is one of the most important maritime remains ever to be preserved.

Another ancient feature on the harbour floor is an undated stone-ramped submarine causeway that links Green Island with the Purbeck mainland. It was probably surfaced with stone flags and is broken by a gap in the centre of the channel. Green Island has extensive traces of Iron Age and Roman occupation including evidence that it was used for the manufacture of shale armlets. Native pottery has also been found on Furzey Island and there is an old record of Romano-British pottery from Brownsea.

The story of the islands is one of eccentricity. Sir Thomas Beecham lived on Round Island in the early 1950s and used the uninterrupted seclusion for writing his biography of Frederick Delius. But the other unpredictable characters all adopted Brownsea. It is the largest island (496 acres) and has a length of well over a mile.

The background to the history of Brownsea is that the island was owned by the monks of Cerne Abbas who built a chapel and a hermitage there. It was dedicated to St. Andrew and the name survived at St. Andrew's Bay until that was drained and reclaimed by William Waugh in the early 1850s. The strategic position of the island was exploited in 1547 when Henry VIII built a castle to protect Poole from seaborne attack by covering the narrow entrance to Poole Harbour. It was a square single-storey building with walls forty feet long and nine feet thick. On three sides the fort had a moat and the fourth, facing seaward, held a hexagonal gun platform. Brownsea was one of a string of coastal forts built by the king as part of the most extensive defence system along the English Channel since the Saxon shore forts of the Romans. To the west, at Portland Bay, Henry built Sandsfoot Castle and Portland Castle, and eastward, on a spit of shingle off Lymington, Hurst Castle was the strongest of them all to guard the important sealanes into the Solent. Brownsea alone was later to become a house but the greater part of the original fort is concealed in the basement of its eighteenth century tower.

Brownsea's real history followed the building of the castle. Queen Elizabeth I gave it to Sir Christopher Hatton who was described as "a mere vegetable of the Court, that sprang up in the night". He was constantly in dispute with the townspeople of Poole and took revenge on them by confiscating the fishermen's traditional ferrying rights between the Sandbanks and South Haven Peninsula of Purbeck. An admiralty court decided against him in 1581 but the fact that the dispute went to law indicates that this communications link between Poole and eastern Purbeck was important from an early time.

When Tudor England was in a state of Spanish Armada nerves, Francis Hawley, the vice-admiral of Dorset who was stationed at Corfe Castle, was ordered with other officers responsible for the coast that no vessels should pass out of his harbours except boats making for other English ports. He was given power to strip suspected vessels of their sails. A result of this order was a shooting incident that occurred in February 1589 when Walter Partridge, commander of Brownsea Castle, rejected a pass presented by the master of the *Bountiful Gift,* a barque leaving Poole Harbour with a cargo of copperas. The vessel refused to stay and the castle battery fired two shots. The master, Walter Merritt, and one of his men, William Drake, were killed and a coroner's inquest at Corfe returned a verdict of wilful murder against Partridge. He later had to stand trial at a special court, was found guilty of manslaughter and sentenced to death "without the benefit of clergy" as the felony was committed at sea. But Partridge, not unfairly, was granted a pardon in December 1590 on the ground that the shots were intended only "to stay the sail ship".

The town of Poole joined the Parliamentary side in the Civil War and Brownsea Castle was strongly armed and garrisoned at an early stage. Four large guns and several chests of muskets were delivered for a force that in February 1645 was twenty strong. When the first phase of the Civil War was at an end, money due to the victor's armies for special services was settled. Poole had successfully held out against the royalists throughout the struggle and £60 was granted to the Brownsea garrison in April 1647.

Colonel Thomas Pride and a detachment of his regiment of the Commonwealth army were stationed on Brownsea in 1654.

His place in history is at the turning point of seventeenth century politics. Charles I, after his forces were finally defeated at

Preston in the second part of the English Civil War, spent weeks at Newport, Isle of Wight, pleading for a treaty. He lied, he evaded, and he procrastinated. That he never intended honouring his concessions is clear from his own admission. His offers were "made merely in order to effect my escape, of which, if I had not hope, I would not have done . . . for my hope is that they now believe I dare deny them nothing, and so be less careful of their guards."

The army saw the achievements of its victory being talked away in a spate of politicians' words. On 30 November 1648 the original colonels' revolt was initiated. Charles had his escape plan thwarted and was removed across the Solent to Hurst Castle on 1 December. The next day the army marched into London. The excuse needed for stage three of the revolt was provided when the Presbyterian members of the House of Commons voted that the king's preposterous suggestions amounted to grounds "for the settlement of the peace of the kingdom". The following day was 'Pride's Purge'. Colonel Pride stationed his men at the door to the Commons and prevented eighty Presbyterians taking their seats. The Independent Rump of the Commons then rejected any idea of reinstating the king and instead set up a revolutionary tribunal. Charles was beheaded at Whitehall on 30 January 1649 and the monarchy and the House of Lords were abolished.

Brownsea was then garrisoned throughout the Commonwealth when there was a need for the defence of Poole Harbour. In 1655 a light boat without decks, described as a "shallop man-of-man", approached some of the boats of George Skutt, Governor of Brownsea Castle. They were taken by surprise but managed to take the intruding vessel and found it had a commission from James, the second son of Charles I, who later became James II of England. The restoration of the monarchy in 1660 led to the end of Brownsea as a castle in the military sense.

The island's next contact with national affairs came on 15 September 1665 when Charles II and his son James, Duke of Monmouth, were rowed round the island. They were resting in Poole after a hasty journey from London to escape the plague. But the visitors did not land on isolated Brownsea Island, the reason being probably that the island's owner was Sir Robert Clayton, one of the wealthiest men in the City of London, who had loaned Charles vast sums. Clayton rarely came to the island but may also have fled from London that summer. At any rate the king had forgotten to repay £30,000 that was borrowed to pay his soldiers. There appears to have been a large house on the island at this time, though by 1800 it was in ruins, and now only two brick walls and the piers that supported a gateway are preserved in the courtyard of an old dairy building west of the castle.

Clayton, as would be expected, attempted to make money out of the island and reopened the sixteenth century copperas works. Copperas is a sulphate of iron, known also as green vitriol, that was used in dyeing, tanning and making ink. As Brownsea's entire industrial history is one of misfortunes, this venture is unlikely to have been successful. Sometime after his death in 1707, Sir Robert Clayton's heirs sold the island to William Benson. He paid £300 and considered he had also bought the castle which, actually, was still crown property. Furthermore, he knew it was. Complaints were made by the people of Poole who asked George II to reclaim the castle: but Benson moved in high places and he outwitted the objectors. Possession being almost everything, and especially so with a castle, he treated the place as his own and promptly started work to add a "great hall" to the fort.

Benson's hobbies were a little ahead of his time and he utilised the island for the growth of rare botanical specimens and planted various species of trees. He also sponsored the arts and printed Samuel Johnson's 'Psalms' as well as erecting a monument to the memory of John Milton (deceased, 1674) in Westminster Abbey. For these two acts he was lampooned by Alexander Pope: "On two unequal crutches propp'd he came, Milton's on this, on that one Johnson's name. On poets' tombs see Benson's titles writ."

By the end of 1741, Benson had suffered a nervous breakdown and had to be restrained. He recovered but his "former love of books had given way to a positive hatred" and he was known as "Mad Benson" until his death in 1754. Benson's friends had included Frederick, Prince of Wales, who visited Brownsea a few months before the owner's breakdown. Frederick, a popular prince, never took the throne as he failed to outlive his unpopular father. Bernard Short wrote in his booklet "Brownsea Island" that many believed Benson practised black magic and that the island was used for necromancy and the meetings of witches' covens:

> It is said that the celebration of the black mass took place in some pine-clad grove. In 1735, a servant girl vanished from the island, and it was strongly rumoured in Poole that she had been sacrificed to some satanic power at one of Benson's hideous ceremonies. Fishermen came back to the town saying that they had heard blood curdling screams ringing forth from Brownsea, and moreover, there had been glimmerings of lights in the woods. Certainly the servant girl from the island was never heard of again. But perhaps she merely

absconded from the island without anyone knowing, and as for the screams they might well have been the shriek of a bird such as a screech owl.

The island entered a phase of improvements when it came into the hands of the Sturt family of More Crichel. Humphrey Sturt, who sat for Dorset in the Commons, took on Brownsea in 1765 and set about turning it into the country estate extraordinary. He built up the castle into a four-storey tower with wings branching off on four sides. The grounds he transformed into ornamental gardens and all across the island he planted trees. By this time there was some semblance of a community as the island had a coastguard station and a public house. Sturt poured some £50,000 into his various schemes and the family kept the island for thirty years after his death. It was sold to Sir Charles Chad who held the island until 1840 and built the cottages called Seymer's House, now in ruins, overlooking the northern shore.

To farming commentator Arthur Young, who never missed an opportunity to make exaggerated claims for the agricultural potential of the infertile southern heaths, Brownsea offered miniature utopia. He wrote in "The Farmer's Tour through England", published in 1770:

> Brownsea, near Poole, consists of nine hundred acres of land, quite wild and over-run with fern, furze and much ling. It was esteemed so very poor and little worth that it was, with difficulty, let to a butcher at Poole for £16 a year; and the only use he made of it was to turn on a few lean sheep now and then.
> In this state Mr. Sturt purchased it, and immediately set about its improvement with great spirit and equal judgment. Besides building the Castle he has planted the sides of the hills with various sorts of firs to the number of a million. These thrive well. The vales and flat lands are improved by degrees, fifty acres laid to white clover and hay seed, that shew how well the land will do for pasture and meadow. The soil is, in general, a black, moory, peat earth, on various strata, either sand, gravel or loam; but the new-laid fields do equally well on all, which shews that the black soil itself is sufficiently good for the purpose. The grass annually improves. I never have seen finer clover—thicker, more luxuriant, or that promised better to be most profitable land. The whole Mr. Sturt has laid is extremely well worth paying twenty shillings an acre.
> . . . there is no production which tends to render a country profitable, agreeable or convenient, but what may be found in great plenty on this happy island, which is really England in miniature.

Brownsea's heyday came when Colonel William Waugh bought the island in 1852 for £13,000. This price was far higher than the earlier sales figures but Waugh had a special reason for wanting the property. His wife had made a hobby of geology and she picked and prodded at the ground with her umbrella to reveal potters' clay. Her opinion of its potential value was endorsed by a professional geologist who reported "a most valuable bed of the finest clay" worth "at a low computation, at least £100,000 an acre".

Waugh was certain that the porcelain of the future would be made with Brownsea clay—"the richest" in the United Kingdom. He was able to back his hunch with the money of others. As a director of the London and Eastern Banking Corporation he had no difficulty in raising £237,000 with the island as security. As an economist, Waugh had doubtful priorities. He not only restored and embellished the castle but wasted a further £10,000 in 1853 on erecting the church which is still standing on the edge of the island woods. An even more wasteful project was the reclamation of St Andrew's Bay which needed countless barge-loads of subsoil and more than a million bricks to add a hundred acres to the island. Its meadows remained watery, and have now fully reverted to marshland.

The western side of the island was devoted to an industrial complex that had to earn sufficient to keep up the ten percent interest repayments on the loans. Brownsea Pottery was built at the southwest corner of the island, opposite Furzey Island, and produced pottery, bricks and tiles. There was a two-storey processing unit with workshops, ranges of kilns, and several subsidiary buildings. The tall brick chimney above the main set of kilns was one of the harbour's landmarks. A short distance away, below Red Hill, was a smaller pottery and stables. A pier was built there but soon replaced by Pottery Pier a little further north. A crescent of cottages for clayworkers was built at Maryland. Further away, on the middle of the northern shore, was the main clayfield where numerous shafts were sunk. A brickworks lay to the east of Seymer's Pier. The whole enterprise was linked by a tramway that ran westward from the brickworks to Maryland, Pottery Pier, the smaller pottery, and then branched into sidings at Brownsea Pottery. The railway kept to the level land beside the shore and was over a mile long.

A surprise came in 1856 whilst Waugh was away in London at meetings of his bank. A number of Poole tradesmen landed on the island and were received by the colonel's wife. They had come to invite her husband to stand for Parliament and offered the seat of Poole. Being deaf, she was at a disadvantage, and thought they had come to demand payment of overdue accounts. The visitors were staggered when she begged for time to pay.

That was the first the people of Poole knew about the impending crash. The difficulties had arisen because the London and Eastern Banking Corporation was on the brink of insolvency. Shareholders turned on Waugh for voting himself huge loans and ordered him to repay the debt. This he could not do and as the Brownsea clay had been suitable not for the finest porcelain but only terracotta and bricks it is doubtful if he was even able to maintain payments on the interest. Waugh fled to Spain and in 1857 the island was offered for auction as part of his bankruptcy proceedings but failed to reach its reserve price of £50,000 and was handed over to the bank. The following newspaper advertisement was published in 1869 and referred to the island by its old name:

BRANKSEA POTTERY AND CLAY WORKS, NEAR POOLE, DORSET. The clay obtained from the pits on the island of BRANKSEA is of the finest quality, and the goods are manufactured with the aid of powerful machinery. The articles offered for sale will be found to bear comparison with the best goods manufactured in any part of England. Every article for drainage purposes may be had. List of Prices forwarded on application to

RICHARD PETTS, MANAGER.

In 1870 the island was sold to Augustus Cavendish Bentinck for £30,000. He took over Waugh's investment and continued the pottery industry until 1887. But the business was being run down and its working force had declined from three hundred to only a hundred men at the close. In 1890 Bentinck died and the island was sold to Major Kenneth Balfour MP. On 26 January 1896, while Balfour was at evensong in the island church, fire broke out in the castle and gutted the interior. Rebuilding was done the following year and the island was next bought by Charles van Raalte in 1901. He twice stood for Parliament at Poole as a Tory but narrowly failed to end the town's Liberal loyalties. He used the island to entertain numerous guests and maintained a band of twenty uniformed musicians who played in the summer evenings on the castle lawn and then in the great hall of the castle during winter. Of all those who came to Brownsea the one whose memory has been most lasting was Robert Baden-Powell.

Baden-Powell in 1907 was still living in the false glory of the charade that had happened in the little Kalahari township of Mafeking. He went against orders, wrote himself a credit note for £500,000, and allowed himself to be holed-up in the place of least strategic importance in the whole of South Africa. He had tricked the Cape Government into allowing him to take some guards into Mafeking to protect stores and used this as an excuse to move his whole regiment into a place where, as he knew, they would be surrounded. Others fought and won the Boer War while Baden-Powell revelled in luxury, dressing up in outlandish clothes, playing polo and writing: "Everything in the garden is lovely." Seldom was a Boer seen and only four white civilians were killed in the entire 'siege'. When the relief column finally entered the town it was given little attention and the commanding officer of an advance patrol told a bystander who he was and what it meant. "Oh yes, I heard you were knocking about," the man replied. One of the officers of the relief column remarked of the relieved: "I have never known men so sulky, or march with such bad grace." Even though the nation went mad after the news "Relief of Mafeking" arrived at Reuter's Fleet Street office at 9.17 p.m. on 18 May 1900, the War Office did not forgive the man who had prevented 1,200 armed men from fighting in the war and there were no special military honours for Baden-Powell. He was the emptiest hero the nation had ever adopted and the myth of Mafeking was written as if it were one of the greatest happenings in our history.

Baden-Powell's lasting contribution to national life started on Brownsea in 1907 when he held a camp for about twenty boys on the southwest part of the island. For ten days they were divided into four patrols, taught games and treated as unarmed boy soldiers. A scout, in B-P's words, was to be: "Trusty, loyal, helpful, brotherly, courteous, kind, obedient, smiling, thrifty, pure as the rustling wind." It is difficult to visualise how the worldwide scouting movement could have grown from such a beginning. Only Baden-Powell with his quick-witted and obstinate driving power, together with an undeserved place in the nation's heart, could have made the idea work. This and the rest of Brownsea's latter day history is well known.

Mrs. Mary Florence Bonham Christie bought the island in 1927 and gradually sealed it off from the world. She relented to pressure in 1932 and allowed five hundred scouts to invade the island for their jubilee celebrations. This was too much for her and the following year she accosted a bait-digger on the beach and said: "If you come here again my servants have orders to throw you, and anybody belonging to you, in the sea." He did return and the warning was carried out by a Scandinavian lady, Bertha Horthung Olsen, who threw his daughter into the sea. A disastrous fire in 1934 killed most of the wildlife and left the island badly scarred for the next twenty years; its damage can even be seen today where dead trees stand amongst the revived woodlands. The flames raged for three days and only a change of wind saved the buildings at the eastern end of the island from destruction; immense columns of smoke became dense clouds that were carried across the Channel and over to France. Mrs. Christie's attempts to keep the island undisturbed then became totally determined and even the naturalist Peter Scott was later banned as an undesirable. Creating a forbidden land caused mystery that appealed to the outside world. Mrs. Christie spent her life in just one of the castle's many rooms and was surrounded by crates with many of her possessions that were never unpacked. Outside the castle stood two old vehicles that had not been used for years: a Morris car and a Ford lorry. In 1940 there were rumours in Poole that the island was being used by a German espionage network. Our own soldiers were later billeted on the island, ate many of the peacocks, and generally decimated the island's animals and birds.

The island's history of eccentricity ended with Mrs. Christie's death on 28 April 1961 and her grandson, John Bonham Christie, presented the island to the Treasury in lieu of death duties. The Government handed it to the National Trust. When the visitors came, a wide area at the west of the island was swept by fire in 1964 and there were fears of a repetition of 1934 when the flames spread across virtually the entire island. Firebreaks were cut and a fire watching and fighting system established: with the island attracting so many (93,282 people landed in 1971) the wilderness is in danger throughout each summer. Of particular importance amongst Brownsea's wildlife is its colony of our native red squirrel. The grey species spread across Dorset in the ten years after the last war and the red squirrel was eliminated almost everywhere. But the greys were not introduced to Brownsea and the island is now one of the last safe refuges of the red squirrel in southern England. They are especially common in Beech Valley on the island. Disease is the one threat they may be facing.

The heronry in the northern woods of Brownsea is the second largest in Britain and has more than ninety nests in most years. Throughout the breeding season and into the autumn these birds can be seen feeding on the tidal mudflats all across Poole Harbour but their numbers diminish in winter. The herons also feed in the valley of the Frome and are occasionally seen flying in from the sea at Durlston Bay. Even the bittern is sometimes seen in Dorset and two or three were found in Poole Harbour during the prolonged frosts at the start of 1963.

Most of the northern half of Brownsea is managed as a nature reserve by the Dorset Naturalists' Trust and visiting is restricted to small organised groups. The Trust's secretary, Miss Helen Brotherton, can see the whole north shore of the island from the windows of her house on the opposite shore at Parkstone. She, with the help of working parties of volunteers, has in many ways replaced Mrs. Christie as the guardian of a unique piece of Dorset. The careful protection of Brownsea is in contrast with the laissez-faire management of the landscape on the Purbeck mainland where only a single acre is owned by the National Trust. Purbeck is one of the most beautiful corners of England and deserves better treatment than it in part receives.

Hindsight That was the situation in 1972 — but times can change for the better! I'll detail the 8,500-fold increase in National Trust acreage on mainland Purbeck, and other environmental plus-points, in the up-datings at the back of the book.

BRANKSEA POTTERY WORKS.

"Branksea Pottery Works" drawn by G.F. Nicholls and published in the Illustrated News of the World of 22 May 1858. I wrongly assumed this to be a print by Philip Brannon when I compiled my book, *Brownsea — Dorset's Fantasy Island* (1986) and have been corrected by J.P. Howe of Munster Road, Parkstone.

CHAPTER XIX

Official Protection

THE PURBECK landscape is protected by various Government orders and designations. This chapter is simply a list of the principal legal safeguards which have been placed on the countryside, its wild vegetation and ancient sites.

Area of Outstanding Natural Beauty

The whole of Purbeck is designated as an "area of outstanding natural beauty" by the Dorset Area of Outstanding Natural Beauty (Designation Order), 1957, made under section 87 of the National Parks and Access to the Countryside Act, 1949. This designation was made by the National Parks Commission and confirmed by the Minister of Housing. Apart from giving the area the strictest of planning controls this Act also allows the local planning authority to plant trees to improve the landscape and to restore or improve.the appearance of derelict land.

National Nature Reserves

Three national nature reserves have been established in Purbeck on land leased by the Nature Conservancy. They have been mentioned in detail in chapters sixteen and seventeen. These reserves are Studland Heath and Little Sea (429 acres, established in 1962); Hartland Moor (640 acres, established in 1954 and extended later); Big Wood, Arne (8½ acres, established in 1954). National nature reserves have complete legal protection as they would be acquired compulsorily if their status was threatened. The Nature Conservancy also has a research station at Furzebrook.

Sites of Special Scientific Interest

Another function of the Nature Conservancy, under the National Parks Act, is to designate "sites of special scientific interest". Section 23 of the Act states: "Where the Nature Conservancy are of the opinion that any area of land, not being land for the time being managed as a nature reserve, is of special interest by reason of its flora, fauna, or geological or physiographical features, it shall be the duty of the Conservancy to notify the fact to the local planning authority in whose area the land is situated." Nine such sites have been designated in Purbeck:

Arne: 3,016 acres which is an outstanding example of Dorset lowland heath.

Ballard Down (east end): Originally 126 acres of great ecological interest. The boundary of the area has been withdrawn to 75 acres because of ploughing on the northern slope of the down. Punfield Cove is included and is of especial geological interest for its famous and highly fossiliferous 'marine band'.

Blashenwell Farm pit: 10 acres of tufa deposits containing Mesolithic remains, fossil mammals, shells and plants.

Brownsea Island: 600 acres (the entire island) containing many types of vegetation rapidly disappearing elsewhere in Dorset. The island is also of outstanding ornithological importance. The boundary of this site was extended in 1970 to the low water mark which increased its area from 496 to 600 acres.

Durlston Bay: 33 acres yielding fossil mammals and shells.

Great Wood and Stonehill Down, Creech: Originally 179 acres of semi-natural woodland and grass heath of ecological interest. There are a number of mosses rarely found in chalk districts. Nine acres of Stonehill Down have been lost to ploughing.

Nine Barrow Down: Originally 93 acres of the south-facing slope of the Purbeck ridge above Knitson. The area was reduced to 66 acres to exclude newly ploughed land. The relatively poor chalkland flora on this escarpment contrasts with that on the north-facing slope of Ballard Down.

Poole Harbour marshes: 1,057 acres (mainly in Purbeck) which are of great importance for coastal ecological research particularly in the field of the development of *Spartina* marshes.

Worbarrow Bay to St. Alban's Head: This coast has great geological interest. The site extends westward out of Purbeck and includes the Fossil Forest of Lulworth which is described as 'unique'.

Ancient Monuments

This is a list of the ancient monuments scheduled in Purbeck under the Ancient Monuments Acts, 1913-53, on the grounds that the "preservation of the monument is in the national interest". The bulk of the sites are prehistoric, but the range is wide and includes relics much more recent, such as Swanage town pump.

(NT) signifies that the monument is the property of the National Trust. LA signifies the ownership of the local authority, and RSPB that of the Royal Society for the Protection of Birds. The list is arranged under parishes:

Arne: Two round barrows on Arne Hill (RSPB); King's Barrow, Stoborough; Three Barrows, on the south edge of Middlebere

Heath (east side NT); Round barrows on Stoborough Heath; Three Lords' Barrow, east of Holme Heath; Round barrow in Bartlett's Firs, Stoborough Heath.

Church Knowle: Three round barrows on Knowle Hill; Barrow on Stonehill Down; Round barrow south of East Creech Farm; Round barrow on Creech Barrow; Round barrows on Creech Heath; Icen Barrow; Pillow mounds north of Woolland Grove; East Creech Roman villa; Ridge dykes on Knowle Hill (a preservation order has been placed on part of this site).

Corfe Castle: Nine Barrow Down barrow cemetery (NT); Rempstone stone circle; Round barrow south of Afflington Barn; Round barrow north of Afflington Farm; Round barrow on Brinscombe Heath; Roman site north of Brinscombe Farm; Romano-British farmstead on Kingston Down; Group of round barrows on Corfe Common (NT); Round barrow on West Hill (NT); Round barrow southeast of Kingston Barn; Corfe Castle (NT); The Rings (NT).

East Holme: Three round barrows in Holme Lane Plantation; Two round barrows on Holme Mount.

East Lulworth: Ferny Barrows; Water Barrows; Two round barrows on Rings Hill; Flower's Barrow hill-fort. *All these monuments are inside the Lulworth tank gunnery ranges.*

East Stoke: Round barrows on West Holme Heath (*inside the Lulworth ranges*); Holmebridge (LA).

Langton Matravers: Strip lynchets at Knitson Farm.

Steeple: The Harpstone; Round barrow on Grange Heath; Drinking Barrow; Round barrow in Pomfrey's Plantation (*inside the Lulworth ranges*); Bond's Folly (NT).

Studland: Fishing Barrow (NT); King Barrow (NT); Round barrow at west end of Ballard Down (NT); Three round barrows on Godlingston Heath (NT); Round barrow in grounds of Studland Bay House; Round barrow northwest of Studland Bay House (NT); Three round barrows east of Kingswood Farm (NT).

Swanage: Two round barrows at east end of Ballard Down (NT); The Lock-up and pump (LA).

Tyneham: Round barrows on Povington Heath; Five Barrows; Povington Barrow; Two round barrows on Earl's Kitchen; Two round barrows west of Rookery Cottages; Four round barrows at Thorn Barrow (these burial mounds, although marked by the metal 'star signs', were virtually destroyed by the army in 1971); Two round barrows northwest of Pool Pond. *All monuments in this parish are inside the Lulworth ranges.*

Worth Matravers: Strip lynchets on West and East Man; St Aldhelm's chapel.

CHAPTER XX

Unofficial Placenames

THE MAIN intention of this final chapter is to show that local pronunciation ("the vulgar tongue" as the old historians called it) is alone in correctly maintaining the true origins of many place names. Several as given by the Ordnance Survey maps are wildly inaccurate and lack even the saving grace of having local usage. It is time the present day cartographers became less pedantic and admitted that some of the first surveyors did a poor job when it came to recording local names which they heard from voices with unfamiliar accents. Some of the placenames in Purbeck where local pronunciation differs from the official forms are given below. Bold type is given for the Purbeck form of the names and mapmakers' variants follow in brackets:

Afleet (Arfleet). The name no longer appears on maps, the mill at Arfleet having been demolished and the area consumed by the Norden clay workings, but the old pronunciation is worth preserving in print. It is completely in accord with the original spelling of the name. Treswell gives it as *Aflet* in 1585 and Isaac Taylor has *Affleet* in 1765.

Ameswood (Alms Grove). A small wood on the south shoulder of the Purbeck ridge where the gated road branches down to Tyneham. It was common land, hence the 'Alms' element if one supposes a silent 'L' but Haime's Grove is more likely. The *hames* were curved bars fitted with loops, used to fasten the trace to the collar of a horse. It was pronounced 'ames' in Dorset, as was the name of Haime, a family frequently in East Lulworth from 1758.

Aves (The Halves). The mediaeval open field on the west side of West Street at Corfe Castle, it was called *West Hawes* on a plan of 1585. *Middle Hawes* lay between West and East Streets. *Hawys* was the name of an owner of land at Corfe Castle from the time of Edward I. *Haw* is also an archaic word applied to closes and yards in towns, although this definition does not describe these two open fields. Whichever is the origin, as *w* used to be pronounced *v* and Dorset speech drops the aspirate, the current form of Aves preserves the original word perfectly.

Backington (Baltington). It was recorded as *Baltingeton* in 1287. The meaning is unknown. I tentatively suggest there may have

184

been an earlier form of *Baecingtun*, 'farm of the ridge dwellers', which would accurately describe its situation immediately beneath Whiteway Hill and the hill-fort of Flower's Barrow at Tyneham.

Bollard Head (Ballard Head). If this name is from the OE *bealg*, 'smooth and rounded down' then the corruption does not help explain the derivation. The word *bollard* is itself uncertain but could have applied to the shape of the headland when seen from Swanage.

Branksea Island (Brownsea Island). Both pronunciations have been in use since the sixteenth century. The earliest known form of the name is the OE word *brunc*, probably meaning the '(side of a) hill'. Charles van Raalte opted for 'Brownsea' in 1903.

Brinscombe (Brenscombe). The Ordnance Survey map (six-inch) reverted in the 1960s to the local spelling, justified by *Bryncescomb* in 1286, but the name is *Brunescume* in Domesday Book. The present farmhouse is sixteenth century.

Coombe Kaynes (Coombe Keynes). This village is beyond Purbeck's western border but is worth including as it shows a long memory for correct pronunciation. The family name is spelt *Chaynes* or *Kaynes* in documents from 1286 onwards and seems not to have been mis-spelt by mapmakers until the first edition of the Ordnance Survey in 1811.

Critch (Creech). The survival of this word is amazing as it is almost the pure OE *cryc* (from the British *cruc*) meaning a 'hill or barrow'. This is one of only about a dozen survivals of Celtic placenames in the whole of Dorset. By 1280 the name was *Crich* and the fact that the local tongue has virtually preserved this sound (against the longstanding advice of the maps) is a fine example of the purity of popular etymology.

Eggleston (Egliston). The popular name is purest; derived from that of the owner of the land, between Tyneham and Kimmeridge, at the time of King John—one *Engelini* or *Egelin*. The name is given as *Eggleston* on Taylor's map of 1765.

Goalter Gap (Gaulter Gap). The local name for this part of Kimmeridge Bay is justified by that of *Goulthead* on an estate map of 1795. Attempts have been made to explain the name as coming from *gaulter*, a tool which may have been used to cut shale. This seems unlikely as the pronunciation 'gawlter' does not occur but it is quite possible that the tool was known as a 'gowlter' at Kimmeridge.

St. Alban's Head (St. Aldhelm's Head). I have never heard any native of Purbeck or any Dorset countryman refer to the headland as St. Aldhelm's (the name of a Saxon saint). Whilst realising that the chapel is called *capella Sancti Aldelmi* in mediaeval documents, I regard its use today as affectation. I have therefore kept to the alternative, colloquial, spelling in this book because that, at least, is understood as a placename. John Smeaton, who built the Eddystone lighthouse in the 1750s, called it *St Alban's Head*, as does the first Ordnance map.

Slip (Slepe). Both the official and local names obviously come from the OE *slaep*, 'slippery place', and the name was given as Slepe as long ago as 1244. The name is a nice piece of description for part of the muddy shore of Poole Harbour.

Vitower (Fitzworth). The peninsula on the southern shore of Poole Harbour on the opposite side of the Ower backwater. The local name perpetuates several centuries of recorded forms, from *Vytower* in 1617 to *Vitt-Ower* used by Hutchins's editors in 1861. The meaning, from *Fitoure* of 1545, could have been "disputed shore" but the alternative official form, first recorded in 1571, brings a second choice. Fitzworth was a detached offshoot of the manor of Worth Matravers where the wife of Hugh Fitz Grip held land in 1068. Worth manor passed from the Fitz Paynes to the Fitz Alans in the fourteenth century. "Fitz's shore" therefore seems more likely.

Swanage Turkey

Afterthought   Wareham people used to pride themselves on being cultured and commercial. They reserved their derision for the inhabitants of Swanage which, as a nineteenth century quarry port, they used to call "Turkey". This was also used as a nickname, as in "Turkey Jack" Churchill.

These were strong insults in the first half of the century as the Turks were notorious for castrating their prisoners. As a result of war with Britain between 1807 and 1824 ex-soldiers who had been released from captivity in Asia Minor travelled the English countryside collecting parish benefits, and proving their disability by showing the marks of mutilation. In other words, the people of Wareham regarded the inhabitants of Swanage as barbarians, if not as eunuchs.

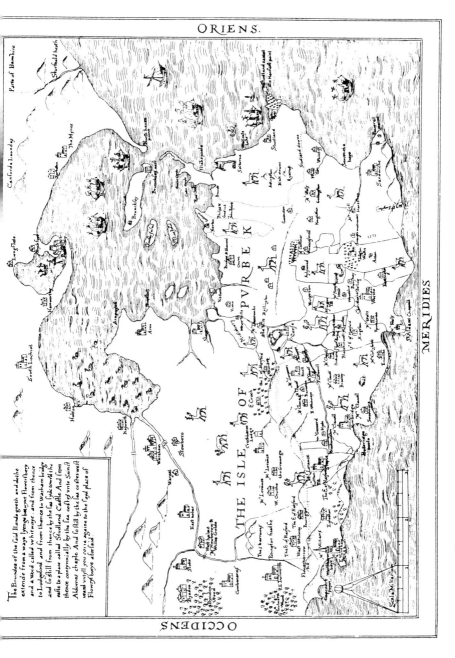

The Boundes of the faid Ilande goeth and dothe extende from a waye lyenge betwyxt Flowerbury and a Wood called whiteaye and from thence to Ludfeford and from thence to Warham bridge and fo ftill from thence by the fea fyde towrd the eafte to a place called Studland Caftle And from thence contynnally by the fea coft yn to Saindt Aldemes chaple And fo ftill by the fea coft weft ward vntyll you come agayne to the fayd place of Flowerbury aforfaid

THE ISLE OF PVRBEK

ORIENS.

OCCIDENS

MERIDIES

Photo-lithographic Facsimile of a Map of the Isle of Purbeck drawn by Ralph Treswell about 1585-6 Preserved at Kingston Lacy.

187

Steeple, Creech Grange, and the Washington connection

Hindsight Having dedicated the first edition of this book to Lieutenant-Colonel Archie Strange-Boston, I followed it up by giving him a drive back in time to all the bits of the Purbeck rights-of-way network down which my old Morris 1100 could be risked. After half a century on the other side of the pond he was keen to find everything of America-in-Purbeck.

Creech Grange was built by Sir Oliver Lawrence, on former Bindon Abbey lands, in about 1545 and extended on the north side about 1600. The Lawrence shields-of-arms are on panels in the barrel-vaulted roof of the parish church at Steeple, showing Lawrence quartering Washington and with the initials "D.L.E." and crest. The Washington crest and Edward Lawrence's initials, dated 1616, appear in the church porch and this English link with the family of the first American president brings Steeple frequent trans-Atlantic visitors. The Dorset connection was remembered in George Washington's time [1732-99] and his elder half-brother was named Lawrence. The other lasting name in these parts arrived in 1691 when Nathaniel Bond bought Creech Grange.

Pieces of twelfth century work survive in the church at Steeple.

The Manor House at Steeple was built around 1600 and rebuilt in 1698 by Roger and Ruth Clavell whose crest appears on a stone panel.

The arms of Sir Oliver Lawrence of Creech Grange − an ancestor of George Washington, the first president of "United States of America" as the Congress of British provinces styled themselves, in revolt, on 9 September 1776. They unilaterally declared "free, sovereign and independent" nationhood on 4 July that year.

Opposite: Creech Grange, from John Pouncy's "Dorsetshire Photographically Illustrated", 1857 − and it is indeed a lithographic photograph rather than an engraved print. Pouncy was pioneering the advance in printing techniques, as he told the world in his set of photographic books which are now exceedingly rare: "The Detail and Touch of Nature faithfully reproduced by a New Process on Stone, by which Views are rendered Truthful, Artistic, and Durable."

"Agglestone, near Studland, Isle of Purbeck, Dorset" by Philip Brannon, 1862, "with Bournemouth Bay & the Isle of Wight in the distance" — which is one of the earliest attempts to usurp Poole Bay and rename it for the new town of Bournemouth.

Attempts for a Purbeck National Park

Hindsight In the years of post-war reconstruction there was a feeling that the wartime slogan "Your country is worth fighting for" had to be given legislative force with an enactment to protect the landscape and public rights of access. Most of the concern centred on the high moors and the pressure for set access areas fuelled by bitter memories of the 1930s, when ramblers and communists made common cause to challenge police and gamekeepers with mass trespasses to Kinderscout, Derbyshire. The estate and the peak itself was to be acquired by the National Trust in 1982, but in the years after the war there was considerable resistance to any legal acceptance of a right to roam across moorland. The opponents of the legislation succeeded in keeping any such provisions out of the National Parks and Access to the Countryside Act, which passed through Parliament in 1949. The only rights for walkers in either national parks or the rest of the countryside

190

would be along highways or across land that had been specifically dedicated for public access.

Purbeck was recommended by a committee chaired by the architect and town planner Leslie Abercrombie [1879-1957] for inclusion in the first short-list of national parks. It would have been unique as the only such park in lowland England, as the rest were in the western and northern highland zones, and the single one in day-trip distance of London. The civil servants dropped the proposal on the grounds of Purbeck's insufficient size to justify the administration, and because its deletion was a sop to the landowners' lobby. Instead the Isle of Purbeck was relegated to an alternative form of designation.

In 1974 I founded the Purbeck National Park Committee to try and revive the original proposals but we met with considerable hostility from just the local naturalists and environmentalists who should have been leading the fight. Their opposition came from a fear that any additional attention drawn to Purbeck would result in still more tourists and outweigh any benefits. One of the American states has a similar problem: "If you love Iowa, don't tell anyone." The Purbeck campaign failed to gain popular support and the committee was wound up in 1976.

"Branksea Castle, Poole Harbour" by Philip Brannon, 1862.

Tanks win ecology battle

Hindsight Having in 1968 founded the Tyneham Action Group, and its successors the 1943 Committee and Friends of Tyneham, I ultimately underwent a volte-face and fought for the Royal Armoured Corps to retain the Lulworth and East Holme Ranges. The insoluble problem that dogged Purbeck's conservation cause célèbre (see page 161) was Whitehall's insistence upon the rule, established after the bureaucratic debacle over another Dorset live-firing area, the wartime Crichel Down bombing range, that decommissioned military land had to be offered back to its former owners or their heirs.

This wrecked my naive hopes of a simple transfer from the Ministry of Defence to National Trust ownership. It opened the way for the poison of modern agriculture to tame what had become the best unofficial nature reserve on the South Coast. I therefore found myself leading deputations to Parliament and the Defence Ministry to campaign against the Nugent Committee's recommendation for the release of the Purbeck tank gunnery ranges.

Ironically I was relieved when it was decided the tanks would stay, though with the concession of a spectacular series of weekend and August holiday paths between Lulworth and Kimmeridge, and that the area as a whole could remain a glorious wilderness. Peregrine falcons continued to breed on the limestone crags of Gad Cliff. It is a sad paradox that the best way of preserving a

Opposite: "North East View, taken from Heath Hill" of Lulworth Castle, drawn by J. Taylor and engraved by James Basire, 1773, showing the seaward panorama towards the Arish Mell Gap. To its left is the western end of the Purbeck Hills, entrenched with the ramparts of Flower's Barrow hill-fort.

LULLWORTH CASTLE, the SEAT of THOMAS WELD ESQᴿ.

reservoir of wildlife is to exclude human beings and fire high-explosive shells. A similar monumental irony is that the Korean de-militarised zone "with one million men in arms on either side" is "a thriving sanctuary for wildlife", to quote Peter McGill in The Observer of 26 June 1988.

Nature rules: National Trust Purbeck

Hindsight There have been more successes, proportionately, for the nature conservation movement in the Isle of Purbeck than in any other landscape in England. That is not to deny that much has been lost, particularly herb-rich older grassland, but the surprise is that such a colossal acreage has been preserved across a wide range of varying habitats.

More wild lowland heath survives in Purbeck than anywhere else in southern England. "The untamable Ishmaelitish thing that it now was it always has been," wrote Thomas Hardy of his Egdon Heath. "Cultivation was its enemy; and ever since the beginning of vegetation its soil has worn the same antique brown dress."

Not that I agree. The heathland flora is not sombre. In the Isle of Purbeck it is as vivid as any in England; the purple of the heather − plus the introduced rhododendron − and great yellow splashes of furze, flowering through most of the year, which fringe bogs that are enlivened by cotton-grass and blue gentian.

There are many more Nature Conservancy signs than in 1972, as National Nature Reserves have spread across Studland, Godlingston and Stoborough heaths, in many cases up to the tree-line of post-war conifer plantings. Overlapping the conservation zone is the eight thousand acre Corfe Castle Estate of Henry Ralph Bankes of Kingston Lacy House, near Wimborne, which was left to the National Trust on his death in August 1981. As well as Corfe Castle itself, the land includes immense blocks of heath and downland, and extends around eleven miles of the Purbeck coast. The National Trust already owned 222 acres of Whitecliff Farm, which prevents the northern expansion of Swanage, and 51 acres of cliff near Belle Vue Farm, south of Langton Matravers.

Until it received Brownsea Island from the Treasury, which had acquired it in lieu of death duties in the 1960s, the Trust owned just one acre of the Isle of Purbeck − at Bond's Folly, otherwise known as Grange Arch, towards the western end of the chalk hills. It is now Purbeck's biggest landowner, with the Ministry of Defence a close second.

Map of National Trust lands

//////	pre-1982 National Trust Land
::::::	National Trust land — the Bankes estate

POOLE

BOURNEMOUTH

Brownsea Island

Shell Bay

Nudist Beach

Little Sea

Hartland Moor — Fayle's Tramway

Studland Heath

Studland Bay

Studland

Agglestone

Old Harry

Corfe Castle

Nine Barrow Down

Ballard Down, obelisk

Bond's Folly

The Rings — Corfe

Whitecliff Farm

Godlingston Manor

Corfe Common

SWANAGE

Langton

Seacombe —

Hedbury Quarry

Belle Vue cliffs

Durlston Country Park

Hindsight   The cliffs south of Swanage were selected in the early 1970s for Dorset's first country park and a significant holding of council land, already highly popular with visitors, was expanded by leasing adjoining fields. This was a Victorian and Edwardian playground with plenty of the history of seaside tourism as well as important wildlife habitats.

In 1974 Durlston Country Park was opened. County planning officer Alan Swindell explained that the management plan had been designed to preserve "the rich ecological pattern" by a "careful balance between people and nature". It includes some of the last sea-cliff nesting sites of the auks, and concentrations of orchids across Round Down. The park incorporates Durlston Head, Anvil Point and a subterranean access problem in the form of cliff quarries at Tilly Whim Caves which were closed through fear of accidents. Inland the park extends half-a-mile, to within one field of California Farm, Durlston Farm and South Barn. On the western edge it joins the National Trust's Belle Vue holding.

The long-running friction between naturalists and climbers has been smoothed by a compromise that creates sanctuaries and areas with a closed season, but allows unrestricted access elsewhere. Some of the climbs rank amongst the most popular in the country and the classic ones have their own names, including Rendezvous Manque between Durlston Head and Tilly Whim Caves, and Traverse of the Gods between the caves and the lighthouse. At the side of the headland is the Subliminal Cliff. Westwards from Anvil Point are Via Christina, Nutcracker Exit, Marmolata Buttress, Sheerline, Bottomless Buttress and Boulder Ruckle Exit.

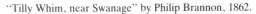

"Tilly Whim, near Swanage" by Philip Brannon, 1862.

"Quarry of the Purbeck paving stone – Swanage, Dorset" by Philip Brannon, 1862.

Destruction of the Cowlease industrial archaeology

Hindsight The veritable open-air quarrying museum that I en-thused about here (see pages 19 to 24) has become prime real estate. David Haysom wrote to the Dorset County Magazine in 1978 with news of the destruction of the Cowlease workings: "During the past twelve months the majority of the remaining workings have been completely obliterated and replaced by con-crete bases for holiday chalets – the crabstones of the old winches having been removed, and the shafts filled to ground level. It is unfortunate that Rodney Legg's plea in 'Purbeck Island' for the preservation of this unique area was not heeded by the local authorities."

Swanworth Quarries

Hindsight   The biggest Purbeck stone-pit in the latter part of the twentieth century, employing thirty and with an output of 400,000 tons a year, is Swanworth Quarries in Coombe Bottom, between Worth Matravers and Kingston. It is operated by Tarmac Roadstone (Southern) Limited and was the centre of controversy in 1988 as its reserves will be exhausted in 1995 and the company wants more ground.

One Kingston resident called it "the grand canyon" and others protested it would wreck the Purbeck holiday trade. Not that I received a single complaint about it in the twenty years I edited Dorset County Magazine, which had a penchant for stirring environmental controversy in Purbeck in particular, so the geligniting of this limestone valley does not seem to have disturbed too many visiting walkers.

Swanworth is the opposite end of the trade from that which graced cathedrals but it fulfils a demand that is hardly likely to go out of fashion – its jagged blocks are the hardcore for roads and sea defences. If there is disappointment for me in continued mineral extraction it is that we fail to grasp the opportunities for creative landscaping. My solution would not be to fill the holes but to shape them into something more dramatic. The countryside is big enough to hold a few adventure playgrounds as the surprise rucks in the green carpet.

"Section & Interior of Purbeck Quarry, Swanage, Dorset" by Philip Brannon, 1862.

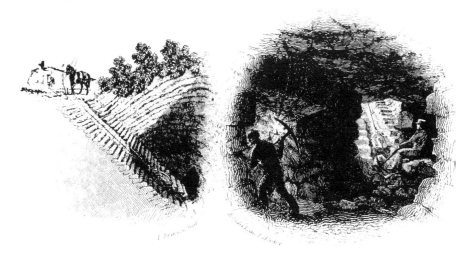

"Clay Pit at Corfe" – at Norden, a mile to the north-west – by Alfred Dawson, 1882.

More holes in the heath

Hindsight "Kimberley must be like this," Andrew Goltz told me in May 1973 when an exploration of the old clay railway at Povington brought him to the lip of an immense open pit. "You could drop the Blue Pool in there several times over."

In 1975 I was able to prove that this biggest hole in Dorset, inside the no-go area of the Lulworth and East Holme Ranges, had been operating for twenty years without planning permission. Dorset County Council then gave retrospective consent to English China Clays, after my publicity, to regularise the position.

In contrast, their application to tear apart the northern end of the Arne peninsula (see page 53), in the area of an old decoy pond and the oak wood of Froxen Copse, had been authorised years before but never acted upon. The council tried to revoke this permission but were defeated after an emotional public inquiry at which the Dartford warbler was the absentee objector everyone claimed to represent.

Counsel for English China Clays was unappreciative of my comments about the issues behind mineral extraction. I criticised the Nature Conservancy Council for non-attendance at a hearing, told the inspector why another potential objector felt compelled to decline giving evidence, and then became the maverick environmentalist who welcomed the creation of more Blue Pools.

The Dartford warbler, I concluded, was the easiest of species to help because it nested in tall gorse, which was one of the few habitats that man could readily replace. Everyone threatened to sue me but none did.

Subsequent clay pits have caused less controversy and several underground workings have come and gone without any at all.

Why it is the Blue Pool

Hindsight The present role of the Blue Pool (see page 41), as a beauty spot among the pines, began in 1935 when T.T. Barnard opened it to the public. The vivid and ever-changing turquoise and blue colour of the pool is caused by diffracted light passing through minute particles of clay that are permanently suspended in water. Miss J.S. Barnard, the present owner of the Blue Pool, pointed out to me in November 1972 that to the surprise of many visitors this blueness is stronger on overcast days, when there is no sunlight reflected off the surface of the pool. The water is also dead. The high concentration of minerals and an absence of oxygen prevents decomposition and for this reason the pool has no vegetable or animal life. There are three acres of water, fifty feet deep, surrounded by twenty-five acres of sandy slopes covered by woodland, furze and heather.

Purbeck pots issued on Hadrian's Wall

Hindsight Archaeologists were surprised to learn in 1972 that black burnished cooking pots found on Hadrian's Wall had been produced by a Roman pottery (see page 42) on the shores of Poole Harbour. It had always been thought that the pots were made locally in the frontier region. Instead they came from one of the furthest corners of England, which says something for the effectiveness of the Roman system of distribution and points towards centralised buying of stores for the Roman army. Such a far-flung trade route had never been suspected. It was discovered after David Peacock, a geologist at Southampton University, carried out a heavy mineral analysis of the clay in the pots and found it had come from 350 miles away in Dorset.

As for the distinctive black-burnish of the pots, R.H.H. Farrar has shown that its decidedly smooth texture was not the result of chemical reduction, as had been assumed, but was achieved in a separate process after the pots had been removed from the kiln.

"Old Harry Rocks" by Philip Brannon, 1862, with Swanage and Durlston Head visible in the distance.

Studland's lost castle

Hindsight Studland has lost its castle as well as Old Harry's Wife (see page 167). Ralph Treswell's map of Purbeck drawn about 1585-86 shows "Studland castell alis Hanfast point" – alias Hand-fast Point – jutting north-eastwards into the sea off the present Old Harry Rocks. Inland from it, from the cliffs above Studland Bay to the cliff-face above the present Pinnacles, he shows a wood. On the Studland side of this there is an enclosure named "Castell Layes". In his more detailed map of the parish, in the Kingston Lacy archives, he shows "ye pinakell" seaward of the castle, but such a chalk stack would have had a relatively short existence and may be presumed to have been washed down. Thomas Gerard, writing about 1624, says " the land stretcheth forth a short prom-ontory furnished with a block-house, for the more grace called Studland Castle, upon which it abutteth" – making it clear there was a castle earlier than the blockhouse.

The editors of the third edition of John Hutchins's county history, looking back from the second half of the nineteenth century, record that on the foreland "three or four guns were usually planted in time of war". Studland Castle would appear to have been on a platform just above sea level immediately on the north side of Old Harry Rocks, and it is quite likely that exploration of the foreshore and the waters close inshore will reveal traces of its stonework.

"Swanage Bay, from Peveril Point" by Philip Brannon 1862.

Hedbury cannon rescued from obscurity

Hindsight The George III gun-barrel that I found at Hedbury Quarry, Langton Matravers, in 1960 (see page 36) has since been mounted on a stone plinth and now points seaward from the cliff edge. Hedbury passed into National Trust ownership, along with the rest of the Corfe Castle Estate, at the death of Henry Ralph Bankes of Kingston Lacy House, on 19 August 1981.

"St Alban's Quarry, St Alban's Head, Dorset" by Philip Brannon, 1862.

St Alban's versus St Aldhelm's

Hindsight   I receive continuing flak, principally from articulate Dorset incomers, for my insistence upon using St Alban's Head as the name for the great headland at the southern tip of the Isle of Purbeck (see page 185). In doing so I am aware that the little timber-less chapel which stands as a sea-mark on the clifftop is dedicated to St Aldhelm, a Saxon bishop of Sherborne, rather than to St Alban – the first British martyr, put to death about 304. Aldhelm died in 709.

In prolonging the error I am perhaps guilty of the affectation that I sense in others. My justification is that generations of mariners have known it as St Alban's Head. So too have their chartmakers, going back to Lieutenant Murdock Mackenzie's "Survey of the South Coast of England" in 1787. St Alban's Head has no community apart from its coastguards and I have always considered it belonged to the seamen rather than us fair-weather landlubbers.

I agree with my correspondents that it is St Aldhelm's chapel, but illogically or otherwise it will, for me, always be standing upon St Alban's Head. I realise this is inverted conservatism, and that eventually the correct style will probably be adopted by the Admiralty chart, but most of what passes for history is an amalgam of misconceptions. That is why the British people have Boadicea as their first hero and can leave the Boudica version to snivelling archaeologists.

Romano-Celtic horse-and-rider

Hindsight My own searches through Purbeck did not unearth an archaeological display-piece until 1988. This is a superb Celtic representation of a Sarmatian horseman; 5,000 of their cavalry were sent to Britain by Emperor Marcus Aurelius after the Romans had defeated this southern Russian tribe in 175 AD. He wears a conical cap and flowing cloak and is carved in relief on a panel of Purbeck marble. Much of the surface is pitted but there are still some highlight patches of polish and the preserved areas include the reins and Celtic-style facial detail.

It was probably cut at the Wilkswood quarries (see page 14). The Sarmatians, distinguished by their peculiar head-gear, are known to have been stationed at Ribchester, Lancashire, but this vigorous carving is a first for Dorset. The stone had been found in builder's rubble from a village near Wareham, having been pulled out of a cow-barn that had been subjected to gentrification, and I was able to buy it.

Saxon bible-page in Purbeck deed

Hindsight Among the vast accumulation of deeds to the Corfe Castle Estate which the National Trust found itself owning on 19 August 1982 — a year to the day after the death of Henry Ralph Bankes — was a 1585 copy of a conveyance that had been bound into a leaf from one of the most famous pre-Conquest great bibles assembled on the instructions of the Venerable Bede in about 712. Bede records in his "History of the Holy Abbots" how he told Ceolfrith to make three such manuscript copies of the bible, one each for his monasteries of Jarrow and Wearmouth — and the third for the Pope.

That copy went with Ceolfrith to Rome in 716 but the abbot died in France and his bible later came into the possession of the monastery of Monte Amiata, near Florence. It was put in the Laurentian Library in that city in 1786 and is known as the "Codex Amiatinus".

The two Wearside bibles were considered to be completely lost but in 1909 Canon Greenwell of Durham came across a leaf in a junk shop in Newcastle. His discovery enabled eleven more leaves to be found, re-used as bindings in the muniments at Wollaton Hall, Nottinghamshire. These were acquired by the British Museum in the 1930s.

One of Ceolfrith's Wearside bibles was stripped apart at Wollaton in the early 1580s,   being used for its vellum as folders for copies of title deeds and other legal documents. These transcripts were made in 1585 when Sir Christopher Hatton bought the Wollaton estate from Francis Willoughby.

Hatton, a favourite of Elizabeth I, sat in parliament for Northamptonshire, though he was losing the queen's attentions in 1584. She had given him Corfe Castle in 1575 and the page from the bible was used to bind one of the copies of the deeds relating to the Purbeck estate. By 1585 Hatton was Elizabeth's key man along all four sides of the square that cornered Elizabeth, Parliament, Mary Queen of Scots and the courts. He was rewarded with Northamptonshire lands, acquired Wollaton in Nottingham, and was given the keepership of the royal hunting forest of the Isle of Purbeck.

The page from Ceolfrith's bible was spotted in a deed box at Kingston Lacy in Dorset by Nicholas Pickwood, the National Trust's consultant on book conservation, who passed it to John Fuggles, the Trust's library adviser, though at that time neither realised that they were handling pre-Conquest parchment.

Emblems of power − the seal of Corfe Castle, and the arms of its last private owners, the Bankes family. Since 1982 the Corfe Castle Estate has sprouted numerous cast-iron signs with the oak leaf National Trust logo

"Seacombe" by Philip Brannon, 1862, showing the cleft in the cliffs south-east of Worth Matravers: on these ledges, leftward towards Winspit, the *Halsewell* broke up with the loss of 168 lives in 1786 (see page 64).

Danish fleet wrecked off Swanage in 877

Hindsight The chapter on wrecks (see page 63) should have begun with the earliest recorded shipwrecks – which changed the course of English history. In 876, following months of fighting, the West Saxons bribed the Danes, who had sailed into Wareham, to negotiate a truce. Saxon money was exchanged for the return of hostages and the Danes also gave Alfred their solemn oath "on the holy ring" to leave Wessex. The enemy departed from Wareham but occupied Exeter instead.

The Anglo-Saxon Chronicle is ambiguous about the sequence and nature of events. The decisive moment was either gale-force winds or fog off Purbeck in 877 when ships were making for Exeter – perhaps reinforcements rather than the original force from Wareham as implied by the Chronicle. Three versions of the manuscript say they "encountered a great storm at sea, and 120 ships were lost at Swanage"; the other two versions have it that they "encountered a great mist at sea, and 120 ships were lost at Swanage". In all probability it was a combination of foul weather with disorientation in thick fog being followed by the gale. The failure of the full Danish force to reach Exeter caused the remainder to accede to Alfred's demands and quit the city for Gloucester, which was in Mercian territory.

Worth and the 'Secret War'

Hindsight Purbeck's contribution towards the winning of the Second World War did not become public property until Brian Johnson's BBC television series on "The Secret War". The people of Purbeck had needed permits to come and go from their own homes and few knew what the scientists in their midst had achieved.

The Telecommunications Research Establishment, which pioneered the development of early warning radio-direction finding equipment that became known as radar, was moved from Dundee to Renscombe Farm, on the west side of Worth Matravers, on 5 May 1940. It was headed by A.P. Rowe and Robert Watson-Watt. Their galaxy of young scientists included Dr Robert Cockburn, Alan Hodgkin and Bernard Lovell – all three of whom would later be knighted.

Cockburn, transmitting from Worth in August 1940, carried out the first interference countermeasures of the war. The transmission was intended, in effect, to bend the direction of the German radio beams (at a frequency of 30 to 31.5 megacycles per second) on which the Luftwaffe was blind-flying to English targets. He recorded the sequence of synchronised German dots and was going to relay them by telephone to Beacon Hill, near Salisbury, but lost the use of the land-line. Instead a simpler broadcasting of the signal known as "Aspirin" effectively widened the beam with boosted dashes and disorientated the German pilots.

In the last week of January 1941 the Germans began a refined system on 42.5 megacycles per second and on the day it came into operation Robert Cockburn commandeered the BBC television transmitter at Alexandra Palace in London. Countermeasure "Domino" jammed the new German signal by re-radiating it back to the attacking aircraft on 46.9 megacycles per second. A second transmitting station was constructed at the Salisbury site, on Beacon Hill, to extend the jamming across the whole of southern England.

On 27 February 1942 the Telecommunications Research Establishment received its best present of the war. The toys that were en route to Worth Matravers, with C Company of the Second Battalion of the Parachute Regiment, comprised the parabolic aerial, receiver and cathode-ray tube of a German Würzburg radar apparatus. The raiding party from "2 Para" had jumped from twelve Whitley bombers on to a 400 feet clifftop, which was covered in deep snow, at Cap d'Antifer, near Bruneval on the Cherbourg peninsula. They and the dismantled equipment were retrieved by landing craft.

Ironically, the operation brought about the evacuation of the Telecommunications Research Establishment from the Purbeck coast to Malvern College, Worcestershire, on 26 May 1942. There were fears that the Germans might mount their own Bruneval-style raid on the Dorset coast. To emphasise the danger, when Reginald Jones and Hugh Smith from Air Ministry Scientific Intelligence arrived, to inspect the radar apparatus captured at Bruneval, it was with revolvers "ostentatiously strapped to our belts".

The final projects perfected at Purbeck included four important radar sets − AI (Airborne Interception; for night fighters), ASV (Air to Surface Vessel; for Coastal Command, to detect submarines surfacing to charge their batteries), Gee (renamed TR to indicate Transmitter/Receiver, which it was not; instead it formed a grid-lattice map from synchronised pulses on a cathode-ray tube in a colour coded pattern that shows the aircraft's location when superimposed on a chart), and H2S (ground-mapping; for Bomber Command to bomb blind, straight through the clouds).

Dinosaurs and the dust-cloud

Afterthought Having presented the asteroid theory to account for the extinction of the dinosaurs (see page 137) along comes the alternative view that the nuclear winter of 65 million years ago was triggered by vulcanic eruptions that have left a sheet of basalt 6,000 feet thick across north-west India.

M7 engine returns to Swanage Railway

Hindsight For the Swanage Railway (see page 33) there would be life after Beeching. His axe, postponed for several years, eventually fell in the early 1970s and the Purbeck branch line was then lifted with indecent haste. It was purchased, however, by Dorset County Council which leased the seaside end to the Swanage Railway Society. Teams of volunteers gradually relaid track and a decade later this had reached Harman's Cross, two miles away in the valley north of Langton Matravers, with the sight, sound and smell of steam returning to the first mile from Swanage Station to a halt at Herston.

The group also began a collection of locomotives though the prize of the Pacific-class engine that carried the 'Swanage' name, on the mainline from Waterloo, eluded them. She is now at Alresford, near Winchester.

Their achievement, in 1988, has been to bring back from America an M7 class 0-4-4T tank engine, number 30053, of the sort that used to work the Purbeck line. She is the only one to survive in Britain, apart from a single specimen in the official British Rail steam collection, and dates from the end of the nineteenth century. For me she is pure Purbeck nostalgia as I travelled the line many times at the end of the steam era. Long before this M7 was brought back from across the water they had been my all-time favourite steam engine: from the point where I started to realise that one was not quite the same as another.

Grosvenor Hotel joins the Durlston blow-hole

Hindsight   Among the casualties in the creation of the Durlston estate (see page 97) was the blow-hole on the headland. As with Thurlestone in Devon and Durdle Door at Lulworth (*th* being replaced by *d* in Dorset's dialect) the name Durlston means "pierced rock". The blow-hole, which Philip Brannon had drawn with a twenty-five feet spurt of water, seems to have been blocked by falling debris during the construction of Durlston Castle.

As for the prestigious Hotel Grosvenor, which was the epitome of Edwardian Swanage, and, I am told, the first building in Purbeck to have a lift, its graceful lines were wiped from the southern panorama of the bay by demolition in the winter of 1987-88.

"Swanage" by John Newman and Co, 1881.

Encombe idyll: kill nothing but time

Hindsight There was too little in the original book about Encombe. It is as near perfection as any Dorset great house and estate, not only for the pleasantly simple south-facing frontage that was completed in 1770, but in its superb situation. The Encombe valley opens on to the sea with a waterfall into Egmont Bight, between Kimmeridge and Chapman's Pool, but it is remarkable for its Golden Bowl, created by a swirl of hills from Swyre Head around to Houns-tout Cliff, that protects not only the house but also its lawns, lake and woods from all the drawbacks of a location a thousand yards from a sea.

William Morton Pitt sold Encombe in 1807 to John Scott [1751-1838], who would be created first Earl of Eldon and was Lord High Chancellor of England just about continuously from 1801 through to 1827. He was described as "almost the ideal of manly beauty". Scott was just about the last bastion in the cabinet against all the reforms that others were reluctantly accepting as inevitable – including those extending voting rights, changing Parliamentary boundaries, and emancipating Roman Catholics. He was never happier "than when among the birds at Encombe" but, his brother William complained, he could "kill nothing but time".

Sir William Scott, first Baron Stowell [1745-1836] was a close friend of Dr Johnson and the pre-eminent draughtsman of international maritime law. His monument is the forty feet high obelisk, tapering in Egyptian needle-style and constructed with blocks of Purbeck limestone from the cliff-quarries at Seacombe, which stands on the 425 feet contour above Quarry Wood at the top of the Encombe valley. Its inscriptions record the laying of the foundation stone by Lady Frances Jane Bankes on 28 May 1835; he was still living and it was raised "in honour of Sir William Scott, created Baron Stowell". The inscription gives Lady Frances's second initial as "I", there being no "J" in the Roman alphabet.

Eldon Seat, on the undercliff of the great inland escarpment of Swyre Head, has a delightful view over the sheltered mini-landscape of the Big Wood and the lake across to Encombe House nestling beneath its trees and the great slope. It is a superb block of

Opposite: "Encombe, the Seat of William Morton Pitt, Esq." drawn by W. Tompkins and engraved by V.M. Picot. It shows the house, in its Golden Bowl, before the arrival of John Scott, the first Earl of Eldon, who bought the estate in 1807.

Encombe, the Seat of William Morton Pitt, Esq.

Purbeck stone, eight feet long and four feet wide, with another massive ashlar as the backrest. They are set on a raised podium, the first stone of which was laid by Lady Elizabeth Repton on 15 October 1835. Beside it there is a memorial to Pincher, the late Lord Chancellor Eldon's last dog, who outlived his master by two years and died in 1840.

At the other extreme of both situation and architecture is the primitive-style rock bridge in the wooded ravine 450 yards south of the house. It is constructed in rustic fashion with great semi-tooled boulders of Purbeck stone, without cement, and has monolithic uprights to ensure it also looks bizarre from a distance. This I take to be a piece of fun by architect George Stanley Repton, the youngest son of landscape-gardener Humphry Repton, who had eloped with the Lord Chancellor's eldest daughter, Lady Elizabeth Scott, on 27 November 1817. The angry father finally submitted to a full reconciliation in 1820, and henceforth, until his death in 1858, the estate had its own gothic architect.

The title has survived, with the Earl of Eldon having as his heir Viscount Encombe, but something caused the estate to lessen the Eldon connection. When Mrs Georgina Bartlett had the public house on the hillside at Kingston it was called the Eldon Arms. In recent years, however, it has changed its name to that of the family rather than their title — it is now the Scott Arms.

"Encombe Vale and House from Eldon's Seat, Dorset" by Philip Brannon, 1862 — with the obelisk to the first Earl of Eldon's brother, William Scott who was Lord Stowell, being glimpsed on the hilltop behind the figures.

Crossbills amid the pines

Hindsight   Crossbills have expanded their numbers throughout the pine plantations of Northumberland, Breckland, the New Forest, and into those of the Frome valley. A flock of about fifteen was reported from Brownsea Island. They are now breeding in the pinelands of the Purbeck Forest which was established across the Rempstone Estate, to the shores of Poole Harbour, in the 1940s. By 1980 the stands were reaching maturity.

Purbeck District Council

Hindsight   The old Wareham and Purbeck Rural District Council became Purbeck District Council in the reform of local government that took place on 1 April 1974.

New bridge over the Frome

Hindsight   A re-routed A351, across the meadows between Stoborough and Worgret (see page 7), has a motorway-style bridge over the River Frome. It was completed in 1988 and the new Purbeck main road now cuts through Stoborough Heath to rejoin the former turnpike coach road. That was brought into the twentieth century at the same time, with a generous scattering of roundabouts, and has started to look like anywhere else in England.

Purbeck cut-off by 1978 blizzard

Hindsight   A taste of pre-Victorian isolation (see page 5) returned to Purbeck for a week in February 1978. All roads in Dorset were blocked by snow in the blizzard that raged from nine o'clock on the evening of Saturday 18 February and continued in growing coldness through the night and the Sunday morning. For fifteen hours the fine snow was driven by force ten arctic easterlies which were impossible to struggle against in a car or on foot – and the conditions on the Sunday morning were such that a building only half a mile away was totally out of sight and the effort to reach it verged on the limits of human endurance. People were stranded in cars all across the county, as was a train in the Bincombe cutting at Weymouth, though it eventually ploughed through into the town, and another pushed eastwards out of Dorchester. Fine snow drifted into lofts and under doors, whilst that from the flatter fields was blown into deep-cut lanes where, according to Sunday Times reporter Brian Jackman, it "was so deep you could sit on top of the telegraph poles". Electricity supplies were cut, as were a high proportion of telephones. As soon as the power went the water supply failed on each side of the Purbeck Hills because it could no longer be pumped into reservoirs on high ground. Radio Solent kept up a succession of news and "What's off" listings, and the police radio became preoccupied with the force's own losses in terms of stranded cars and then recovery units that were failing to find them. It was the blizzard of the century, and over everything, wrote Jackman, "hung the unaccustomed silence of a world without traffic".

Worth Matravers was one of the Purbeck communities that lost all its services, though they breached the white ramparts to reach the Square and Compasses Inn. Those households with Aga stoves and kerosene lamps relaxed into a comfortable self-sufficiency. From one, where a snowdrift had entered the living room, Professor Bryan N. Brooke became the first occasional occupant of Purbeck to break out, via a Coastguard Landrover on Tuesday 21 February. The walls of snow were only part of the problem but the Coastguard rescue markings proved sufficient passport through the police cordons.

Brooke reached Wareham station and London, still in gumboots, in time for a committee meeting, and was in the operating theatre of St James's Hospital, Balham, in time for surgery the following day. His story is in issue 67 of Dorset County Magazine.

"The Hanging Towers, Corfe Castle" by Philip Brannon, 1862.

"Corfe Castle, Dorset" by Philip Brannon, 1862.

Purbeck once had no strangers

Hindsight In showing the extent of change in Purbeck since 1972 I am obscuring the real onslaught of progress which took off with the arrival of the branch railway from Wareham to Swanage in the summer of 1885. When Encombe House was burgled in August 1880 and £15,000 worth of jewellery, silver and gold was stolen from the study of the third Earl of Eldon, the police had no doubt they were looking for a local villain.

As the Dorset County Chronicle reported: "A stranger prowling about could certainly be noticed, for the population of the whole of the Isle of Purbeck is exceedingly sparse, and the unfamiliar face is as a rule pretty well scanned by the man in blue as well as the more general inhabitant."

It would take another century for leisure to bring visitors to Purbeck even in midwinter. As recently as the first edition of this book the locals and devotees were more or less assured of having the coast to themselves in winter. All that has changed and the pressure for pleasure space is inexorable. One fears for Purbeck if its appeal is to be extrapolated indefinitely.

215

"The new Kingston Church" of 1874-80, drawn by Alfred Dawson, 1882. St James s church was the last great flourish of Purbeck marble, virtually on cathedral scale, and the final major creation by architect George Edmund Street [1824-81] who was a skilful mediaeval restorer as well as a Gothic revivalist. He was delighted with the results and called it his "jolliest" job. There are some harsh words about it here (page 13) as at the time Purbeck needed a railway rather than what was in effect a colossal private chapel for the third Earl of Eldon [1845-1926]. Writing in "Purbeck Parish Churches", in 1985, Fred Pitfield praises the impressive interior for its authentic thirteenth century details and the lavish use of Purbeck marble for the shafting of the arcade piers.

Next pages: The song "Swanage" by George Lewingdon, of Ivy Cottage, Poole (see page 97). It was published about 1880. This edition is for the amusement of the people of Rüdesheim-am-Rhein, who have twinned with Swanage, in the hope that the author of "Sound Ideas" and "Music and Language with Young Children" – Merle Chacksfield of Rabling Road, Swanage – will sing it like a Rhine maiden on her next visit to the West German wine town.

SWANAGE,
Song,

Written and Composed

BY

GEORGE LEWINGDON.

Author of

LIFT UP THE ROYAL STANDARD & *SONG* BOURNEMOUTH.

Price 3⁸

PUBLISHED BY
GEORGE LEWINGDON.
SWANAGE

SWANAGE.

Written and Composed by
G . LEWINGDON.

Arranged by J. SMITH . Organist. Poole.

2

219

stone   and   shin_gle   free   With   lof _ _ ty
ebb   and   flow_ing   tide   Where   ves _ _ sels

hills   of   Col_our'd   sand   And a   deep   re _ fresh_ing
lay   in   west_ern   gales   And   all   in   safe_ty

sea.
ride.

4

3. At Pev _ 'ril point a dou _ ble reef Of jag _ ged
4. Near to this is Durl _ stone head A splen _ did

rocks are seen And there you find the
fore _ _ land there Where rug _ _ ged rocks in

u _ _ nio beds with spar both red and green
bold re _ lief Stand tow _ _ 'ring in the air

'Twas here the Dan _ _ ish ships were sunk For
There's Til _ _ ly whim and An _ _ vil cove What

221

his _ _ t'ry tells us so A glo _ rious
charm _ _ ing spots to see Where snug _ glers

vic _ _ t'ry Eng _ land won A thou _ sand years a _
hid their bran _ dy kegs From off the deep blue

go.
sea.

"Ancient Manor House of Downs Hay" by Alfred Dawson, 1882. The name has since reverted to its mediaeval spelling, Dunshay Manor. It has been the home of artist George Spencer Watson [1869-1932] and sculptor daughter Mary Spencer Watson [born 1913]. Dunshay lies in the valley to the south of Harman's Cross.

Two faces of Purbeck, sketched by Alfred Dawson for the 1882 "Picturesque Rambles in the Isle of Purbeck" by Charles Edmund Newton-Robinson [1853-1913]. Scoles Farm, in the valley south of Corfe Common, dates from 1300 and is the oldest inhabited building in the parish of Corfe Castle. The other drawing shows a heathcropper setting off with a wheelbarrow, probably to dig peat for his fire, from a hovel on Studland Heath.

Also by Rodney Legg

Editor *Dorset — the county magazine* [issues 1 to 114, 1968-87]
Purbeck Island [original edition of this work, 1972]
A Guide to Dorset Ghosts
Ghosts of Dorset, Devon and Somerset
with Mary Collier, Tom Perrott
Afterword *Coker's Survey of Dorsetshire* [for the 1980 second edition of the 1732 work]
Editor *Steep Holm — a case history in the study of ecology*
Annotator *Monumenta Britannica* with John Fowles [first edition as two volumes 1980, 1982: volume one re-issued as an expanded first American edition, 1981]
Exploring Ancient Wiltshire with George Osborn
Old Portland with Jean M. Edwards
Romans in Britain
Purbeck Walks [three editions: 1983, 1985, 1988]
Old Swanage
The Dorset Walk with Ron Dacombe, Colin Graham
Stonehenge Antiquaries
Guide to Purbeck Coast and Shipwreck
Hardy Country Walks
The Steep Holm Guide
Lulworth and Tyneham Revisited
Walks in West Dorset
The Blandford Forum Guide
Dorset's War 1939-45
Cerne's Giant and Village Guide
East Dorset Country Walks
Blackmore Vale and Cranborne Chase Walks
Exploring the Heartland of Purbeck
Brownsea — Dorset's Fantasy Island
Purbeck's Heath — nature, claypits and the oilfield
Wincanton's Directory [two editions: 1987, 1988]
Mysterious Dorset
Walks in Dorset's Hardy Country
National Trust Dorset with Colin Graham
Lawrence of Arabia in Dorset
Dorset Encyclopaedic Guide
Literary Dorset

224

Index Of People

INDEX of PEOPLE

Hanham, T.B., 94
Hardle, Robert, 132
Hardy, Eliza, viii
Hardy, Thomas, ix, 31, 46, 96, 194
Hardy, William Masters, 5, 27, 71
Harris, Bob, 39
Hatton, Sir Christopher, 172, 205
Hawley, Francis, 172
Haysom, David, 197
Haysom, W.J., 40
Henry III, 10, 14, 16, 17, 132
Henry IV, 132
Henry VIII, 9, 11, 23, 171
Henshaw, Patrick, 46
Hodgkin, Sir Alan, 207
Homer, Miss M.S., 152
Howe, J.P., 180
Hutchins, John, 18, 186, 201, 210
Hyde, Thomas, 43, 53

Isabella, Queen, 130

Jackman, Brian, 214
James I, 59, 131
James II, 173
Jarman, Edward, 95
Jenkins, Harry, 88
Jenner, Dr Edward, 102, 103
Jesty, Benjamin, 102, 103
Jesty, Robert, 103
John, King, 10, 128, 129, 131, 158, 185
Johnson, Brian, 207
Johnson, Samuel, 174, 210
Jones, Rev M., 64
Jones, Dr Reginald, 208

Kearley, Alice, viii
Kearley, John, viii
Keats, John, ix
Kent, Earl of, 130, 131
Kerr, Barbara, 43
Knight, T.E., 71
Knolles, Robert, 63

Lander, Frank, 69
Lander, Thomas Chinchen, 35
Lavery, Thomas, 75
Lawrence, Sir Oliver, 188
Lawrence, Col. T.E.,iv
Leland, John, 23
Leofric, Bishop, 9
Leontas, Rosemary, vi, viii
Lester, Rev L., 123
Lewin, Stephen, 45, 56
Lewingdon, George, 97, 216, 217
Lincoln, Robert of, 56
Lovell, Sir Bernard, 207

Mackenzie, Lt. Murdock, 203
Malmesbury, William of, 126
Maltravers, Sir John, 130, 131
Mansel, Eustace, 64

Mansel, Maj. John, 61
Mansel, Sir Robert, 60
Mansel-Pleydell, J.C., vi, 145, 146
Marston, Miss L., 148
Masters, William, 5
Maton, W.G., 59
Mauléon, Savaric de, 129
Maxwell, Donald, 4, 61
McGill, Peter, 194
McQueen, Ian, 130
Melhuish, Miss J.M., 161
Merritt, Walter, 172
Miller, Henry, 75
Miller, Jack, 75, 163
Miller, Joseph, 72
Miller, Walter, 72, 75
Milton, John, 174
Monmouth, Duke of, 173
Mortain, Count of, 56
Mortimer, Roger, 130, 131
Moulder, Mrs A., 76
Mountjoy, Lord, 59
Mowlem, John, 31, 95, 96

Neve Foster, Dr C. le, 22
Newman, John, 209
Nicholls, G.F., 180
Norman, John, 27
Nugent, Baron, of Guildford, 192

Oliver, John 95
Olsen, Bertha Horthung, 178

Partridge, Walter, 172
Peacock, David, 200
Penistan, Morley, 151
Pennie, J.F., 109, 111
Perren, John, 75
Petts, Richard, 177
Phipps, James, 103
Pickard, Rev George, 74
Pickwoad, Nicholas, 205
Pierce, Richard, 64, 65
Piercy, Rev M., 69
Pike family, 41, 44, 46, 49, 50
Pitfield, Fred, 216
Pitt, William Morton, 12, 210
Pittman, Lt.-Col. Thomas, 124-126
Pomfret, Peter de, 130
Pond. Benjamin, 79
Pope, Alexander, 174
Portman, Edward Berkeley, 87, 88
Portman, Maurice, 149
Powell, T.P., 55
Powys, Llewelyn, 75
Pride, Col. Thomas, 172, 173

Rawles, Jos, 4, 5
Redding, Cyrus, 12
Redvers, Baldwin de, 128
Reid, Clement, 104
Rendell, Stan and Joan, vii
Repton, G.S., 12, 212
Repton, Humphry, 212

Riches, Mrs A.F., 78
Richmond, Prof. Ian, 58
Robinson, C.E. [Charles Edmund Newton-Robinson], 25, 67, 223
Romilly, Sir Samuel, 89
Rowe, A.P., 207
Russel family, 161
Russel, John, 64
Russell, Lord John, 88
Ryder, Richard, 150, 153

Saville, R.J., 123
Schoofs, Capt., 69
Scott, Lady Elizabeth, 212
Scott, John, 12, 210
Scott, Peter, 179
Scott, Sir William, 210
Sherren, Wilkinson, 127
Short, Bernard, 174
Simpson, Alexander, 75
Skutt, George, 173
Smeaton, John, 37, 186
Smith, H.P., 82
Smith, Hubert, 77, 78
Smith, Hugh, 208
Southborough, Lord, 163
Speed, John, 158
Spencer Watson, family, 222
Stainer, John, 149
Stanhope, Lord, 85
Stenton, Prof. F.M., 96, 126
Stephen, King, 128
Stevenson, William, 45
Stickland, Jesse, 29
Stickland, William, 66
Stowell, Baron, 210
Strange-Boston, Lt.
Col. Archie, iv, 188
Street, George, 13, 31, 32, 216
Sturt, Humphrey, 175
Suttle, E.W., 135
Swanland, John, 64
Swindell, Alan, 196
Sydenham, Richard, 92

Tatchell, Leonard, 150
Taylor, Isaac, 184, 185
Taylor, Phillip, 73
Thomas, Abbot, 63, 64
Thomas, Gareth, vi
Thomas, Henry, 75
Thompson, W., 140
Thomson, Nelson, 28, 39
Tregonwell, Lewis, 87
Treswell, Ralph, 187, 201
Treves, Sir Frederick, 95
Tubbs, William, 48
"Turkey", nickname, 186

Uffen, Robert, 136

Vancouver, Charles, 40
van Raalte, Charles, 177
Vespasian, 111, 114, 115
Vye, Harry, 72

Wallace, Percy, 66

"Pembroke Tower, Corfe Castle, Dorset" by Philip Brannon, 1862.

"Entrance to Corfe Castle − External View, Correction Tower on the Right" by Philip Brannon, 1862.

Index Of Purbeck Placenames

"Interior View of Gateway, Corfe Castle, with Corfe Castle Church & Town beyond" by Philip Brannon, 1862.